Seeing the Dead, Talking with Spirits

Seeing
the Dead,
Talking
with Spirits

Seeing the Dead, Talking with Spirits

SHAMANIC HEALING THROUGH CONTACT WITH THE SPIRIT WORLD

Alexandra Leclere

Destiny Books
Rochester, Vermont

Destiny Books
One Park Street
Rochester, Vermont 05767
www.InnerTraditions.com

Destiny Books is a division of Inner Traditions International

LIBRARY OF CONGRESS CATALOGING-IN-PUBLICATION DATA

Leclere, Alexandra.
  Seeing the dead, talking with spirits : shamanic healing through contact with the spirit
world / Alexandra Leclere.— 1st ed.
    p. cm.
  ISBN 978-1-59477-083-8
  1. Leclere, Alexandra. 2. Spiritualism—Biography. 3. Spiritualists—Biography. 4.
Spiritual healing and spiritualism. I. Title.
  BF1283.L43A3 2005
  133.9'1—dc22
                                                                    2005015854

Printed and bound in the United States

10 9 8 7 6 5 4 3 2

Text design and layout by Virginia Scott Bowman
This book was typeset in Caslon, with Lithos and John Handy used as display typefaces

With unconditional love and joy I dedicate this book to
my children, Tania, Tristan, Terence, and Talia,
who sustain me, and to Georges, because he is there.

Contents

Acknowledgments

Special thanks to Anne Dillon who was essential in manifesting this book. Thanks also to Diane Foster Grella and Sandy Weiss for their support. John Perkins, Penney Leyshon, Melanie Noblit-Gambino, Rosalyn Bruyere, Don Cardinal, and Jan Brugal are some of my teachers who I must thank for having blessed my path. The staff of Inner Traditions have been wonderful to me. Finally I want to thank all of my clients who are also my teachers and keep me in the light. May this book be a reflection of all the love and joy I have received.

Foreword

IT TOOK A GREAT LEAP OF FAITH FOR ME to move from writing books on indigenous people to exposing the shadow side of my life in *Confessions of an Economic Hit Man.* The shamans were behind me, urging me to take this leap; they had taught me about the powers of intent, courage, and focused energy, and of how to use them to transform ourselves and our communities.

We have arrived at a time in history when we know that human societies must change. The world we have created is not sustainable. We cannot continue walking a path where so few control so much of the material wealth and so many are relegated to extreme poverty. We cannot continue to glance from side to side as we walk this path and persist in the belief that the things we see—the animals, insects, plants, and all the other non-human entities—are "out there," separate, apart, and independent of us. Our only hope, if we are to survive as a species, is to change. We must transform ourselves; we must change the way we look at the world and our actions. We must revise our concepts of economics, science, and ecology and shapeshift the structures that govern us.

In order to step onto this new path, it is necessary for us to step outside the walls that have limited our ways of thinking, feeling, and living. And this transition must occur on both personal and societal levels.

Most indigenous peoples I have known prophesize that we have entered a time that offers the hope for transformation. Native cultures throughout the Americas, Africa, the Middle East, Asia, and Australia have predicted that the first years of the twenty-first century are a time of great opportunity. They tell us that the potential exists for raising human consciousness to levels never before experienced. They are very clear: higher consciousness is what is required in order for us to transform—and to survive. These prophecies, as well as the individual teachers who shared them with me, prodded me to make that leap of faith and write *Confessions of an Economic Hit Man.*

Alexandra Leclere has taken a similar leap of faith. Her *Seeing the Dead, Talking with Spirits: Shamanic Healing through Contact with the Spirit World* is a book about transformation. Writing it required great courage and a deep belief in our limitless possibilities. One of her goals is to open you to the possibilities for re-creating yourself and, in so doing, conceiving a new and better world. This book tells the story of one woman's heroic journey, the obstacles she encountered, the discoveries she made, and the doors she opened; in opening them, she empowered her core self to walk through those walls and step out onto her new path. Through telling her personal story, Alexandra also inspires the rest of us to follow. She empowers us to take our own heroic journey.

As you read Alexandra's book, I encourage you to move deep inside your own core self. I urge you to explore your dreams and to know that you have the ability to materialize them. And I exhort you to include in your personal dreams the dream that the prophecies will be realized. Together we will heal ourselves and the societies we have created; we will manifest a world our children and grandchildren will be proud to inherit.

JOHN PERKINS, author of
Confessions of an Economic Hit Man and
*Shapeshifting: Shamanic Techniques for
Global and Personal Transformation*

PROLOGUE

A Session

WHEN SHE MADE THE APPOINTMENT over the phone, Beatrice explained that she wanted to find out more about the strange things that were happening to her. She had intuitions and strange dreams. A friend suggested Beatrice call me because of my work with the Spirit World. My initial assessment after our telephone conversation was that Beatrice was "breaking through," becoming aware of her spiritual self.

As I was driving to the appointment, my spirit guide gave me information about what would happen. I "heard" that I had to remove energy from Beatrice's heart that was causing her trouble. She had a heart condition that I was going to heal. I was "told" that I would be given instructions about exactly what to do.

As I drove up to The Oaks, where I had my office, I enjoyed the magnificent view over Long Island Sound. The trees made a collage of greens as the sound of waves softly kissing the shore drifted toward me.

When I walked into my small corner office, the sunlight greeted me through the mansion's windows. One window is round; the other is rectangular. In the middle of the room two chairs faced each other and a small mattress lay on the floor.

Beatrice arrived. She sat in one of the two chairs while I walked around the room with an abalone shell that carried burning sage from South Dakota. In her forties, Beatrice looked very chic, her short hair cut

1

at an attractive angle and her coordinated sweater and skirt both made from cashmere. Her happy smile completed the picture of an upscale woman.

I went to the window and said the Lord's Prayer and then a private prayer to the Creator. My instructions became clearer. Sitting across from Beatrice, I was to reach forward when I got the signal, pull out something from her heart, and throw it out the window.

I calmly put an offering of tobacco on the windowsill. I sat down across from Beatrice, who was chatting cheerfully about nothing important, making small talk. She looked to be the picture of health.

"Why did you want to see me?" I asked quietly.

"I feel so confused. I haven't been very happy. Strange things have been happening. I just haven't been myself for almost two years now. I don't know what to do. Oh, my poor husband, and my children," Beatrice began to sob. Her whole demeanor changed.

"Is there something wrong with your family?" I asked gently.

"No, they're fine! It's me. I don't know what to do," Beatrice continued sobbing.

I "heard" from the Spirit World that I needed to reach forward now, grab the "something" from her chest, and throw it out the window. As Beatrice sobbed harder, I saw a hideous shape form on her chest; it grew larger as she sobbed more.

"Don't be afraid. I'm going to grab something in front of your chest," I said quietly. I reached forward and grabbed the something and threw it out the window.

Beatrice stopped crying.

"How did you know I had developed a heart problem? A cardiologist is monitoring me. Over the past two years it has gotten worse and worse," Beatrice told me.

"I think your heart problem is over now," I informed Beatrice.

Then I invited Beatrice to lie down on the mattress. I sat next to her on the floor. She closed her eyes and relaxed as I guided her meditation. The words that I spoke to her were words that I "heard" and was repeating out loud. I "saw" a six-year-old child.

"Do you see anything in your mind's eye?" I asked Beatrice.

"I see a little girl. I think she's six years old," Beatrice said. She described the little girl I "saw." Guiding Beatrice, I helped her connect with this happy child who was full of love and wonder. This child was her younger self. Beatrice had lost touch with the love in herself for herself and others. Sometime during the guided meditation, when Beatrice was feeling full of love, I saw some dark energies rise off her body. I waved them away from her with my hands. I never touched her.

The session ended, and Beatrice slowly sat up. She felt elated but a bit dizzy. Beatrice left feeling calm and happy.

She called me a couple weeks later. Her regular electrocardiogram showed that her heart condition had stabilized. She was told that she no longer needed to come in every month to have her heart checked. Two months later, when she had her next electrocardiogram, her heart condition had completely disappeared. Beatrice had not done anything about her heart condition except to have a session with me.

1
Yoga in Paris

MOST PEOPLE DON'T THINK OF YOGA when they think of Paris. There are a lot of other "more French" things to do. It was different for me because I lived there. I had married a Frenchman, Georges, and now had three beautiful children under the age of five. Tania, Tristan, and Terence were my life. I didn't do anything but take care of them.

When my former roommate Kim suggested doing some yoga, I immediately agreed. I thought yoga would be a great way to reconnect with myself as a person, to be not just someone's mom. I felt this would be beneficial to the children as well.

We lived in a beautiful, chic area of the city. Sundays, late in the afternoon, I would take the Metro to the Gare du Nord station, then walk down the Boulevard Sebastopol to the Sivananda Yoga Center. It wasn't in the best part of town, but even near the gray train station I enjoyed walking down that tree-lined boulevard. Paris is unique in that every part of it carries charm and beauty. I loved Paris, and still do.

There was no elevator in the yoga center's building, typical of Paris at that time. We had to climb seven flights of stairs and then do yoga! I would meet Kim at the class.

Actually, Kim was far more involved than I was. She was still single and could devote more time to her yoga studies. I just followed along, glad to have some time away from my mothering duties and to pretend that I was single again, even if just for two or three hours.

I loved going to those Sunday-night yoga classes where, among other things, I learned to stand on my head. After the class we would participate in *satsang:* first we sang Sanskrit mantras and then we sat cross-legged on the floor, in front of an altar with a flame burning. We were supposed to stare at the flame in front of the altar for twenty minutes. It was horribly uncomfortable and difficult and, in the beginning, my legs would go numb. My mind was always raging with a million thoughts of things I had to do, but during the satsang I could do nothing. I forced myself to stay there and be still. This is part of the—shall I call it—beauty of meditating in a group.

Several times Vishnu Devananda, the head of the organization, came to Paris and spoke to us. We went on a yoga retreat with him in the French countryside. It was magnificent to get up at six in the morning and meditate; quite a change from being up all night with a baby! On returning to Paris we were given our own personal mantras at an initiation ceremony. This all seemed to be lots of fun compared to dealing with three demanding children, so I participated enthusiastically.

A couple of days after I got my mantra I was having trouble remembering exactly what it was. For me this whole experience was fun, therefore I didn't take it very seriously. However, one night Sivananda, the revered founder of the Sivananda organization, came to me in a dream. I can still visualize his face as he spoke to me in that dream. He told me how to say the mantra correctly and reminded me that it was a very powerful tool that I had to use properly. I never forgot my mantra again, and I began to look upon the whole yoga experience as something much more profound.

I continued doing the meditation at the center in Paris and it became increasingly enjoyable. It was my time to "do nothing," a rare and beautiful moment for a mother. And yet, as I began to take the practice more seriously, it turned out to be a bit more than I had bargained for. During meditation I began having out-of-body experiences that frightened me. They caused me to worry about being available for my children. How could I be there for them if I was out of my body? The yoga people told me that I had to follow my path, that my children would be taken care of. This frightened me even more. I prayed to God to let me take care of my babies while still pursuing the meditation. And so it was that, while I continued to meditate, I never left my body again.

Parallel to my yoga practice, my children grew, and I pursued a career in television. I began as a television scriptwriter, working on a messy table with my children jumping all around me. As a freelance writer, I never wanted to refuse a job, and it seemed that I would always get the most work during school holidays. I nevertheless persevered until I realized one day that someone was changing the words of my scripts.

When I discovered that the producer is the one who gets the last word regarding script changes (yes, some directors will take issue with this, but hey, it's the producer who pays and therefore it's the producer who gets "final cut"), I decided I wanted to become a producer myself. That way, no one would change my scripts.

Meanwhile, I made some contacts internationally, and I was asked to represent companies selling television programs to France. I never really enjoyed distribution, but it was a lucrative business, and it supported my production work.

Thanks to my regular meditation and my mantra, I eventually opened my own company, AOM International, Inc. I always repeated my mantra before any and all business meetings, which were rapidly becoming an integral part of my job.

The first time I had an important meeting with a French television network executive, I was a basket case. In the morning I tearfully explained to my husband how hard it was for me to go see this executive because I needed to get the rights for several programs, and there was absolutely no reason I should get them. I felt like an orchid with no roots, just hanging on a tree branch; I had no large company to back me up.

In the waiting room outside the executive's office I repeated my mantra silently, over and over again. The moment to meet the executive arrived. I was calm, if not very confident. To my great surprise, the executive had covered her desk with orchids. I couldn't believe that someone in an office would have so many orchids! I understood the wink of destiny, *le clin d'oeil du destin*, as the French would say. My courage in place, I made my pitch.

Needless to say, I got the rights to the programs I wanted, and from that moment on my company grew. My children were now old enough for me to feel comfortable about leaving them with a nanny, and soon I was busy traveling around the globe selling television shows.

THE JET-SET LIFE

It was another perfect day in Monte Carlo, and I was staying at the magnificent Ermitage Hotel. Its Old World opulence and royal decor made me feel like a queen. It didn't matter to me that I was there on business as part of a television market. My room looked like it could have been in my favorite part of the Louvre: the area where period rooms are reconstructed, complete with the appropriate furniture. I rolled over in my comfortable bed and snuggled deeper under the down quilt. I could have stayed there forever, but when the phone rang again and again, I knew I had to answer it.

"Il est six heures et demi, madame. C'est votre reveil," a gentle male voice intoned. He was giving me my 6:30 A.M. wake-up call.

"Ah, oui. Merci. En fait, vous pourriez m'envoyer un portier d'ici une demi-heure. Malheureusement je dois partir aujourd'hui," I sleepily replied. "Please send me a porter in half an hour. Unfortunately I must leave today."

"Biensûr, Madame," the voice agreed. "Of course."

I would now have to get up, get washed and dressed, *and* pack my suitcase before the porter arrived. I was exhausted and decided to give myself five more minutes of heaven, dozing peacefully in bed. Breakfast would just have to wait until I arrived at the airport in Nice. Anyway, the delicious dinner that had ended way too late the previous night, as all Mediterranean meals do, would keep me hunger-free for a while.

Half an hour later I heard crisp knocking at my door. Frantically I looked at the beautiful gilt clock. Seven! Oh, no! I had to get to the heliport to catch a flight to Nice to then catch a flight to Paris, to then catch a flight to New York! I sprang into action and ran to the door.

"Oh, je suis désolée, Monsieur. Je me suis endormie." I explained to the porter that I had fallen asleep as I ran to my suitcase to begin packing it.

"Ne vous inquiétez pas, Madame," he said. *"Si vous voulez bien, vous pourriez aller vous préparer. Je vais m'occuper de tout."* He assured me that I could just get ready in the bathroom and he would take care of all the rest, including the packing.

Now that's real service! I thought, as I grabbed a tailored suit and raced to the bathroom. I looked at myself in the mirror. A tall, thin, attractive, blond, blue-eyed young woman looked back at me. *Hmm,* I thought. *Even exhausted I don't really look my age.* And despite that incredible meal the night before, I still fit in my suit. *Why do the Monagasque chefs love cream sauces so much? And why can't I resist them?* I wondered. By the time I came out of the bathroom my suitcase was packed and ready to go. The porter and I went down to the lobby where I spent exactly two seconds checking out. With warm smiles wishing me "bon voyage" I hurried out the door to the waiting taxi. The driver already knew where I was going.

In record time we made it to the Monaco heliport. All the passengers—big-deal television executives—were already on board. The hotel had called and managed to delay the helicopter—for me! As I was climbing into the helicopter I overheard one of the businessmen muttering, "Who is this person we're waiting for? I'm going to miss *my* flight."

At that moment I really felt that I had "arrived." I had become one of the important few for whom helicopters were held; even more important than those important businessmen whose company I was among. I felt like a bona fide member of the jet set.

There was definitely an attractive side to the globetrotting business of television production and distribution. I loved traveling and enjoyed dressing up in nice clothes and going to cocktail parties and dinners with interesting people, including heads of state.

It seemed that anyone who worked in the entertainment business was some sort of amusing character or other, and that contributed to the glamorous fun of all it all. There were also the fabulous meals in all the world's best restaurants, not to mention the best hotels. For my distribution business, I had to go to conventions in Cannes, London, San Francisco, Paris, New Orleans, New York, Las Vegas . . . Poor me!

I no longer had the time to write scripts—or produce anything! My job suddenly became all about distribution, as it became increasingly clear that my responsibility was to enable the distribution, which would enable the production, which would enable the writing that I had wanted to do in the first place! It ended up that I wasn't doing what I truly loved: writing. But it sure proved to be fun traveling around the way I did.

My world changed when my husband, Georges, took a job in New York. Moving from Europe back to the States didn't seem like a big change at the time because we would be leaving for only two years; we collectively decided to do it. But now that I had finally gotten my television production and distribution company up and running full throttle in Paris, I wasn't about to drop my carefully developed European base. I figured I could just commute back and forth between America and Europe. I actually believed that I could spend a lot of time with my husband and kids in the States and pop over to Paris occasionally to check in on my business.

Once this plan went into effect, however, I found I was completely unprepared for the misery that I experienced when in Paris. (Mother hen that I am, I should have realized that this might happen.) The romantic notion of living on both sides of the "big pond" became completely lost in what can only best be described as my sorrow of loneliness.

When by myself in Paris on business, I avoided our old friends, because being with them and their children made me feel even more desolate. I hadn't spent much time cultivating an active social life on my own; I had spent all my time working or with my family, with the end result being that it now seemed that my job had total control of me.

On top of that, I had to be in Paris more than I had anticipated. To buy more time in the States, I worked Saturdays in my Champs Elysées office until two o'clock in the morning. Sundays would also find me at my desk. To add a little spice to it all, terrorists were leaving bombs in various places along the Champs Elysées. The terrorist bombs didn't worry me, because I was then, and remain today, fatalistic about death. One day in Paris I walked through a shopping area just twenty minutes before a bomb exploded and killed two people. If I had been killed in that explosion, that would mean it had been my time to go.

Georges never told the kids when I was flying home, because he didn't want the children to be alarmed if I missed a flight. One day, upon my arrival in New York, I went to pick up my kids at school. I remember walking into the classroom and seeing Terence, age seven, standing alone next to the window waiting for our nanny to pick him up. He turned around and looked at me before turning back to the window and mumbling to himself, "It looks like Mommy. I must be dreaming." Then he shyly turned around to look at me more closely before running into my open arms. That did it for me. I thought that my own child hadn't recognized me! I decided then and there to stop my long-distance life.

But changing my life was not so simple. I opened a branch office in New York, but with my main office in Paris, I just ended up having more work. It seemed that I was single-handedly supporting two offices full of employees who were too dependent on me. I wasn't even writing, which was what I really enjoyed. Something had to give!

God decided to help me get my priorities straight. I got pregnant. I decided to have that baby, my fourth, and as a result, my life was forced to change. Baby-in-belly and I traveled happily together for a few months until my doctor said, "No more airplanes."

LIFE IN NEW YORK

I phased out the distribution part of my business and closed my company in Paris. With baby at my breast, I kept my small New York company semiactive. The two years that our family had planned to stay in the States turned into eight. These were years of putting Georges and the children first and squeezing my business life into narrow margins around their schedules.

In the midst of my hectic suburban-soccer-mom life, sandwiching my production work in between chauffeuring children, I began to feel exhausted. Yet I also realized I was attempting to do too much. Had it not been accompanied by severe menstrual bleeding, I wouldn't have given the exhaustion a second thought. The bleeding became such a nuisance that I finally saw a gynecologist.

I sat on the examining table, my legs mercifully out of those awful stirrups, looking at the doctor who had just examined me.

"You better think about this surgery. I put people in the hospital with higher iron counts than you. Hey, you don't want to drop dead in the street one day, do you?" The doctor smiled at me.

"I just don't like the idea of a hysterectomy," I told her. "It's a major surgery that will change my life."

"No it won't. You don't want any more children, right?" she cheerfully replied.

"No. I already have four," I answered cautiously.

"There you go. What else do you need a uterus for? If you really want, I could leave your ovaries in, but I'd rather take them out too, while I'm at it," the gynecologist added. "Remember, you don't want to drop dead in the street."

"Okay. I'll consider it," I lied, thinking I would never set foot in this doctor's office again. I went back to my home and into my office. "Drop dead, indeed. Over my dead body," I joked to myself. Although the bleeding was severely annoying, I reasoned that I would just have to put up with it a little longer. I would just have to remember not to schedule anything the second day of my period, or the third for that matter. Those were my Niagara Falls days.

"I can handle it," I assured myself, as I tried to concentrate on my work.

I called Sarah at the network that was considering my cartoon series. After several meetings with her and much talk, it seemed like they were interested in my proposal. Sarah was going to present it officially at their next development meeting. I was eager for some good news.

"Hi, Sarah? It's Alexandra. How are you?"

"Hi, Alexandra. I'm fine. Things are really busy here. Sorry I didn't get back to you. I was meaning to call you," she apologized.

Liar, I thought. She never called me back. I always had to do the calling.

"No problem," I answered her cheerfully. "Did you have that development meeting you were expecting to have?" I asked hopefully.

"Yes. Everyone loves your project. The concept is terrific. There are a couple of suggestions that people made about developing it a bit," Sarah answered.

I was flooded with joy. The light was finally shining down on me. My luck was in the process of changing for the better, now and forever. Hallelujah!

"Great! I'm so glad they liked it. Sure, changes are fine. What do they want?" I asked.

"I wrote down what they said, and I can send you a copy of that. You'll have plenty of time to develop it because we don't have any funding to produce the series right now. You know we are working on another project that is really utilizing all of our resources at the moment," Sarah explained.

"Oh, sure. I understand. But the development will be funded, right?"

"No, we're really strapped for funds right now. But if you develop this on your own and incorporate our suggestions, your project will have a much better shot at our next development meeting, when we're done with the big production we're working on right now," Sarah said.

"When will you be in a position to do something on my series?" I asked with trepidation.

"Oh, I'd say in about a year from now. If you could contact me then . . ." Sarah continued talking but I wasn't listening anymore. I felt shot through the heart! A year from now! And then they would consider it! Finally, mercifully, the conversation ended.

After I hung up the phone I began to look through the papers jumbled on my desk, trying to find another project to focus on. *Okay. This project goes on the back burner. Hmm, looks like I can't take this other one here any further right now. How many rejections can one television project get? A heck of a lot,* I concluded. *I wonder why they don't give out awards for the largest number of rejections a project can get. I'd probably win that one,* I thought ruefully.

I looked in the mirror. A tall, exhausted, moderately out-of-shape, middle-aged blonde looked back at me. My blue eyes were barely visible under my tired lids. I was grateful that camera phones didn't exist, that Sarah hadn't been able to see me. I was dressed for soccer-mom duty and chauffeur service. Not that long ago I had had a great figure and looked significantly younger than my chronological age.

What has happened to me? I wondered. *Did someone beat me with an aging stick? Maybe an ugly stick, too.*

In all honesty I still didn't really look my age, but I felt it. I didn't even consider myself a true television producer because I wasn't producing *anything*. I felt stagnant and frustrated because I couldn't get a production beyond the initial planning stages. Every topic I chose seemed to go nowhere. My one great hope was this animated series that I had worked so hard on, developing the characters and even getting an artist to draw them. That series had just gone into deep freeze with one phone call. I had shopped it around, and Sarah was my last resort. Telling me to develop it on my own for a year was a nice way of saying "no" in television language.

And yet, once again the universe smiled on me. Out of the blue, someone presented me with a contract to develop a prime-time television series. I couldn't believe it! This was a once-in-a-lifetime opportunity that

I couldn't pass up. I hired the best attorney to negotiate my position in the production as well as my remuneration. It was going to be incredible! Granted, it was still in project form, but I was going to be a major part of it and would have been paid good money. I was tremendously happy that this incredible windfall had come my way. But just when the contract was about to be signed, something happened. Oh, cruel fate!

Georges got a job offer he felt he couldn't refuse; the job was based in London. To me, at the time, it seemed as though my first responsibilities were to my husband and family. The memories of the loneliness I had experienced when commuting to Paris were too vivid. I had to support this new move. I passed on the contract. I was London bound.

PREPARING FOR LONDON

The whole idea of moving to England made me shudder. Georges had announced this job possibility, and then—one-two-three—he had signed the contract and gone off to London, leaving me to feel as if I was peripheral to this important relocation decision.

My gut told me it was a bad idea. I loved London, and I had loved living in Europe for seventeen years. I just felt that this was a bad career move for my husband, never mind the personal sacrifices I would have to endure.

Georges expected me to tag along, and that is what I dutifully did. In my opinion, life sucked! In the flurry of all the preparation for the move, I didn't have time to think about the recommended hysterectomy; I was too busy taking care of other people's lives and needs. On top of the preparations at home, it was my responsibility to spend time in London *before* the move, finding schools for the children and a place for us to live. It's not surprising that under these conditions I began to suffer from migraine headaches.

We also had made the decision to rent, rather than sell, our house in the States, and that proved to be an unusual challenge. Our house was a terrible mess and had to be thoroughly cleaned. My absences to London were covered by babysitters who made sure that the children were well. But the house became a disaster area as a result of my being away.

When it came time to have our "open house" I did the best I could, and then frantically prayed that the house would be rented. As luck would have it, some people did decide to rent our house. Hallelujah!

We took the house off the market. Then, after believing for months that the house was rented, the offer was withdrawn. The real-estate agent had never gotten around to doing the paperwork, and our future tenants had found something else. Once again I was busy cleaning and praying, "Please, God, have somebody rent our house!" It was harder to find tenants at this point, because the busy house-renting season in Westchester County, New York, was over. But we finally found some new tenants, and the papers were signed. Once more I rejoiced.

On the day before we were supposed to move, we had planned a good-bye party: the movers were scheduled to arrive the following day, and the tenants were due to move in in two weeks' time. The morning of the party, my husband flew in from England. As I drove him home from the airport I told him about the guests who were coming to the party.

"Everyone we invited is coming! Isn't it wonderful to see how many good friends we have? They're all planning to visit us in London. I actually think they're all coming because they want a place to stay! I got the extra tables delivered yesterday from the catering place. They were really accommodating this time. I also have lots of food. The weather looks like it will cooperate for once. People will start arriving around one o'clock. By the way, did you remember to pick up the liquor at the duty-free store? If you didn't, I think we'll have enough anyway. You look really exhausted! Are you feeling OK? Maybe you should take a nap so you'll be in good shape for the party. And don't forget the movers who are arriving at eight tomorrow morning. We'll all need to be in good shape for that!" I chattered happily on.

"Something happened," Georges muttered.

"Something happened on the flight?" I inquired.

"No, at work," Georges replied.

"Things haven't gotten better, huh? Well, hopefully everything will work out fine when we're all together in London," I said cheerfully.

"We're not going," Georges announced.

"We're not going?" I asked.

"To London," Georges responded flatly.

"We're not moving to London?"

"No," Georges answered.

"What happened?" I demanded.

"I quit my job. It was so bad that I thought it was better to quit it now before you and the kids moved to London. It would be harder then. I didn't want us all to get stuck there," Georges answered.

"When did you do this? I talked to you on the phone last night! You didn't tell me anything then!" I wailed.

"I wanted to tell you this in person," Georges told me as we drove into our driveway. Two hours later our first guests arrived.

Our house was rented, it was too late for me to take advantage of that fabulous career offer, *and* Georges was unemployed! To top things off, our children, who had originally hated the idea of moving to London, were miserably depressed when they found out we weren't moving after all. I had resigned from all the positions I had in volunteer organizations. I had been honored and thanked, and it would have been embarrassing for me to stay on after that.

I thought that our farewell party would be sad, but I had no idea that it would be *this bad*. Georges immediately flew back to London to wrap things up there. I had to focus my energy on finding a place for us to live.

Now that we were not moving, I decided to pray fervently to get our house back! If only I had shown more faith that things would work out for the best, I wouldn't have been so stressed. It got me thinking about the bigger picture. After conferring with a lawyer and another real-estate agent, I made sure our would-be tenants found a new place, and we were able to remain in our home.

Around that time someone e-mailed me a story entitled "The Burning Hut." It struck a nerve. In the story, a shipwrecked man on a tiny island scavenges what he can to scratch out an existence. Painfully he builds a miserable hut where he sleeps and keeps whatever he has managed to gather. One day a bolt of lightning comes down and sets his hut on fire. Unable to do anything, the man calls out to God.

"God, why are you doing this to me? What little I had was in that hut!" he cries. Two days later a ship appears. The man is saved.

"How did you find me?" the shipwrecked man asks.

"We saw some smoke," the captain answers.

A little faith can go a long way. It's just so hard to remember that when you're in a crisis.

In the middle of all this back-and-forth turmoil, I still had problems with hemorrhaging. But, more than ever, the timing was wrong for a hysterectomy. I felt like a trapped rat. I probably would have had high blood pressure if I had had enough blood.

2
Beginning My Journey

MY BODY DIDN'T AGREE WITH MY PRIORITIES regarding a hysterectomy. I kept hemorrhaging and getting weaker. In desperation, I went to see two other gynecologists. The second one was an unpleasant replay of the first. The third one I saw was admired because he only recommended surgery as an absolute last resort. He received me the same day I called for an appointment. After a thorough examination, which included a sonogram, he explained that I had two fibroids, and they were placed in such a way that only a hysterectomy would take care of the hemorrhaging they caused.

I was back to square one. *There must be another way*, I thought as I promised the doctor to schedule the hysterectomy soon. This time, I really believed I had to do it.

There must be another way, I kept thinking. I remembered Dr. Bernie Siegel. After my father had died of cancer ten years prior, someone gave me Siegel's book *Love, Medicine, & Miracles*. I was intrigued and went to some of his workshops. There I witnessed the benefits of guided meditation. Now, years later, I wanted to use that tool. Even though suburban motherhood had usurped my meditation practice, I still remembered the benefits I had enjoyed in Paris, and then later as a traveling businesswoman. Like riding a bicycle, I hoped it was something that one didn't forget how to do.

MEDITATION IN NEW YORK

At home, full of good intentions to "pray away" my fibroids, I sat down crossed-legged and stared at the candle flame flickering in front of me. I was so uncomfortable that I had to use a timer to make sure I didn't jump up after five minutes. I still managed to find a multitude of reasons to interrupt my meditation. Nevertheless, I was determined to *make this work*. I reminded myself that at Dr. Bernie Siegel's workshop I had met people who had healed themselves of cancer this way. What were a couple of puny fibroids compared to that?

Gradually I built my meditation practice up to twenty minutes a day, always timing myself. I began my meditation by repeating the mantra I had been given by Vishnu Devananda while practicing Sivananda Yoga in Paris. After a while, I would close my eyes and imagine the fibroid on one side of my uterus disappearing. I would imagine it being washed away, layer by layer, and then eliminated through my urine. I was sure it was getting smaller and smaller. Day after day I continued my meditation. After a while I was sure that one fibroid was gone, because my hemorrhaging had abated.

A true television producer loves to be in production. We live for the excitement of pulling it all together. The lights, the cameras, the actors — they are all pure adrenaline flowing through our veins. I didn't think I could do a show about meditation, but alternative medicine was something else again. There was more action. I also felt encouraged because I believed I might learn something that would help with my remaining fibroid, and so I decided to develop a talk show about alternative medicine.

Acupuncture, reflexology, applied kinesiology, and Reiki were all fascinating to me. These approaches to healing needed to be brought to the world, and I wanted to be the person to do it. I decided to make a pilot. I was wondering whom to cast as the female lead when I serendipitously met Susan Bruin, an actress and a healer, at a cocktail party. She knew all about this stuff. It seemed like a good omen that the talk show's perfect host should just randomly appear at a social function. Maybe life was getting better, I hoped.

As Susan's co-host I cast my son Terence, who is a professional actor. His girlfriend, Ellen, also a professional actor, was already interested in yoga and loved the idea of the series. Terence also seemed to enjoy learning about alternative medicine. My son Tristan, a professional television technician, helped with the filming and editing, while daughters Tania and Talia became my assistants. Georges was the stage manager. I called my series *Around the Corner*, because I believed that help was always just around the corner.

Writing and producing *Around the Corner* was great fun. After hours of editing, I screened the whole show and realized how bad it really was. I decided to use it as a practice run. I was undaunted as I produced a pilot for a redesigned series.

The new pilot, *Heavy Breathing*, was good. It took a completely different approach to alternative medicine that incorporated humor. I tried to market it. I even went to the National Association of Television Program Executives, the big television market, trying to find some outlet for it. There was none to be found. In retrospect, I think the show was ahead of its time.

While I was busy making my two pilots, I let my husband use my company as a structure within which he could do business as a consultant. When he changed my logo without conferring with me, I knew we were having communication difficulties. I had hired a professional team in Paris to design my logo, which I loved. Now, in one swift move, it had been replaced, and by the time I saw the new one, it was too late to do anything about it. Obediently I changed all my letterhead paper, but my heart wasn't in it.

There were other things that Georges presented to me as faits accomplis, and I blindly agreed to sign rather than rock the boat. Somehow facades were so important. I felt that I had lost my company, and after the rejection of my pilots I went into a tailspin.

Although my hemorrhaging had abated somewhat while I was working on the talk shows, it now came back with a vengeance. I kept remembering the gynecologist who warned me that I might drop dead in the street. I was exhausted, depressed, and had no will to fight anything anymore.

Reluctantly I scheduled a hysterectomy for a couple of months in the future. I didn't care about mutilating my body, or the hormone imbalance I would have to endure after the surgery, or all the other reasons why this surgery was questionable. I would have "gone under the knife" right away, but my son was graduating from college soon, and I didn't want to be laid up or out of commission.

I never shared my health condition with anyone but my husband. He didn't seem to know what to do with the information and offered no opinion. I chose to ignore it also, until the date of the surgery.

A DOOR CLOSES; A WINDOW OPENS

In the course of producing *Around the Corner*, Susan had mentioned a friend of hers who was a "healer's healer." I was intrigued by the concept of a powerful healer. According to Susan, this woman seemed to have magical powers. Never admitting to myself that I was on the brink of physical collapse and that I had scheduled surgery for a major operation, I made an appointment to see Penney Leyshon about my migraine headaches, which had reached epic proportions.

I had mixed emotions as I approached her typical Upper West Side building for our meeting. Full of anticipation and ready for change, I was nevertheless so depleted and depressed that I had to drag myself up the four flights of stairs to her apartment. I felt the excitement and fear of embarking on a new adventure. I took a deep breath, rang the bell, and waited on the dark landing outside her door. Light flooded over me as Penney opened her door. From the window behind, sunlight lit up her curly blond hair like a little halo around her head. She peered at me with her crystal-clear blue eyes as she invited me in. I felt that I had known her my entire life.

As I entered, I looked around Penney's apartment. The walls were covered with beautiful, colorful abstract paintings and collages. They seemed to vibrate with life.

"These paintings are incredible," I exclaimed.

"That's my work," Penney said. "They're full of energy and angels."

"Angels," I mumbled. I was enchanted. "Well, umm, as I told you over the phone, I have horrible migraine headaches. In fact, just this past week

I had one every day, and the prescription medicine I take for them didn't help. They seem to be worse than ever and have become unbearable." I never mentioned my fibroids or my anemia.

"It happens sometimes that my client's problems get worse before they arrive here. Often a healing starts as soon as an appointment is made. Take off your shoes, belt, and watch, and go into the next room and lie on the mattress. I'll be right in," Penney smiled.

As I lay alone on the mattress in Penney's healing room, I suddenly felt completely defeated and hopeless. My enthusiasm about meeting this super-healer was gone, and I felt like a heap of rubble. Although I hadn't been suffering any pain when I arrived, now my head hurt unbearably, and I was miserable. Something drew my attention to the bright light coming in through the small window behind me. Painfully, I propped myself up on an elbow and turned to look at it. In a pathetic voice I whispered a prayer to the light: "I don't know what's going on, but all I really want to do is help people." Feeling a little better, I lay down again.

A little while later Penney came in and sat on the floor next to me. First she asked me to lie face down; later I turned to lie on my back. Occasionally Penney told me to shake my hands and my feet, or she wiped something away from some part of my body. Sometimes she asked me to breathe deeply. Penney occasionally put her hand on me gently and then removed it. The whole session lasted twenty minutes.

"Okay. That'll do it," Penney whispered. "You can get up slowly when you're ready. You might feel a little dizzy."

I did feel light-headed as I got up. I walked out of the healing room and sat down to put on my shoes. Gradually I began to feel euphoric. My headache was gone.

"Wow. I feel wonderful," I said to Penney.

As I left she smiled and said, "Be sure to drink lots of water. You've begun a purification process."

I felt terrific. I was so energized I couldn't sleep for the first two nights. I watched several movies a night because of this insomnia. On the third night I realized that I was actually staying awake because I was afraid of facing something in my sleep. Something was coming up. I was petrified!

Slowly the terror took form. Years ago Dr. Bernie Siegel had led a guided meditation to our most frightening place. For me it was outside the door of a school building when I was about seven years old. I don't know what was inside, but it terrified me. Now that horrible fear had returned; I was consumed by terror. These strange emotions seemed unfounded, but they were still overwhelming. I didn't understand what was happening.

I woke my husband. "Georges, wake up. I don't know what's going on, but I'm afraid." He watched with concern as a tremendous feeling of grief engulfed me, and I began to sob uncontrollably.

"I've never seen you cry like this before. What's wrong?" Georges asked with alarm.

"I don't know," I sobbed. I didn't want to be hugged, and I didn't know why I was upset. I just kept trembling with heartfelt grief. Helplessly Georges watched me weep for no apparent reason.

After a while it was over. I didn't know what had happened, but something tremendously heartbreaking and dreadful left me that night. A great weight was lifted. From that moment on I began to really care about being alive again. I wanted to take care of myself.

It's hard to see the forest for the trees, and it took me a while to realize that Penney might be able to heal me of my fibroid condition. As I struggled with a "Niagara Falls day" I called Penney to set up an appointment specifically for my fibroid. While she was tentative about being able to heal my physical condition, I was absolutely certain that she could.

"We'll see what happens," Penney agreed.

Once again I climbed the four flights of stairs to her apartment. Excitedly I walked in to be healed for once and for all of this problem. Penney greeted me warmly and conducted this second session pretty much as she had the first one.

"You might have one last major hemorrhaging, but then it'll be over," Penney told me during the session. I left feeling euphoric, and within two months my symptoms had disappeared. I no longer had to schedule my life around my period. I could tell that my iron levels were up because I had so much more zip. Rather than confirm the date for my surgery, I cancelled it. A year later the gynecologist who was supposed to perform the operation reluctantly confirmed that I no longer needed it. He didn't understand how going to a healer could help, but he had to recognize that my iron level was normal, obviating the need for surgery.

I was back in business again. My son graduated from college. In the fall I was ready to start a new life. My new mission was to produce a documentary about Penney, and about healers in general. There are so many women like me who were subjecting themselves to potentially unnecessary hysterectomies simply because they weren't fortunate enough to know any healers. And what about other surgeries? I wondered if anyone could be healed of anything by a healer. Who are these healers? Where do they come from? How does this kind of healing work? I wanted to learn it all and bring it to the world. Penney prefers to call herself a facilitator because, like most healers, she doesn't believe she effectuates the healing. She feels that the healing comes from God, and she simply facilitates it. The working title of my show was *Healers: Fact or Fiction*. I was going to prove to the world that healers were definitely an important resource for healing.

I expected to learn a great deal from my research for this show. I never expected to become a healer myself.

A PAST LIFE

I continued to have sessions with Penney every few weeks. I did this because I enjoyed seeing her, and I always left feeling good. I'm sure many things happened that I didn't really notice, shifts that just happened gradually. One visit did have a surprising effect. It was supposed to help me be more effective in realizing my television projects. Because Penney is so generous, the session lasted well over an hour.

According to Penney, that is why it had such an unusual effect on me. The day after the session I was taking my usual route home, driving by an elementary school. A school bus drove up in the opposite direction and stopped just as I was passing it. Once it passed my car, it put a stop sign out. Before I knew it, a siren had gone off, and I was being pursued by a police car. I stopped right away, confused. *Why am I being stopped like this?* I wondered. *I did nothing wrong.* In my rearview mirror I watched the policeman walk up.

"License and registration," he demanded.

"What did I do, officer?" I inquired sweetly as I got out the papers for him.

"Didn't you see that stopped school bus?" he answered brusquely as he walked off.

Yes, I saw the bus, I thought to myself. *I saw it stop after I was past it. What is this cop talking about?*

When the policeman returned I said, "The bus wasn't stopped when I passed it."

"Yes, it was. I saw it," he answered curtly.

"I swear it was still moving as I passed it. Maybe you looked up and saw it after I was already past," I offered.

"No, I know what I saw," he said as he handed me a ticket.

All of sudden I was overcome with wild emotions. "But I didn't do it!" I insisted as I began to cry. I was horrified that I was crying in front of this policeman, but I couldn't stop. Unimpressed, he waved the ticket in front of me.

"This is horrible! I can't believe this! It's not right!" I began to obsess as I tearfully took the ticket.

The policeman looked at me with concern. "It's only a ticket, lady," he said. "It's not so bad."

As I drove off I was inconsolable. I began to sob and berate myself for having done something so wrong and so bad. But what had I done? Nothing! When I got home I was in such emotional pain I wanted to hurt myself physically to ease the searing ache. On the one hand I knew that my reaction was absurd, but on the other I couldn't control my emotions. I thought I had gone insane. My emotions were totally inappropriate for a traffic ticket! I didn't know what to do or where to turn. As a last resort I reached for the Bible and randomly chose a passage. It spoke of wealth. That made me remember the business session I had just had with Penney. According to her, my attitude toward wealth was preventing me from succeeding. *Maybe all this has something to do with my session with Penney,* I thought. But what would a random traffic ticket have to do with my attitude toward wealth? And why was I falling apart like this? I called Penney. Fortunately she answered the phone.

"It sounds like a past-life experience coming up," Penney said.

"A past-life experience?" I echoed. I knew that a past-life experience was an event in a previous life. And while I believed that it was possible to have lived before, I never thought *I* could have a past-life experience, not to mention a spontaneous one.

"Yes, it's something you've lived through before that you need to get rid of now," Penney explained.

"What can I do?" I implored Penney. "I feel horrible. I'm in so much pain. It's so bad, I can't stand it! It hurts so bad I want to feel physical pain instead."

"Take a bath or drink a lot of water. You live near the shore, right? You could go for a walk along the water's edge. That would help. You'll get over it," Penney assured me.

I hung up feeling as though I had just seen the light at the end of the tunnel. It felt good to know that I wasn't crazy and that this experience would end. But I still felt so miserable! By now I was sobbing.

Outside the rain was falling hard. I drank some water and thought about taking a bath, but I knew I had to get outside. I covered up and braved the rain. The wind blew in strong gusts and the waves crashed violently against the shoreline as I fought to move forward. I was grateful for the heavy drops of rain falling hard on my face. They would mask my tears. To my great surprise, a story unfolded in my mind. It came complete with colorful images and vibrant pain.

It was the Middle Ages. I was a queen in beautiful Kidwelly Castle in Wales. I was left alone with my beloved son to defend my castle. Rather than retreat with everyone, I insisted that my son stay with me to defend the castle, because I would not give it up. We both shared a deep love for our home. The barbarians arrived and broke down the gate. They defeated us and took over the castle. There was unspeakable carnage. Then, in front of me, they held my son and poked out his eyes so he would never see this castle again. Reliving this horror made me feel all the emotions of that moment. I was overcome by grief and guilt. What had I done to my son? All this suffering had been caused because I had valued material possessions more than human life. To this end I had put my son's life at risk.

As I walked through the pouring rain, I began to gain more perspective and the emotions became less intense, more like those belonging to another person. By the time I got home I had managed to mentally distance myself from the horrifying grief that had besieged me. As I calmed down, I began to reflect on the whole story of Kidwelly Castle.

I had visited the castle just two years before with my husband and daughter. At the time I had felt tremendously close to it. The castle consisted of broken walls and some odd stairs here and there; grass grew in and around the whole thing. I was surprised that I didn't need the visitors' map to know what all the rooms were, but I chalked it up to having a very good sense of orientation. When I read the story of Kidwelly's queen, I felt an emotional bond with her, and I understood her zeal to defend her home at any cost. This, too, was easy to dismiss as just random empathy.

Another curious thing related to my son Terence. From birth he had been obsessed with castles, building them at every opportunity. It was more than a simple interest; it was a burning passion. His fixation now made sense in the context of this past-life memory. He was ready to do anything to provide a castle for his mother. And something else that seemed bizarre and inexplicable now seemed to have an explanation. He would taunt, "Poke my eyes out. Poke my eyes out." It always gave me the chills, but he wouldn't stop it.

All of this confirmed the reality of the past life I had just experienced. It was my first past-life regression. It was horribly painful, but it certainly explained why I would be fearful of being wealthy in this life and attaching myself to signs of material gain. It had cost me my son's eyesight in the past, as well as my own life, and I had learned that that was too high a price to pay. Releasing this past-life block would free me from the barrier that prevented me from enjoying wealth in any form.

However, there was one piece of this puzzle that didn't fit. Why would a traffic ticket trigger a past-life regression to a castle in Wales? According to Penney, I was not only facing the reason for my fear of wealth, but I was also facing being unjustly accused. That's why I had been so desperate to avoid the ticket. In that same past life I had been unfairly divested of my rights by an intruder. Penney thought that it was possible that the policeman had been the leader of the Kidwelly Castle attackers so many years ago. Now I needed to exonerate myself from this current travesty of justice to vindicate that past-life experience.

But where was Perry Mason when I needed him? Anyway, getting a lawyer didn't make sense to me. I decided to defend myself. After a couple of court date postponements due to my travel schedule, I finally had to face the music. At last I was going to trial to contest the unfair ticket.

I was obsessed with proving my innocence. It seemed as though exonerating myself from these charges would free me from my whole life's experience of injustices, not just the Kidwelly Castle atrocity but so many more instances when I had been victimized. If I could overturn this ticket, I would be a victim no more!

The cards were stacked against me. Passing a school bus is considered a serious offense, especially in this school-oriented community. The punishment usually included points against the driver's license plus a hefty fine. But I didn't care about all that. It was the principle that counted.

The day of reckoning arrived. I dressed in a sober, attorney-like way and brought cutouts and illustrations of what had actually happened. The judge scheduled for that day had never overturned a ticket for that particular violation. My only hope was that the ticketing officer wouldn't show up because the judge traditionally sided with the police officer involved. As I sat waiting I looked around for that cop. He wasn't there. Then, right before my name was called, he came in. My chances of proving my innocence were zero. Shaking internally, I came forward. The prosecuting attorney took me aside and spoke to me. I told him I was innocent and showed him my artwork. He seemed unimpressed. I insisted on my innocence. I was a model citizen in our town, and I had a perfect traffic record. The prosecutor spoke to the judge. He spoke to me again. He spoke to the judge once more. The back and forth was endless. Once again, the prosecuting attorney spoke to me gravely as he told me the case had been dismissed.

I had won! Anything was possible. Terence must have benefited from this release in some strange way, too, because afterward he stopped saying "Poke my eyes out" and was no longer obsessed with castles.

3

Meeting Jesus

HEALERS CAN BE SELF-TAUGHT, like Penney. More often they are trained by someone who, like Penney, has discovered a way to heal. These original, natural healers instruct others in their precise techniques. A good example of this is Reiki. The founder of Reiki, Dr. Mikao Usui, wanted to find the way in which holy men from earlier times had healed people. After many years of study, he went to a mountain and fasted for twenty-one days. On the twenty-first day he was shown bubbles of all the colors of the rainbow. In these bubbles were the Reiki symbols, the same symbols found in certain Tibetan writings. Today people are able to take courses and receive certification to become a Reiki Master, allowing them to practice this healing technique on those in need.

Craniosacral, polarity, reflexology, and applied kinesiology therapies are other energy-healing techniques that have a formal certification process for trainees. Some nurses are taught therapeutic touch as part of their medical training. These modalities all work with the energy in the body. And, in most techniques, there is some kind of recognized connection to the Spirit World.

The healing experience varies from one modality to another. Some healers, like Penney, almost never touch the client. Others lay hands on various places on the body, and others do movements similar to massage. I decided to meet as many healers as I could and personally experience what each one did.

My first healer was a craniosacral practitioner named Hilarion Thorneywell. In craniosacral practice, the nervous system is treated as a hydraulic circuit. By applying pressure at different points on the body, the flow of energy is liberated, which allows healing to happen. Hilarion's specialty is removing the trauma that lodges in a person's muscles after automobile accidents. When I was thirteen I was involved in a serious accident. I went over a 135-foot cliff with my parents in our Valiant. My parents were trapped in the car, and I had to scramble out of it and up the cliff in the pouring rain to hail some passersby to save them. We all got out with just a few bruises. It was a miracle. Although I never felt traumatized by this accident and in fact I had almost forgotten it, I thought it would be a good idea to have Hilarion work on me with the intention of removing any residual trauma.

I was feeling happy as I hopped onto Hilarion's massage table, and I felt very relaxed as she began applying pressure to various parts of my body, beginning with my liver, because she could tell that I had a lot of anger stored there. According to her, anger usually settles in the liver.

Gradually I began to feel very mellow. After about thirty minutes Hilarion was standing behind me, and I "saw" Jesus Christ appear next to me, his sacred heart emanating beautiful white light. He seemed to be offering me his heart and the beautiful light. I was overwhelmed. Jesus had long dark hair, a beard and mustache, and was wearing a blue robe over a red tunic. He seemed to be surrounded by white light. The sight of him was so extraordinary that I was speechless. I felt encompassed by his light. My heart seemed to connect with his, and I entered a state of amazing bliss. I was calm and happy. Everything was perfect in the glory of that light.

"Are you all right?" Hilarion questioned me.

"I see Jesus," I whispered. "He's offering me his sacred heart."

"Oh," Hilarion caught her breath. "That's remarkable," she said with feeling.

"Do you see him?" I whispered.

"No, I don't," she answered.

I could say no more. I wanted to stay forever in that beautiful presence of Jesus. It was pure, unconditional love. It seemed as though nothing else existed. Exhausted by the experience, I finally closed my eyes to rest. When I opened them again, Jesus was gone.

I'm not Catholic, so I had no reason to imagine Jesus with his sacred heart. The image I saw wasn't even one that was familiar to me. I was astounded and transformed. The feeling of serenity, love, and well-being was overwhelming. It was beautiful, and all-encompassing.

It was more than two hours after we began the session when Hilarion finally helped me off the massage table. She brought me something to eat and drink.

"Are you sure you're all right?" she asked me gently.

"Yes. It was beautiful," I answered dreamily. "Does this always happen during your sessions?"

"No. In fact, this was a quite unusual session. I've never had anyone experience anything like that before. It's fortunate I didn't have any clients lined up after you. A session usually takes only an hour," Hilarion said with wonder. "Can you walk now?"

"Yes, I'm fine," I wobbled on my legs. "Do you know why I saw Jesus?" I asked.

"No, I don't. But something is happening. You'll have to wait and see." I wandered out in a dream. It felt like I was walking on a cloud.

The next day I went to the library and looked for the image I had seen of Jesus with his sacred heart. I thought perhaps it was a painting I had seen somewhere. Even with the help of the librarian, I couldn't find that picture of Jesus. I tried the Internet, and right away I found the exact image, which I printed out in color. The next time I searched for it on the Internet, it was gone.

I don't know what happened during that session with Hilarion. I do know that something profound and life changing took place. I didn't know how it would manifest itself in my life, but I knew things were going to be different.

4

Visions

IT WAS THE TUESDAY BEFORE THANKSGIVING. My kids were gathering in Westchester for the long weekend. For the first time ever I had agreed that we would go to a friend's house for the big meal.

I returned home after shopping and listened to a phone message from the retirement residence in Ohio where my mother lived, telling me that she might be taken to the hospital. When I called back, Mom was already in the hospital, in intensive care. I knew I had to go to Ohio. The earliest flight I could get was on Thanksgiving Day. Driving on the Wednesday before Thanksgiving, when I'd probably be stuck in traffic much of the way, wasn't an option because it seemed dangerous to attempt alone. I would have to wait for the flight on Thursday. I was grateful that my family wouldn't have to miss my favorite dinner of the year, although I probably would.

THE FIRST HEALING

I caught the flight, dropped my suitcase at the hotel, and went to the hospital. I'm the kind of person who feels uncomfortable around sick people and hates hospitals. *I could never be a doctor or a nurse,* I thought as I walked down the nearly empty hallways to the intensive care unit. It was a large white room with different machines that seemed to be randomly distributed around the room. Everything was sterile and cold and quiet except for small sounds the machines made. There were several beds, some occupied, some empty. I asked the nurse where I could find my mother. She indicated a bed that was farthest away from her, almost hidden in a corner of the room.

I walked up to the bed and saw my mother. Vomit had dried to her chin and sheet. She didn't recognize me. I was shocked. Just a few days earlier she had spoken to me lucidly. Now she didn't even know who I was. This beautiful, intelligent woman who spoke eight languages fluently just three days prior now couldn't say a word. Tears sprang to my eyes as I gently cleaned her chin. I noticed that her arms were tied to the bed. The shock of seeing her in this condition turned into anger. I needed to know what had happened, and I needed to know it right away. I marched back to the nurse.

"What happened to her?" I demanded, trying to keep my anger in check. "Why is she tied up?"

"Let's take a look at her chart," the nurse answered calmly. She slowly looked for Mom's chart and glanced through it. "According to the tests they did it looks as though she didn't have a stroke. I can't really tell what is wrong with her."

Not a stroke, I thought. *Then what's going on? Why doesn't this idiot nurse know more? Who's in charge?*

"Why is she tied up?" I demanded.

"She must have been combative earlier," the nurse answered.

"She seems quiet now. Why don't you untie her?"

"I don't have the authority to do that," she answered vaguely.

As sweetly as I could, considering I felt like punching this perpetrator of my mother's suffering, I asked, "Who do I need to talk to for more information about my mother?"

"You'll have to talk to her doctor. That would be Dr. Chinbauble," the nurse answered slowly as she read Mom's chart.

"How can I reach him?"

"I suggest you call his office tomorrow morning. Find out when he'll next be in, and you can make an appointment to see him. His office is in the building next door," the nurse said helpfully.

"Tomorrow morning? To make an appointment? Where is he right now?" I demanded.

"Oh, you can't reach him now. He's out of town. Just call his office in the morning and you'll find out when he'll be in," the nurse quietly responded.

And while I'm waiting I'll take two aspirins, I thought. *This nurse is like some kind of bad joke.*

"What am I supposed to do right now?" I asked, feeling increasingly desperate.

"You can sit and wait with her," the nurse replied, offering me a chair to take into the room.

I thought, *She expects Mom to die and just wants me to sit here and watch her fade away.* I couldn't do that.

"Why is she tied to the bed?" I demanded again.

"They must have a reason. Probably so she won't fall out of bed or pull out her catheter. It's for her safety," the nurse told me, calmly changing her story.

"I'm here right next to her now, and I'm going to untie her," I declared.

"I suppose it's okay, as long as you're here," the nurse reluctantly agreed.

I returned to my mother and untied her arms. She smiled at me. I wanted to cry and scream and pummel the nurse and everyone else who had put my mother in this horrible situation. I held Mom's hand, and spoke softly to her.

"Hi, Mom. It's me, your daughter Alexandra. I've come to be with you. How do you feel?"

Mom just stared at me blankly.

After a few hours it was getting late and the nurse insisted I leave. I didn't want to, but I was exhausted. I didn't know what to do or where to turn. Mom was now asleep, and I felt useless sitting next to her in that unforgiving ICU. I decided that I had gotten as much information as I could from the nurse about my mother's health. The next step was to track down her doctor to get some action. I would need all my strength for that, which meant I needed to get some sleep myself. I wasn't going to let my mother die, abandoned in a corner of some ICU.

I went back to the hotel and called home. No one answered. I called Penney. No answer. I was on my own. I tried to call home again. Again, no answer. Of course, they were still at Thanksgiving dinner. I thought about food. I remembered that the restaurant in the hotel was serving a special Thanksgiving Day meal. Rather than stay in my dreary room, I ventured downstairs to seek food and company. I found neither. The restaurant was closed. Everything in this small town was closed. The receptionist finally took pity on me and prepared a cold plate that I took up to my room. My cold Thanksgiving dinner was turkey and stuffing and cranberry sauce and even a bit of pumpkin pie. *A veritable feast*, I thought.

Georges called as I entered my room. The family had enjoyed a wonderful Thanksgiving. I felt left out and alone. Quickly I got off the phone. The cold plate didn't look appetizing anymore. I tried to sleep but couldn't; my mind was too busy planning my next move. My instinct was to call Penney and ask her to save my mother, but down deep I knew that wasn't the answer. *What can I do? What can I do?* I asked myself over and over. Sleep wouldn't come, and I began to pray. I prayed with all my heart and soul to God to have mercy and to please save my mother. I prayed that no one should die like that, tied up and abandoned in a hospital room.

Early the next morning I tracked down my mother's doctor. He wasn't pleased to see me. He tried to explain that my mother was simply aging. I wouldn't have any part of it. This was the same doctor who had told me a couple of years ago that she had Alzheimer's disease when, in reality, she had had a chemical imbalance in her system. I badgered the doctor with more questions about the tests he had done and the others he planned to do.

"I don't plan any more tests. She doesn't show any evidence of a stroke, so we can rule that out. There really isn't anything else to do," he told me. I was furious. During the night I had remembered that a few years ago, following surgery for colon cancer, Mom had improved right after the operation but then had become disoriented. A Dr. Newman was in charge of her in the rehabilitation unit of the hospital. She had run some tests and discovered that Mom's calcium level was high. Dr. Newman had ordered a potassium drip, which had made all the difference. In a couple of days Mom was her old self. After that incident I tried to get my mother to change doctors, but she insisted on remaining faithful to Dr. Chinbauble. Now I asked Dr. Chinbauble if he had tried the potassium drip that had once saved my mother from incoherency.

"No, no. It won't make any difference," Dr. Chinbauble told me.

"Why don't you try it?" I insisted.

"Look, I'm her doctor, and I know what to prescribe for her. A potassium drip won't make any difference," he repeated.

"You won't know if you don't try it," I implored.

Dr. Chinbauble was losing patience with me. In order to get rid of me he agreed to review her chart when he had time and perhaps order the potassium drip.

As soon as I got to the ICU I asked how I could change my mother's doctor. They told me that she had to do it herself. *Were these people crazy? I thought. She doesn't know her own name. How can she make a decision about her doctor?*

"I've got power of attorney in the event that she can't manage her own affairs," I announced solidly. "I'm exercising that power right now. I want Dr. Newman to be in charge of my mother."

"You'll have to speak to Dr. Newman about that," the nurse told me dryly. She obviously considered me a great nuisance.

I called Dr. Newman and got her right away. That was a good omen in my mind. She said that she would evaluate Mom's chart, and seemed to think it might be reasonable to try a potassium drip.

I sat with Mom some more until she fell asleep again. I was praying fervently in my mind and my heart. *Let this potassium drip bring the miracle of health to my mother,* I prayed. After a few hours I was so exhausted that I had to leave.

I went to the arboretum, a park where I had enjoyed tremendous freedom as a college student. It was wonderful to be among the trees in the crisp cold air. I breathed in energy and exhaled exhaustion. I looked at the water running in a creek. There wasn't much of it this time of year. I remembered photographing the creek for a college project: depicting the Tao by showing water in various forms. As I looked at the beauty of nature around me, I felt close to God and all living things. I prayed harder for my mother. I prayed with every fiber of my body.

When I returned to the hospital Mom was receiving her potassium drip. I said a silent prayer of thanks. I spent the rest of that day and the evening with Mom. By evening she was beginning to talk. She still didn't know who I was, but at least she knew her own name. In the late evening when she was asleep again, I left for my small hotel room. I was grateful that she was showing some signs of improvement.

The next morning when I arrived Mom greeted me by name. I wanted to cry in thanks to God for the miracle he had given us. By that afternoon Dr. Newman decided to move Mom to a regular room.

When Mom was taking her nap I once again went to the arboretum. It seemed to embrace me with its calm energy. I cried gently as I said a prayer of thanks for the miracle that had just occurred. We were incredibly blessed.

Back at the hospital, it was amazing to see how quickly Mom remembered everything. She was back to her old self, for better or for worse. I laughed to myself as she ordered the nurses around. She was doing so well that Dr. Newman wanted to send her home in a couple days. I felt so relieved.

The nurse who had been in the ICU a few days earlier came down to visit. Having heard that Mom was up and around, she wanted to see it for herself. She had expected Mom to die.

Finally, the night before I was supposed to leave and Mom was supposed to go back home, I had dinner with a high-school friend of mine, Prue, who still lived in town. I hadn't contacted her before because I had been too busy dealing with my mother. Now I wanted to briefly connect with this dear friend. When Mom went to sleep, I went to Prue's. It was a joyous meal.

The next morning I went to the hospital to see Mom. In the hallway I saw Prue. *Isn't that sweet of her,* I thought. *She came to visit Mom.* That wasn't the case at all. Prue's husband, who had had dinner with us the night before, was now in the hospital. He had experienced pain during the night and came to the emergency room to have it checked out. Now they were waiting for the results. I couldn't believe it. I had left their home around midnight and he was fine. *Life is so fragile,* I thought.

Fortunately, by the time Mom was ready to leave the hospital Prue's husband was also: it turned out to be a false alarm.

I flew home feeling happy with a job well done. My mother was back at home being her feisty self. When she was checking out of the hospital she had been resentful about the staff speaking to me rather than directly to her. Mom had no idea that she hadn't even known her own name a few days earlier. Even the fact that she still couldn't spell her name easily didn't trouble her, and gradually she regained all her abilities.

What bothered me was that Mom seemed really angry with *me*. I had left my family in the middle of an important holiday to save her life, and she was angry with me? If I hadn't gone to Ohio, Mom would have died. How could she be angry with me?

Shortly after her release, Mom was preparing to host her French club. She asked Georges and our daughter Talia to create an invitation in French for her, which they did. The next day our local Baskin-Robbins called to say Mom had sent us a cake. From time to time Mom had sent ice-cream cakes for different occasions.

She's probably sending Georges and Talia a thank-you cake, I thought ruefully. She seemed downright hostile toward me since her return home, so I was sure the cake was not intended for me.

I drove to Baskin-Robbins to pick up the cake. It said THANK YOU on it, no names. I asked the store clerk shyly, "Who is this cake for?"

The young clerk, reading the cake, said off-handedly, "It says thank you."

"I understand that. What I want to know is, to whom exactly was the cake sent?" I inquired. "Can you check the order, please?"

Rather annoyed, the clerk looked up the order and said, "It says it's for the Lecleres."

"All the Lecleres?" I continued my interrogation, amazed that Mom might really want to thank me for saving her life. "Are you sure it's not specifically for Georges or Talia Leclere?"

The clerk looked at me with more annoyance. "It's for everybody," she said, and turned around, ending the conversation.

I was joyful as I drove home. How could I have imagined that I wouldn't be included in this wonderful thank-you cake? Of course Mom would include me. I had tears in my eyes as I chided myself for being a selfish daughter. As soon as I got home I called Mom.

"Hi, Mom," I said gently.

"Yes," she answered dryly.

"I wanted to thank you for the cake you sent," I said with love.

"What cake?" she asked suspiciously.

"The Baskin-Robbins cake you sent. I just picked it up," I said warmly.

"Why are *you* thanking me? It's not for you!" Mom barked at me. "It's for Georges and Talia. They wrote the invitation for me. Why would I send *you* a cake? You never did anything for me."

I was struck to the core by her cruelty. Didn't she realize I had saved her life?

"I came to see you when you were sick," I offered sadly.

"Oh, that. It was nothing important," Mom declared.

"Okay. Well, I'll make sure they get the cake. Good-bye." I hung up, devastated.

It took me years to realize that Mom really didn't want to live. Ever since my father had died five years earlier she had been waiting to die herself. She often said she had accomplished everything she needed to do in her life. She had raised her children and remained married and cared for her husband for fifty-one years. Now, when an opportunity had appeared, Mom had prepared herself to die. I had stepped in between her and death without asking her permission.

I learned much from my mother's near-death experience, but the most important thing I learned was the power of prayer. Every fiber of my being had wanted my mother to live. I had no other thought in my mind and no other focus. I had always believed that miracles could happen through prayer, and now I had lived that miracle. Against all odds my prayers had wrenched my mother from the grips of death. I wondered at this incredible gift that is accessible to us all.

INTUITION

Back at home I continued researching healers. I came across Diane Goldner's book, *Infinite Grace*. She wrote about her experiences as a skeptical journalist researching energy healers in the United States. Her book presents an excellent discussion of energy healing in the United States today.

Diane and I were meeting for lunch at a small organic-foods restaurant in Greenwich Village. I was delighted to find a parking space in front of the restaurant. I put coins in the meter, reminding myself I had two hours for lunch. The inside of the restaurant was designed like a barn, with rustic dark wood tables and chairs, and the upstairs table we had was very comfortable. I soon was totally engrossed in our conversation; she was telling me all about the experiences she had had while gathering material for her book.

"So you have psychic ability?" I asked Diane.

"We all do," she answered. "We just don't develop it. You're psychic, too," she announced.

"No, I'm sure I'm not the least bit psychic," I laughed in response.

"You never know." Diane smiled as she continued telling me about her psychic experiences.

All of a sudden I jumped up from the table.

"My car! I've got to put some coins in the meter. It's just outside. I'll be right back!" I called over my shoulder as I ran down the stairs.

There was a ticket on my car! I was furious. Fifty-five dollars down the drain! I looked around for the ticketing villain. There was no one to be seen. Ticket in hand, I sadly walked back to the table where Diane was waiting.

"I got there too late. Too bad for me," I tried to say as lightly as possible. "I should have remembered to put some money in the meter sooner."

"You see? You are psychic. You knew just when you were being ticketed," Diane continued.

"No," I said. "I just randomly remembered that I needed to put money in the meter."

Undaunted, Diane continued. "When did the meter expire? It's written on the ticket."

I looked at my ticket. "The meter expired half an hour ago," I said.

"So you didn't *just* remember it was time to put money in the meter," Diane explained.

"No, I guess not," I admitted slowly.

"At exactly what time were you ticketed?" Diane asked.

"It says 2:35 P.M."

"What time is it now?" Diane asked.

I looked at my watch. "It's 2:38," I said, thinking ruefully that I had just missed avoiding the ticket by a few minutes. I really wasn't getting her point.

"When you remembered the meter, it was because you were receiving a ticket at that very moment. You see, you do have psychic ability. I don't think fifty-five dollars is too much to pay to find that out," Diane laughed.

I was amazed but very skeptical. It had just been a coincidence.

When I left Diane to go home, I still couldn't understand how I missed seeing the ticketing officer, or at least his or her car, when I ran downstairs. Usually they are either dropped off to ticket an area, or they are double-parked and walk up to the meters to check whether they have expired. I kept trying to imagine an officer walking up to my car but I couldn't get the image. Suddenly, in my mind's eye, I "saw" a police car drive up, stop abruptly, ticket my car, and then drive quickly off. I thought this was impossible. *It takes time to check out the meters, and it has to be done by foot,* I thought. *This is all ridiculous stuff,* I scoffed.

I told my husband how quickly I had been ticketed, but before I could say anything else, he commiserated with me.

"There's a new device in police cars now. They can be flying down the street, and when they pass an expired parking meter the device goes off. They pull over, write a ticket, and drive away," Georges said. "All this in a matter of seconds."

I was astounded. I had "seen" in my mind's eye exactly what happened.

Maybe Diane is right, I thought. *Maybe everyone has some psychic ability, including me.*

CLEARING OUT THE PAST

Among the many healers I met, I was quite impressed by Rosalyn Bruyere. Her book about energy healing, *Wheels of Light,* was incredibly informative. It discussed energy within and around the human body. I went to see her New York representative, Theo Kyrkostas, a certified energy healer and an ordained minister in Rosalyn's organization, The Healing Light Center Church. Theo told me about his cousin Chris, who had been diagnosed with terminal liver cancer. Medical doctors had given him two months to live. Twelve years later, Chris was jogging every other day to maintain his good health. He attributed his recovery to Bruyere's expertise.

We sat in Theo's living room as he explained about energy healing and the methods Rosalyn had taught him. After a while, Theo felt that the best way for me to understand the process was to experience it. This seemed like a good idea to me, too. We walked upstairs to Theo's healing room. I stretched out face down on the massage table. It felt good to have energy flow through me as Theo gently placed his hands on my feet first and then on other areas of my body. He didn't massage or bear down on my body. He just held his hands gently for several minutes on each area.

Even though I don't like being touched by strangers, I really enjoyed the gentle flow of energy, and I slipped into a kind of dream state. During the session we didn't speak much. Every once in a while Theo would ask me how I felt. I always mumbled "good." Before I knew it, the session was over. I left feeling full of energy and information about the miraculous recoveries people had enjoyed, thanks to energy healing. As I walked out the door I was unaware of the unpredictable effect Theo's demonstration would have.

A few days later I was meditating in front of a candle flame when, just like a film that was being projected in front of my eyes, I saw myself as a small child being abused by my baby-sitter, Mrs. Gray. It was hideous. I couldn't make this horrible movie stop! I called Penney to find out what to do.

"Nothing," she answered. "Just wait it out."

I began to cry. I didn't want to see this! What I was "seeing" was confirmation of what I had always suspected: I was a victim of sexual abuse. This explained why anytime something about sexual abuse came up, it I always felt terribly uncomfortable. I couldn't bear to hear or talk about it. I had attributed this to normal revulsion but now understood why I had such a violent reaction to the subject. I was a victim of it myself.

I had never liked old Mrs. Gray and had tearfully told my mother that I didn't want her baby-sitting me, but my mother sent me to her anyway, telling me what a great sitter she was. Now I knew why I was so glad when she died. All these years I had buried the memory of that horrid abuse and had been left with only a miserable feeling of being a dirty, bad girl. Now I sobbed, "watching" her sexually abuse me as a child, and I felt my tears were cleansing me. I felt so sorry for the poor little girl that I had been.

Over the following days I recognized that I felt cleansed and much stronger than before. I felt that I had the power to no longer be a victim of anyone. I also had a sense that the nasty secret was gone! There was no reason to feel ashamed. I knew I had done nothing wrong, and even realized that I had tried to save myself. By telling my mother I didn't want Mrs. Gray to baby-sit me, I was trying to show my mother that something was wrong. But instead of hearing me and responding to my distress, she told me I was bad because I didn't love Mrs. Gray as she believed all the other children did.

After those first days of tears, there were no more emotions attached to that incident. I looked at it in the same way someone might consider any minor childhood event. It was just something that had happened, rather as if I had fallen and cut my knee. No big deal.

I never told Theo about this revelation and subsequent cleansing. I was too shy about my personal life to share this kind of information with someone I barely knew. I did ask him if he had "seen" anything about me during our session. He said that all he saw was a car accident. It took me a long time to be able to tell other people about the abuse I suffered. It's not information I volunteer easily because it's intensely personal, and it's not a part of my life today. I can, however, speak about it when it is appropriate.

I'm including it in this book because those of us who were abused shouldn't be ashamed of it. We aren't to blame. We are helpless victims who have survived aggression. We should feel proud of our survival capabilities. In discussing my experience, I want to empower others to speak out, too.

SEEING MY FIRST GHOST

To really understand energy healing, Theo encouraged me to attend a weekend workshop he ran for healers, a kind of refresher course. I thought I was going as an observer.

At the workshop Theo began by building up our energy through a series of exercises called qi gong (pronounced "chi gung"). I clumsily followed along. Fortunately, Theo was very patient as I struggled to follow the fairly rapid and confusing movements he made with his arms and legs. Everyone else already seemed to be familiar with them. *I was never any good at aerobics, either,* I thought to myself. As Theo encouraged us to feel the energy field around us, I waved my arms more or less appropriately and mumbled about my energy, just like I saw the others doing. Truth be told, I didn't feel anything.

Not feeling energy was the beginning of my fog. Soon I felt completely overwhelmed as Theo talked about chakras and colors and energy directions. I thought I would never get it straight. How many chakras were there? Which is red or blue or whatever other colors they're supposed to be? Everyone else there was a working energy healer and knew all this backward and forward.

When it came time to practice on each other, Theo insisted that I participate and learn to channel energy through my hands. *Uh oh,* I thought. *No hiding my ignorance now.*

"Everyone can do this," Theo proclaimed. I wasn't so sure.

We did energy chelation on each other. This technique, developed by Rosalyn Bruyere, channels energy to someone who is sick. In our case, one of the students lay face down on the massage table while three of us put our hands gently on her body where Theo indicated that we should. We were supposed to invite energy to enter through our feet and let it rise up through our bodies to come out through our hands. I concentrated on bringing up the energy. I had no idea if anything was happening. I tried again to feel the energy. All of a sudden I could feel heat coming through my hands. My palms actually felt warm. The person on the massage table said she felt something. *Hallelujah! What a kind person,* I thought.

At the end of the workshop Theo wanted to conduct a closure ceremony for three of his friends, a woman and two men. They had just lost a loved one. Theo had told us earlier that the deceased was the mother of one of the three people who were seated in a circle, but he never said who. A fourth chair held the deceased's keys and a candle.

The healers in attendance and I formed two circles around the chairs and walked around the chairs in opposing directions, occasionally switching directions at Theo's command. It seemed pretty chaotic, with people bumping into each other because they couldn't get the directions right. I was just trying to follow everyone and keep track of which direction I was supposed to go in when suddenly Theo instructed us to stop where we were.

"Would anyone who knew Evelyn like to say something about her?" Theo inquired.

One of the seated men began speaking sadly about the deceased. He ended by saying, "Evelyn was a kind person. She contributed a lot of love and nurturing to many people. Now she is at peace."

"I hope Evelyn's spirit is with us today so she can hear your beautiful words," Theo said softly.

I thought to myself, *I wish I could see her.* Boom! Evelyn, the deceased woman, appeared to me! Just like that. I could see her as clearly as I could see everyone else in the room. Evelyn was standing next to the woman seated in the circle. She was trying to comfort her by caressing her hair and putting her arms around her. The seated woman had no idea Evelyn was trying to hug and comfort her. I was thrilled to be able to see this ghost, because I was sure all the healers around me could see Evelyn, too. After feeling so lost all day trying to remember chakras and colors and channel energy, I felt that finally I could do something just like these important healers. I was so proud that I could see this ghost that I blurted out, "I know she's here! I can see her."

After the ceremony I turned to the healer next to me.

"Did you see Evelyn, too?" I whispered to her, sure that her answer would be Yes.

"No, I didn't," the healer replied, rather annoyed that I asked her. I was surprised, but said no more.

I nonchalantly approached different healers and asked them the same question. It turned out that I was the only person who saw her. It was astounding to me, but I really had seen her! I had always thought it was possible for people to see ghosts, but I never imagined that I would. Theo approached me with enthusiasm and support.

"So you saw Evelyn?" he said.

"Yes, she was standing next to the woman and trying to console her," I answered.

"That makes sense. Evelyn was Mary's mother," Theo said. "That's really great! I'm sure the fact that you saw Evelyn here will make Mary feel better."

I felt pretty good about it, not at all frightened or worried. I actually thought it was pretty neat.

When I went home, I told my family that I had clearly seen a ghost. They accepted this as something strange and kind of exciting. They weren't shocked, horrified, or afraid. To them it seemed to fit with all the research I was doing. It was all part of an incomprehensible world that they didn't live in. I myself accepted this gift as something wonderful and exciting. I felt like I was entering the world of healers; I still imagined that most healers were clairvoyant. I didn't take into consideration the fact that I was the only person in that group of healers who had actually seen the deceased. It never struck me that I had an exceptional gift.

In the days that followed I didn't "see" any more ghosts, but I didn't go to anyplace where I might want to see a dead person's spirit. I started seeing something else. I began seeing a Native American in complete ceremonial dress standing next to me. He was usually slightly to my right, facing me. It was very unsettling to say the least. I was prepared to see dead people at funerals, but a phantom Indian was something else. He never left my side. I mentioned this to my husband, who smiled and ignored the subject. I felt uncomfortable about seeing this person, so I tried to ignore him. The next time I saw Penney, I nonchalantly asked her if she saw anything around me. She said she didn't. I didn't want to talk about it to anyone, including Penney, because I was afraid someone would think I was having hallucinations or that I was crazy. Nevertheless, as hard as I tried to ignore the Indian next to me, he just wouldn't go away.

5
Leaving Home

AS I CONTINUED MY RESEARCH ON HEALERS, Penney suggested I meet a "raw healer," named Foxes of all things, to round out my research. According to Penney, a "raw healer" was someone who had natural talent but wasn't specifically trained. I was meeting a lot of healers from different disciplines, but they all had certificates from some more-or-less established organization. Even Penney had a certificate as a shiatsu massage therapist, although she practiced her own type of healing. Foxes had natural energy and was self-taught. I was intrigued.

THE WARNING

A raw healer with a name like Foxes sounded pretty interesting to me. Maybe he was dashing and handsome and suave, with mystical powers on top of all that. And why "Foxes" instead of just plain "Fox"? Unfortunately Foxes lived upstate; I had plenty of local healers to check out before traveling that far. And I was very busy with Penney. In fact, I had organized my whole life around her—well, the little bit of time I had away from my family obligations. A husband and four children always need something, and I was trying to be Donna Reed, a perfect wife and mother.

I considered Penney my official healer, and all my "free time" and energy went to her. I worshipped Penney Angel, as I called her, and hung on her every word. She had healed me and believed in me. She freed my soul. When Penney told me over the phone that she wanted to move out of the city, I insisted on helping her. She agreed because, as she later put it, "When I was on the phone with you, a spirit came into my window. You're magic."

Together Penney and I drove all over Westchester looking for the right apartment, a place where she could set up an artist's studio and paint. I also offered her a room in my home. I knew Georges wouldn't mind sharing our home because, even though he didn't particularly believe in healers, he did like houseguests. One summer, on Georges' invitation, we had twenty-seven guests stay with us for various amounts of time.

Penney liked the energy of my place, and I felt that I learned a lot simply by being with her. Penney taught me a whole new way of interacting with people. She had a perception of people and an effect on them that was profound.

After searching for a while she decided not to move from her New York apartment, but that she would take me up on my offer of a room. I was delighted. We set up a barter system whereby she would use the room in exchange for occasional healing sessions for my family and me.

Penney seemed to see things in me that I never knew existed. When I told Penney that I had seen the deceased Evelyn at her memorial service, she said, "I'm not surprised. You're so magical." I didn't think there was anything magical about me, but I liked being around someone who thought I was.

Penney brought her easel and palette and set up her studio in our guest bedroom. She drove out a couple of times a week and painted for a few hours. Whenever Penney wanted to come I made sure I was at home, whether or not we had also scheduled a session. Penney never asked me to do this. I didn't realize that I was not only giving Penney all of my spare time, I was also giving her all my power and energy. I don't think Penney recognized it either. It was exactly what I had done when I had unwittingly given my company to my husband by deferring all decisions to him. It left me powerless. Even though Penney often told me to not give my power away to everyone, I still did it unconsciously. It was automatic.

Some of us are born caregivers. We want to nurture everyone, just like Donna Reed. Others are takers. They love to be nurtured. Usually the caregivers connect with the takers. It sounds like a happy combination, but the reality is that the caregivers end up giving too much and feeling used as a result. The takers end up taking more than the caregiver ever intended to give. The takers sorely resent the whimpers of the wounded caregivers when the givers want to be, at the very least, thanked for their efforts. The takers don't think they owe anyone anything because the caregiver gave them something. Takers don't give excessively of their time, talent, and treasure. They usually have a well-established comfort zone around themselves that allows them to give of themselves, but at no personal expense. They just assume that if someone nurtures them, the caregiver is not overextending him- or herself.

I was a caregiver in a family of takers. And I did feel bad when no one thanked me for my efforts. Isn't that the typical mother's song? I always deferred major decisions to my husband, believing that he would love me more if I did.

It was a pattern that I had picked up as a child. When I was growing up, the youngest in the family, my parents were always right. Early on I learned that by "caregiving" them, deferring to their point of view and following their orders, they would be nicer to me. If I didn't, the consequences were severe and often violent. It was a no-brainer.

My number-one best friend from college, Margaret, enabled me to continue this pattern of giving away my power. Our friendship was based on our unspoken agreement that she was better than me. Not much better, but better nonetheless. We were both smart, but she was smarter. We were both popular, but she was more popular, and so forth. If a situation came up where I was undeniably better, for example, in singing (she couldn't sing at all and I was in the prize-winning chorus), we both agreed that the activity in question was stupid, unimportant.

This continued throughout my life. I believed that I would be loved if I deferred to the wisdom of those around me. I often found myself the hardest worker in a group, which allowed the group to thrive, but I never received any credit. If I were put in a visible position, it would be as vice-president of an organization, usually enabling the president to look good. I then expected to be appreciated for my sacrifices. I never was.

We give up power when we let someone else take charge of a situation that we can handle. Every time we know we can do something, instead of taking action we tell someone else how to take action for us, or we simply defer to someone else's idea of what to do, and thus we empower that person. That act of empowering someone strips us of our own power, especially if we overextend ourselves and have no more time or energy to identify and manifest our own dreams.

Take the example of a mother who teaches her young son to dress himself. Gradually she empowers him to dress himself by showing him how to do it and by cheering him on. As she does this, she becomes less important to him. In the end, the son can dress himself. He never thanks his mother for teaching him as he runs out the door to meet his friends. In the same way, men and women constantly "caregive" others and receive no thanks in return. In the case of the mother and her son, it is part of her job description to educate her son, and if she plays her cards right, in the long run he will appreciate her teaching. In situations involving two adults, a caregiver will do the same kind of selfless nurturing, maybe write a report for a colleague, and then feel bad when they get no reward.

Another way that people give up their power and energy often passes unnoticed—when a caregiver is passive in front of a taker. The taker begins accepting help graciously offered by the caregiver. Gradually the help becomes expected. This isn't the fault of the taker. Because the caregiver is so good at convincing the taker to take, the taker honestly believes that the caregiver enjoys giving. Caregivers might even believe this, too, until they're asked about their own hopes and dreams. They usually haven't had enough time (power, energy) to identify those dreams. The next step is for the taker to make slight demands on the caregiver. The caregiver enjoys being recognized, and readily helps out the taker, even though it might be tremendously uncomfortable because the caregiver has overextended him- or herself to such an extent that he or she is physically or emotionally exhausted, or both. Regardless of the uncomfortable positions caregivers find themselves in, they still go overboard to accommodate takers.

Giving away my power was bad enough, but I also gave away my energy. I didn't just defer, I also put my personal effort (energy) into serving the nurtured person. I actively participated in manifesting the nurtured person's dream. With Penney, I was putting all my power and energy into helping her manifest her dream of having a comfortable studio to work in. Where was my dream in all of this?

I must say that Penney herself is an incredible giver, and not in the least a taker. She has devoted her life to making the lives of others better, often at her own expense. She never was trying to take anything from me. I was so intent on giving to her that I made it clear to her that she was doing me a favor by accepting everything I gave her. I'm sure that Penney had guidance that instructed her to allow me to be this way, because it was part of my journey and what I needed to learn.

Ultimately, I was so concerned with nurturing everyone around me that I didn't have anything left for myself.

I knew a bit about energy from the research on healers I was doing, but I didn't know about power or how the two were related. I knew we all have energy within and around us. Some of us have more energy, some have less. We usually recognize this when we feel good with some people and depressed and exhausted after being around others. This all is a result of our exchange of energy with the person we're dealing with. I certainly wasn't aware of how to control any of it.

All of us take in energy. We have different ways of holding on to it and using it.

People give away their power by allowing someone else to control their lives. Whenever I deferred my own desires to allow someone else to manifest his or her own wish, by supporting that wish I would give away my power of decision and my energy of action to that person. I convinced myself to do this, choosing to be a martyr and good friend by walking the extra mile for that friend. It became a way of life for me. One extra mile turned into another and another.

The problem with giving someone my energy, or letting someone just take it, was that the individual usually would use it for his or her own purposes, which often didn't include me, not for a common cause. It was as though I was saying to someone I liked, "Here, take my energy. Now love me!" But there would be nothing left to love, just a pitiful empty heap. Unfortunately, I didn't realize this until much later. I also didn't know how to refill myself with energy. I just knew how to feel depressed about it.

Penney wanted to thank me for helping her look for an apartment. She gifted me with a tarot card reading by a friend of hers, Boris Plansky. I thought this would be exciting and lots of fun. The two tarot card readers I had been to years ago had found good things to say about my future. It was great to have positive things to look forward to, regardless of whether they were true.

Penney left us alone in her apartment while Boris did the reading. I watched this large, bushy-haired man as he mumbled hello. He first had me throw pennies to cast a trigram for the I Ching, announcing that he always began this way. I obediently threw the pennies. Without writing anything down, Boris named the trigram and made some rapid comments about it that I didn't understand or remember. After all, I hadn't come here for an I Ching reading. Then he pulled out his tarot deck. He handed it to me, I happily shuffled the cards thoroughly, and then handed them back. He sat across from me looking nervous and concentrated. Boris obviously took his job seriously. As he put the cards down, he announced dramatically, "Armageddon! You're going to face Armageddon this year!"

I was shocked. What was he talking about? This wasn't good news! *Armageddon, indeed!* I thought, as I sat in shocked silence.

Boris put down more cards. "It's the ultimate battle for you. The world as you know it will never be the same. This is an X-rated reading. Not for children, this kind of fight. Yes, you're going to break away from your family life. Everything's going to be upside down." Then he proceeded to give me details of what appeared to be my future demise.

My entire life was based on my family. Boris was telling me that this year would bring an end to all that. My life's foundation as I knew it would crumble. It was up to me to persevere through these changes, fight the good fight, and come out into a new way of being.

I hated hearing this! My life wasn't perfect, but I certainly didn't think it was reaching crisis proportions. Armageddon? The fight of my life? Was there no hope of wonderful, fun things to come? It was like a slap across the face. No sugar coating from this tarot reader! *Who wants to hear this kind of stuff anyway?* I thought. I had come to hear good things that would make me feel optimistic about the future. Instead, I was being told this could be the worst year of my life. I began to detest Boris as he continued to tell me more horrible details. I was in too much shock to make him stop. When he finished the reading, he practically ran out the door. I left feeling totally numb, trying to forget everything Boris had just told me but nevertheless believing every word.

The next day, when I had recovered somewhat from the shock of it all, I was furious with poor Penney.

How wicked she was to subject me to that crazy tarot card reader, I thought, forgetting that she was trying to be nice by offering me this reading. *She's supposed to bring good things into my life. She should have known the kinds of things that jerk would tell me. Who wants to hear awful things about the future anyway? What a rotten gift,* I pouted.

All of a sudden I didn't want to be around Penney. I didn't have the courage to tell her how I felt, so I just told her that Boris wasn't nice about the reading, and that I didn't like it.

Although I was still angry with Penney for subjecting me to such a distressing event, the next time she was due to come to paint at my house, I was waiting for her as usual. When she didn't show up, I was afraid something awful had happened. I was right. She had been in a terrible accident en route to my house. Penney had only injured her knee but her car had been totaled as it slid into a wall next to the highway.

I felt very bad for her. She was unable to come out to paint now because she couldn't walk easily and she didn't have transportation. In ultimate caregiver mode, I offered to drive into the city and chauffeur Penney out to my house. She wisely declined my offer. I couldn't be with her even if I wanted to, and I wasn't sure I wanted to be around her anymore. I wanted to forget that horrible tarot reading, and being around Penney would have reminded me of it. I was lonely and confused. I decided to collect my energy and work on my television project about healers. I wanted to get away, and I finally called Foxes at his home in upstate New York.

HEALER IN THE ROUGH

Although Foxes lived about two hours north of my home in Westchester County, he was going to be in my area for a meeting that coming Saturday in the late afternoon, and he accepted my invitation for lunch. The universe had its own plan for me.

I'll never forget that Saturday when I prepared lunch for Foxes. I was almost giddy with enthusiasm at the prospect of meeting a powerful healer. I imagined him to be tall, handsome, and dashing, with mystical powers. Then I began to think that, rather than being suave, he was probably more a Davy Crockett type. I remembered Fess Parker, the actor who played Crockett on television. I loved watching that show as a child, and now the real Davy Crockett was coming to my house! This was going to be fun. Although I usually serve gourmet French cuisine for my guests, because that's all I know how to cook, I decided not to prepare a fancy meal for Foxes, the rugged backwoods healer. Davy Crockett would prefer a basic hearty stew. I didn't use any of my usual spices. Georges was alerted to this visit, and he opted to be part of it. I was annoyed, because of his negative attitude toward healers; he didn't believe in them.

Foxes came in through the side door without knocking, true to his name. He met Georges, who was standing in the kitchen, and I came in after they had awkwardly introduced themselves to each other. Foxes didn't look at all like Davy Crockett. In fact, the only similarity between the two was their height, except that Foxes seemed *too* big. He was very large and appeared menacing to me, with piercing blue eyes and a smirking mouth. He had coarse, frizzy brown hair pulled back into a ponytail, and he seemed to be perpetually hunched forward, ready for a fight. Nothing about him seemed appealing. Instead of Davy Crockett I had gotten Hulk Hogan's worst enemy! I thought I had made a mistake by inviting this odd middle-aged man into my home. At that point, I was glad Georges was there.

"Lunch is ready, so why don't we just sit down right away," I said cheerfully, thinking, *If we eat quickly he might leave faster.*

Foxes lumbered over to the table and sat down. I was surprised at the soft quality of his voice; it didn't match his intimidating demeanor. He also had a sophistication about his language that belied his outward appearance. I began to feel more comfortable with him. We spoke about healers and the healing arts. I drank up every word.

After a while Georges took over the conversation, as he usually did. Not only was he dominating the exchange, he was discussing the scientific approach to energy healing, comparing energy healing to science fiction. Georges, trained as a scientist, had a great deal of trouble accepting anything that wasn't scientifically proven. He wouldn't say it outright in front of a guest who was presumably a healer, but it was clear that

Georges thought all of this healing stuff was nonsense. His attitude made me want to end the meal. It also seemed to me that Foxes and Georges had forgotten I was there. This afforded me the opportunity to once again inspect Foxes' exterior, and I became annoyed at the whole thing. I had had enough. First Davy Crockett turned into a goon from the World Wrestling Federation and now I had to listen to "healer bashing" from my husband. A tension headache was building at the back of my head. By dessert, as Georges and Foxes were chummily loading on ice cream and devouring an entire pie, I was debating how I could discreetly leave the table to get some Excedrin when Foxes said to me, "You've got something at the back of your head. Do you want me to get rid of it for you?"

"Oh, you see something there?" I asked. I thought both he and Georges had forgotten I was there.

"Yeah. There's like a dark cloud forming. I can make it disappear if you want," he answered.

"Well, as a matter of fact I *am* getting a headache back there. I was just going to take some Excedrin for it," I admitted.

"Why don't you let me try?" Foxes insisted.

"Yeah, I suppose, why not?" I agreed.

"Let's do this over there," Foxes stood up and began walking toward the living room.

"Okay," I agreed, and followed him in a daze.

Georges stood up and announced, "I think I'll take a nap." He yawned widely and went into our bedroom. Later he would say that Foxes hypnotized him to make him go away. I doubt that to be true, because Georges is always sleep deprived. He often has trouble keeping his eyes open after a heavy meal.

Foxes and I went into the living room. I stood in front of him as he held his hands behind my head, not touching me. The pain in my head became excruciating, and I was just about to scream at him to stop. I needed a couple extra-strength pain killers! Suddenly the pain left as Foxes said, "There it goes."

I looked at Foxes with renewed interest. Maybe there was more here than met the eye. Foxes sat down and made himself comfortable. Intrigued, I sat down to talk to him further.

"You know how I decided to have lunch with you?" he queried.

"No," I answered.

"When you called, and we were talking on the phone, I looked out my window and I saw two foxes playing together. That's what made me decide to come here for lunch," he confessed.

How bizarre, I thought, *but how romantic. Davy Crockett would do something like that.*

"Do you often take your signals from nature?" I asked.

"All the time. I'm a tracker," he said proudly.

I had no idea what he was talking about.

"What do you mean, you're a 'tracker'?" I ventured.

"You know, like Tom Brown Jr. You ever heard of him? He's written lots of books about tracking," Foxes continued.

I shamefully shook my head no.

"Well, Tom Brown Jr. was taught by an Apache scout to track animals," he explained.

"You mean follow animals' tracks on the ground?" I announced proudly, trying to avoid the fact that I didn't know what an Apache scout was. "That sounds like fun," I lied.

"Tom's tracked people, too," Foxes explained.

"Like criminals?" I asked. Finally, something I sort of understood.

"Yeah. He even got shot doing it," Foxes said.

I was impressed. I didn't know anybody who did things like that except for the fictional Davy Crockett.

"Tom calls the Apache scout 'Grandfather,' which is a sign of respect. Grandfather met Tom when he was a young boy and taught him all about nature and the Apache ways," Foxes went on. "I've studied with Tom."

"So you're an Apache tracker, too?" I asked.

"Oh, no. I've learned something about tracking, but not from the Apache. I know other tribes better," Foxes said.

"So you know a lot about Indians?" I asked. Maybe he could explain something about the Indian chief whom I constantly saw next to me.

"Some. I've had some experience. That's where I got my name," Foxes said proudly.

"Why is it plural?" I ventured.

"It's short for Fox's Paw. I think that sounds weird so I just have people call me Foxes," he said, as though having a plural name wasn't weird.

He could have just called himself plain old Fox, I thought.

"What's your real name?"

"That's it. I'm going to have it legally changed as soon as I can," he announced.

Okay, I thought. *Anyone who wants to legally change his name to Foxes can't be too shocked by my next question.*

"Do you ever see things, like spirits?" I asked innocently.

"Sometimes I see things," Foxes answered.

"Do you see anything around here?" I asked, thinking of my Indian chief.

"Out in the backyard I saw some Indian activity or settlers or something like that. I'm not really sure. I wasn't paying attention," Foxes said.

Oh, dear, he didn't see my Indian, but he did see something strange in the backyard, I thought. *I might as well share with him what I see next to me all the time.* I felt like we were two patients in an insane asylum sharing our craziness.

"This sounds sort of strange, but sometimes I see an Indian standing next to me," I said. "Nobody else can see him. Just me." I held my breath to hear Foxes' reply. Would he tell me I was crazy?

Without blinking an eye Foxes said, "What does he look like?"

Reassured, I tried to describe my Indian chief but couldn't. I finally tried to draw him with his feathered headdress. It felt wonderful to talk to someone about my companion. Foxes didn't act as though there was anything unusual about having an Indian chief in full ceremonial garb standing next to me all the time. It seemed perfectly natural to him, although he didn't seem to know why I had my companion, or who he could be.

Foxes then changed the subject back to his experiences with tracking. After a few hours I became saturated by Foxes' conversation. I wasn't an outdoorswoman and I couldn't relate to his interest in identifying animal tracks out in nature. How many episodes of *Davy Crockett* can you watch in a row? And Foxes' adventures weren't the least bit as exciting as any of Davy's had been.

I began to worry that Foxes would never leave. I had invited him for lunch, not the whole day, and I had other things to do besides listen to him talk about himself! I wanted to turn the television off. Finally Foxes stood up to go, and I felt relieved. Just before walking out the side door, he paused and came toward me. As he approached I had an instant of panic, afraid he would decide to stay longer, but he just gave me a quick hug good-bye. In the instant of that brief hug my whole body lit up. It was a feeling of ultimate perfection, better than sex. Then he left. How could I react this way to someone who, just two minutes earlier, I couldn't wait to get rid of? He was gone now, but I could still feel the hug.

A few days later I called Foxes, allegedly to research my project on healers. I really wanted to talk to the person who had given me such a powerful hug. As we spoke, I felt incredibly comfortable.

"I know things about people," Foxes crooned to me over the phone. "It's a gift I have."

I couldn't pass that opening without jumping in and asking, "What do you know about me?"

"You are a very interesting and complicated person. You show a facade of happiness, but you have an undertone of dissatisfaction," Foxes said.

That sounded right on the mark. *And* he thought I was interesting. I didn't notice that his analysis could fit pretty much anyone, and I asked, "Why would I be dissatisfied?"

"You aren't?" he countered.

"Well, maybe I am a little bit. But why?" I asked in a guarded manner, realizing that most people are dissatisfied with something.

"You need to find out who you're supposed to be," Foxes declared.

"You mean I don't know what I'm supposed to be doing?" I wondered aloud. That really struck home.

"Yeah. It's hard for you because your energy level is older than your real age. There's something like a big shroud over you preventing you from finding your way," Foxes continued.

That sounded true. I generally felt frustrated and exhausted, and I often wasn't sure what to do next. Because I had stopped organizing my life around Penney, I felt lost. What a mess! And Foxes could see it all.

"Oh," I said in a noncommittal way, just to keep him talking. His voice sounded like a lullaby. *Can he really see into my soul?* I wondered.

"It seems that your personal frustration is making you annoying," Foxes continued.

That one woke me up. "Annoying?" I said aloud. This didn't sound nice anymore.

"Yes, sometimes that happens. It's not your fault because that's not your true self," Foxes crooned on. "It's a result of your personal frustration because you're simply echoing your parents. You're not living your real life. That's where the dissatisfaction comes from. That's why you're not happy," he ended.

He was right that I felt frustrated and dissatisfied.

"What can I do?" I asked, completely immersed in his voice.

"You should try meditation. That and conscious introspection will help you. It will enable you to have revelations, which will allow you to become your real self. I can help you with that," Foxes' soothing voice reassured me. I was intrigued, plus I remembered that hug.

"You could, huh? It's too bad you live so far away," I said. "Any plans to come down here again soon?"

"No, I don't get down to the city that often. I like to stay up here where it's really beautiful. The air is clean. Have you ever been up here?"

"No, I don't think so," I said. "It's pretty far away."

"It's not that far. The drive up is easy. I'll fix some lunch for us. We can continue our conversation in person," Foxes encouraged me.

I agreed to go meet him for lunch two days later at his home in upstate New York. When I hung up, I realized we had been on the phone for two hours talking about life in general and, more specifically, about how I could live *my* life more effectively. This was amazing, because I hate talking on the phone. Nevertheless, here I was, sitting in my office for over two hours totally mesmerized by Foxes' voice. I wanted to become my true self and throw off my shroud. Foxes would be there to help me. The two days before our meeting seemed interminable.

Full of anticipation, I left to make the long trip to see Foxes. I was looking forward to seeing him in his environment, the great outdoors. But first I had to get there. With each painfully slow mile the congested traffic inched along. The drive seemed endless, and the memory of that incredible hug faded. I now felt that this would be a one-time trip. I also began to question the validity of the trip itself. *Don't I have anything better to do with my life than spend four hours driving to see some weird freak?* I thought. I realized that I really didn't, and continued my journey. My fondness for Foxes disappeared completely while I waited for a traffic accident to be cleared off the road.

To make matters worse, rather than give me directions to his house, Foxes wanted me to call him from a mini-mart nearby. He would then come get me, and I would follow him. *Who does he think I am? Some kind of idiot who can't follow directions?* I thought as I drove into the gas station parking lot, annoyed that my journey was not yet over. *And how dare he tell me I'm annoying?* He's *annoying!*

I called Foxes on my cell phone and got an answering machine with a stranger's voice. I rechecked the number and tried again. After four calls, including one to Penney to make sure I had the right number, I left a message on the strange answering machine. Penney assured me that Foxes was usually pretty good about keeping appointments.

That really would take the cake, I thought. *I spend all this time driving up to meet this weirdo, and he stands me up.*

Foxes had left my expected arrival time very open and I had left extra early in the morning. So even though the trip had taken two hours longer than I'd expected, I knew I wasn't too late for lunch. I decided to wait just fifteen more minutes before starting the long drive home when finally Foxes called me back on my cell phone. It had been almost an hour since I first got to the mini-mart. By the time Foxes picked me up I was furious. Who did he think he was? I wasn't pleased!

Foxes hadn't heard the phone, he explained, because he had been in his backyard, building a sweat lodge with a friend. *What kind of a person invites someone to lunch and then isn't there to hear the phone ring when the guest is supposed to call? And who was that voice on his answering machine? This man definitely has no manners,* I thought. I never confessed to him the number of times I called, or that I had called Penney to check his phone number. I already felt enough like an idiot.

I followed his van to his house at the foot of the Adirondacks, wondering why I had even bothered to come in the first place. We parked, and Foxes led me up a hill to see the sweat lodge. Foxes planned to spend New Year's Eve, just three days away, in the lodge, praying for world peace. *What a ridiculous way to welcome in the New Year,* I thought.

Foxes introduced me to his friend Dan and showed me the lodge. I was tremendously annoyed and saw no value in this small hut. The prospect of going into one seemed unthinkable. Foxes was planning to build a fire in front of it where he would heat stones that he would take into the lodge to keep himself warm. Cruelly I mentioned that the weather prediction for New Year's Eve was for below-zero temperatures. Foxes looked uncomfortable, and I felt good. The idea of anyone spending that special night in a small hut by himself seemed a stupid waste of time. To do it in sub-zero weather seemed totally insane. *And to meet with this jerk I had to drive four hours and wait for an hour at a gas station? I'm the crazy one,* I reflected to myself.

"The lodge looks pretty good, Dan. Are you sure you don't want to come out here with me?" Foxes tried coaxing his friend to join him there on New Year's Eve.

"You know I would if I could, Foxes. But Debbie—" Dan turned toward me, "she's my girlfriend—has made some plans for us. I can't get out of them," he added sadly.

Smart girl, I thought. *And smart man, too.*

"I guess that's why it's good I don't have a girlfriend," Foxes answered him as he pointedly looked at me.

I returned his look with a cold stare. *Couldn't care less,* my eyes said.

"Well, lunch is ready," Foxes said lightly. "Let's eat. You should join us, Dan." After protesting mildly, Dan acquiesced, and the three of us walked down the hill to Foxes' home.

The house was large, dilapidated, and dirty white. I wondered if there was a front door as we entered through a filthy pantry into an even filthier kitchen. No wonder Foxes had come in through the side door of my house. *That's all he knows,* I thought.

The inside was a feng shui nightmare. Clutter, debris, and squalor were everywhere. It reminded me of what I had seen as a teenager at a church work project when we had gone to a ghetto in Columbus, Ohio. Everything was dirty. Everything looked broken, too. The sink was full of dishes and dirty pans. None of the dishes matched, and most were badly chipped.

The floor looked like it hadn't been washed in years. The small table was cluttered with things and the chairs around it didn't match each other or the table. They looked so decrepit that they seemed dangerous to use. The walls needed painting and were covered with grime. It wasn't even clear what their original color might have been. Foxes, twice divorced, lived here with three other middle-aged divorced men. *This doesn't look like a home. It looks more like Heartbreak Hotel,* I thought to myself.

I went to the bathroom and found that it rivaled any in the Third World for filth. On my way back to the kitchen I peeked into the living room. I shouldn't have. It was an extension of the rest of the squalor. A wasp's nest attached to a severed tree limb in a corner caught my eye. I realized it must have been someone's idea of decoration, but I also wouldn't have been surprised to find that some wasps had just gone ahead and made a gigantic nest in this mess.

Back in the kitchen, something struck me as being wildly out of place: on the refrigerator were family-type photos. Someone was trying to make this eclectic collection of people into a family of sorts. This group of lonely, middle-aged men thrown together by circumstance seemed very sad.

Foxes immediately apologized for the place. He said he had moved in four years prior and was hoping to get his own place up north a bit. I couldn't believe it had taken a grown man four years to want to move out of this place. I certainly never wanted to come back, and I wondered again why I had come in the first place.

At Foxes' invitation, Dan and I awkwardly sat down around the cluttered kitchen table. My broken chair creaked ominously as I eased into it, making me wonder if I would gracefully end up on the floor. Foxes handed us chipped plates and random-sized forks as he pushed aside the papers and who-knows-what else. I tried not to think about how clean it all might be. I felt lucky that I had been to China and had developed the ability to eat anything under unusual conditions. I was sure this was another test of that ability.

To my great surprise, however, Foxes had made an excellent French cassoulet. It turned out that he was a gourmet cook, specializing in French cuisine. *I guess I could have made him a gourmet French meal instead of that boring stew,* I thought guiltily. As I savored the delicious cassoulet, I chided myself for judging a book by its cover. Foxes definitely had a refined side. I felt more comfortable with him because of this "French connection." It's one thing to make a French meal because he knew of my

French connection; it was another thing to make an unusual and difficult recipe.

After our late lunch Dan left, and Foxes invited me to the qi gong class he taught. I hadn't planned to stay so long, but I wasn't ready for the long drive back. Harvesting a little energy through qi gong seemed like a good idea. I also wanted to learn more about Foxes and see him in teacher mode. We took my car because Foxes' van didn't run well.

As we were driving over dark, rolling, narrow roads, Foxes pointed out some lights in a formation in the sky.

"Stop the car. Let's have a closer look," Foxes commanded.

We stopped to look at this oddity looming above us in the dark night sky.

"It looks like warning lights for an airport," I said logically. "They're in a pattern."

"Yeah, but there's no airport here," Foxes said.

"There's no airport?" I echoed, incredulous at the sight of the stationary lights. "What could they be?"

Suddenly the lights were gone. They hadn't flown away. They just disappeared as though they had been turned off.

"It must have been a spaceship," Foxes explained. "We see a lot of them up here."

"Spaceship?" I repeated. "This must be a pretty amazing place."

"It sure is," Foxes agreed.

We got to the community center where Foxes taught his classes. The large room was practically empty when Foxes started. The two students and I took our places facing Foxes. He led us through a series of qi gong positions. We would get into a position and then hold it for an eternity. Then we sat on the edge of our chairs, eyes closed, with our arms and legs lifted in a qi gong posture. Suddenly, I felt an exquisite instant of incredible ecstasy. It was the same way I had felt when Foxes had hugged me. I opened my eyes and looked at Foxes. Was it coming from him? Foxes wasn't anywhere near me. He had his eyes closed in the front of the class. I realized that it was energy that made me feel that ecstasy!

Qi is the Chinese word for energy. Qi gong is the Chinese practice of building up personal energy, in much the same way that yoga does. The exercises we were doing were specifically designed to fill us up with energy. I never realized how depleted I was until I filled up doing this qi gong. That's when I realized that the power of Foxes' hug was really his transfer of his personal energy to me. He carried so much energy that it pretty much blew my fuses. The same thing was happening at this qi gong class. Understanding this made me feel more in control. Now I just had to find a qi gong teacher at home.

No one showed up for Foxes' tai chi class, and the qi gong students had to leave, so Foxes showed me some hand-to-hand combat moves that are the foundation of tai chi. Although it is now considered "the Chinese yoga," tai chi was originally a martial arts form. As we turned in the movements, I felt the heat and excitement of incredible emotion. It was so much fun, all this energy.

Finally it was time to go home. Somebody was coming by to be interviewed about renting a room in Foxes' house. I tried to imagine the kind of person who would want to live in that squalor. It would have to be someone pretty desperate. As far as Foxes' reason for living there, I began to see it differently. I wondered if he felt he needed to be there with these suffering people. He, a great healer, was helping them, healing them, just like Jesus, who would go to unsavory places to help the troubled. Foxes' day job, incidentally, was as a carpenter and painter.

We drove back to Foxes' house in perfect harmony. Full of grace for this strange man, I felt guilty about the bad energy and thoughts I had brought to his sweat lodge when I had first arrived. I now saw his effort to spend New Year's Eve there as a heroic, selfless gesture to save the world. I asked to go back to see the lodge again.

Under the moonlight I said a prayer of safekeeping for my newfound friend. It was a magic moment under a full moon. Just then car lights showed up at the house. The potential tenant was there. Reluctantly we walked in silence to the house. Foxes asked me to stay for the meeting, and I did.

After meeting the potential tenant, a poor woman desperate to leave her abusive husband, the roommates all turned to me and asked me what I thought. *Why should I have a vote on this?* I wondered. I thought the woman was nice and would be a good tenant, and I told them that. The other tenants agreed to have her move in. Foxes walked me to my car, gave me a hug, and said that he would call me soon.

All the way home I was floating in heaven. The hug hadn't been a magic one like the first one, but it didn't matter. What an intoxicating evening with such an intriguing healer! With him, I had seen a sweat lodge and a spaceship. Most of all, I had again felt that exquisite rush of energy while doing qi gong.

THE NEW YEAR BEGINS

For New Year's Eve, Georges and I decided to go to our local country club with our daughter Talia. We hadn't been very diligent recently about organizing parties at home or getting ourselves invited to parties. I guess part of this was due to my interest in the healing arts and my newly discovered ability to see dead people. It all seemed too weird to share these discoveries with others who would find it equally weird or weirder, and I was so interested in these new topics that I didn't really want to talk about anything else. I was isolating myself more and more. Our club always had a great New Year's party and I really felt the only way to welcome in the new year was with a party.

Our evening was fun. We all danced and we made noise as the clock struck midnight. But then after the party Georges and I had a huge argument. I was crushed. *Why is he so mean to me?* I thought.

A few days later, I was feeling very edgy and dissatisfied. I called Foxes. He told me about his night in the sweat lodge. Everything had gone well, and he had spent a beautiful night.

He probably had a better time than I did, I thought. We talked a bit longer, and Foxes invited me up to see him again so that I could experience his healing work. We hadn't had an opportunity to talk about that when I had visited him before.

I wanted to escape somewhere, so I decided to go experience some more magic in Foxes' part of the world. My traveling companion was a book on tape that reflected my cheerful state of mind: *On Death and Dying,* by Elisabeth Kübler-Ross. It turned out to be quite uplifting. I was amazed at the beauty of the afterworld she described. It calmed me. Driving up there this time didn't seem so difficult as I enjoyed listening to this divine book.

When I arrived Foxes greeted me warmly in his kitchen, and I noticed for the first time the abundant sunlight streaming in through the window. Someone had actually washed the dishes that were piled in the dish rack. I wondered if the new tenant was responsible for that. For some reason the kitchen didn't appall me anymore.

I sat down confidently in my broken chair. Foxes sat across from me in his, and we talked. It was easy to talk to him. He encouraged me with simple questions and seemed to have all the time in the world to listen to my answers. I felt like the center of the world. Spontaneously I told Foxes the story of my New Year's Eve fight with Georges. This was a first for me. I had never shared private information like this with anyone, even my close women friends. I had been taught early on by my mother that I should never talk about family matters to outsiders.

One of my most memorable childhood experiences of how sharing personal information could lead to disaster happened to me in kindergarten. During show-and-tell I told them that I had overheard my daddy say he might take a job in Columbus, Ohio, about three hours from our home. Little did I know that this information was then passed from teacher to teacher around the school. It concluded with the principal calling my mother and asking her if she was planning on divorcing my dad. My mother spanked me.

"You're a bad girl. You're not to ever tell anyone anything that happens in our family, ever!" she warned. After that I never shared personal information with anyone, period.

When I got married, Georges unwittingly continued the theme of "never share information." He was supplementing his salary as a television reporter with personal appearances as a celebrity. I would often accompany him on these. One evening, at a dinner party with Georges' colleagues, I spilled the beans about one of Georges' celebrity appearances, and later that night Georges told me how important it was to his career that his colleagues not know about them. I understood perfectly then that marriage was like living in my childhood family: I should never share any information regarding my private life with anyone outside the family. And after that I never did.

Until now, that is. Here I was talking up a storm with a relative stranger about my argument with Georges. I was explaining how hurt I was by his meanness and how hard I tried to be a loving wife. I noticed that Foxes seemed disappointed that my focus was my husband, but I continued anyway. All of a sudden Foxes announced that I had to resolve this issue before I could do anything else with my life, and he offered to conduct a healing. He explained that up to that point he had simply been assessing whether he should conduct a healing or not. Spirit apparently finally "told" him that it was a "go." It was time for me to go home to pick up my daughter from school, but I didn't want to pass up the opportunity to have a significant healing by this powerful healer. I made some phone calls so that my daughter would not be stranded, and I was ready for my healing.

We went into the living room, which still contained the suspicious wasps' nest in the corner. Foxes had me lie down on a dirty, threadbare rug. There was nothing inviting about this cluttered room, which was crowded with broken couches lining the walls. The dirty windows allowed no light through. As instructed, I shut my eyes and tried to relax. Foxes got out his paraphernalia. I knew there was a blue jay feather, because Foxes put it in my hand to hold, and I smelled cigarette smoke when he blew it in my face.

"You have a hole in your chest," Foxes announced. "We need to fill it."

That was news to me, but what did I know? After that I drifted off. Foxes never touched me. I don't know what he did, but I felt wonderful during the healing. My whole body felt light and I felt young and beautiful. When the healing was over, I opened my eyes. I was full of joy and love. I felt terrific!

Then Foxes explained what I should do. For the next three days I was supposed to meditate morning and night to fill the hole in my chest with joy. On the third day, I should find a stone and dig a hole seven inches deep and seven inches in diameter at the top, cone-shaped. I should do this near my favorite tree. I should also write all the pain, illness, and negativity I wanted to get rid of on a piece of paper and prepare an envelope for it. On the fourth day at sunrise Foxes instructed me to first burn some incense and then say a good-bye prayer to all my illnesses and pain as I put a leaf in the hole. Then I should offer a prayer of joy to the Creator as I burned the envelope. I should ask to be of some service to the world, and the Creator would help me seek and find my vision, beyond a shadow of a doubt. I should bury the ashes and then put a stone over the dirt. This spot would then be a place of prayer and a shrine of worship for me, as well as a place to go in moments of grief. I would be investing my spiritual energy there. If ever I should move, I needed to dig up the seven inches of dirt and put it in a bag to keep until I found a new place to put it. Before I traveled I needed to say a prayer and take a pinch of the dirt with me. I actually still carry a pinch of that soil in a locket that I wear around my neck.

Sitting at his kitchen table, I looked at Foxes. The sun was pouring down on us, and I was filled with love. I told Foxes, "As God's warm light pours over me, I will shower you with unconditional love." Foxes smiled and blushed. My words surprised me; they seemed to flow of their own volition. This wasn't romantic love. It was God's pure love that flows through all of God's creations.

Now it was really past time for me to go. Foxes gave me the blue jay feather. I left feeling wonderful. What had happened? What a strange afternoon. I felt like a beautiful new person. I was full of love for everyone! I was full of energy. My heart was full of song. The trip back flew by. I was extraordinarily happy. Who was this strange man? This uneducated construction worker living in squalor had opened up a channel of love and happiness that I had never experienced before.

When I got home I was wonderful and loving to my whole family. They were pleased to see me in such good form, especially Georges. I seemed to love him more than ever, too. I loved the whole world.

After dinner that evening, I eagerly began my meditation.

THREE DAYS OF MEDITATION

That first evening as I began my meditation, lying on the floor of my office, I was happy. I saw visions. Penney appeared to me. She wanted to see how I was doing. Most of all I saw Foxes, and I felt his presence. The next morning, day one, I also was full of visions during my meditation and that night I had a repeat of wonderful visions of light.

I was in a great mood all the time. I was laughing and singing. Nothing bothered me. My family adored me this way. I was a new, fun mom who was great to be around and who never seemed to be overwhelmed or in a bad mood.

The second day my morning meditation was again wonderful. During the day I began writing the list of things I wanted to get rid of. At night I eagerly went to do my evening meditation. I was waiting for my visions to begin, to see something in my mind's eye, but nothing appeared. I waited patiently with my mind completely blank. All of a sudden I "heard" heavy footsteps, as though a man wearing heavy boots was walking in. There was nobody in my office. The door was closed.

As the footsteps neared, I "saw" black boots of a man step over me and straddle me, facing my head. I couldn't see anything beyond the tall black boots. I heard him unzip his pants and then felt him urinate on my face. I couldn't move. I was furious. In reality nothing was happening. No human being was there, but I heard and felt this abomination. When he was finished, I heard him zip up his pants and leave. The door was never opened. There was no moisture around me. Yet I had had this very real experience. I got up totally confused. This wasn't any fun! What was going on?

The next morning I apprehensively did my meditation. Nothing happened, and I didn't "see" anything. I was grateful that nothing bad happened. As soon as I could, I called Foxes. It was our first conversation since my healing; I described my unpleasant experience.

"How did that make you feel?" Foxes asked.

"Furious. I couldn't move, but I was mad!" I answered. "What happened? All the other meditations were so good!" I described seeing Penney and other positive things.

"Sounds like this was either a past-life experience or some bad spirit who came by. You know, when you start to open up to the Spirit World," he explained, "it's as though you have a target painted on your ass. Everything is going to try to get you. I remember one time I woke up and was wrestling with a huge monster in my bed."

"What did you do?"

"I found out why it happened. You can also protect yourself," he added.

"Protect myself? How can I do that?" I asked, thinking he could have told me all this sooner.

"You can smudge out the room before you meditate," Foxes explained. "Have you ever smudged?"

"Well, yes, just once. Someone gave me a big smudge stick and I tried to smudge out the house for springtime. The whole thing got out of control and I burned the carpet and the fire department came," I admitted. "It was pretty embarrassing, especially when I had to explain what I had done. They got a good laugh out of it, and it cost me fifty dollars."

Foxes laughed. "That's okay. Next time you visit, I'll show you how to smudge. It's not hard. For now, just use any kind of incense. I've got to run. Call me again to tell me how it's all going," Foxes said as he hung up.

I wished I had called him before. Maybe I could have avoided that awful experience. I loved hearing his voice. That night I burned incense all around my office before settling down to meditate. My meditation this time brought me some powerful visions of color.

The next morning at dawn I went to the hole I had dug the previous day near my favorite tree. I burned the envelope containing the list of all the things I wanted to get rid of and put the ashes at the bottom of the hole. Very solemnly I covered the hole and put a big stone over it.

I was wondering if the blue jay would have any meaning for me. Foxes hadn't been sure it would be because I had dropped its feather from my hand during the healing session. Later that day as I was pushing a shopping cart through the supermarket, I had to stop quickly when something fell down in front of my cart. It was a framed illustration of a blue jay! Spirit gave me my answer!

The next several days were very joyful; I had extraordinary feelings of new love for everyone around me. I was living pure joy.

6

Meeting My Guide

AFTER THE POST–NEW YEAR'S HEALING I received from Foxes, we began having great conversations on the phone. Gradually the topic shifted from me to my project on healers. I had been researching this television project for months and had written a presentation for it.

TEACHER IN THE ROUGH

It turned out that Foxes considered himself an authority on the subject of healers and the healing arts. However, in our conversations, instead of listening to me and encouraging me to talk, he began sermonizing about anything and everything; it was the world according to Foxes. It seemed to me that he saw himself as some kind of spiritual guru and saw me as his disciple.

I'm not sure about the veracity of everything Foxes told me, but he certainly had a lot to say.

He loved to go on and on about what was really meant in the Bible and about how everyone has misinterpreted it. Foxes was raised Catholic and took issue with the literal and single-minded approach presented by that sect, although he was still a Christian. We spent hours on the phone, talking about his opinion of the origin of the healing arts. The subject fascinated me, but I also just liked to listen to his voice. Our conversations enabled me to stay in the world of healers, so different from my everyday world. I must have been learning something, too, but my rational self was out the window. He mesmerized me.

In one of his tirades Foxes supported some of his information by quoting a local woman who was a deep-trance medium.

"A what?" I asked. The good thing about Foxes was that, because he considered me a complete neophyte, I could ask questions about anything without embarrassment.

"A deep-trance medium. That's someone who goes into a trance and then information comes through them. Later, they don't remember what happened while in the trance. It's a kind of altered state," Foxes explained.

"Altered state" was another confusing term for me, but I decided to wait on that definition.

"Where do the messages come from?" I asked.

"They come from the Spirit World. It's a way that spirits have to communicate with us," Foxes answered. "It's information to help us in our lives."

The ease with which Foxes talked about this made me feel more comfortable about the Native American I saw next to me all the time. My Indian was obviously part of the Spirit World. Still, I didn't want to acknowledge to anybody other than Foxes that I "saw" anything around me; people might think I was crazy. I believed it was one thing to "see" a dead person who everyone knew had once been a living being, but to "see" a strange Indian who came out of nowhere was insane. Maybe I was just imagining him. Nevertheless, wherever I went, this Indian chief was next to me. At home, driving my car, at a friend's house, he was there. When I flew to Europe with my husband, the Indian was close by as I entered the plane. I could not deny his presence. I told my husband about this development, but he listened to this as he did to everything else I told him about my adventures with healers; he ignored it. I was on my own with this phenomenon.

"You know the Indian chief I told you about when you came to my house?" I asked Foxes.

"Yeah, what about it?" he answered.

"I still see him," I continued.

"So?" Foxes questioned.

"Well, what do you think about that?" I ventured.

"Have you found out anything about him?" Foxes asked.

"No. I thought maybe you could help me with that," I offered.

"*You* see him. *You* do the research. What do you expect me to do about it?" Foxes barked, annoyed.

I didn't understand why he was so grumpy. He had been so much nicer the first time I had mentioned it. Now he didn't seem to want to talk about it. I felt hurt.

"I thought you might know what kind of Indian he is," I continued.

"I'm not going to do all your work for you," Foxes muttered.

I was surprised at Foxes' rather hostile answer. He was usually so soothing and comfortable. As a rule, Foxes was pleased when I asked him questions about healing and healers. Our relationship was based on his superior position as the healer savant and I as the student. Now he was acting cruel. *How could someone who had led me on this path so lovingly turn so mean*, I wondered.

"But you know all about Native Americans. I've never met any, and I don't know anything about them. I don't even know where to start looking for information. Why don't you want to help me?" I insisted.

"Have you ever heard of coyote teaching?" Foxes questioned.

"No, what's that?" I answered, thinking I didn't really care to learn, either. Why learn about coyotes when I needed information on Indians?

"Coyote teaching means you have to search everywhere to find the answer yourself. You don't just go to someone and get an answer. You go out and look for it. I've got to go. Call me later. Good-bye," Foxes ended our conversation.

I felt bruised by Foxes' dismissal, but I also felt challenged. I was going to find out who my companion was on my own, and I was going to start right away!

The only problem was that I had no idea where to start. Meditation seemed as good a place as any, so I settled down in front of my candle flame to discover where to look for information about my Indian chief. During my meditation I "heard" the words *go to the library*. That seemed like a pretty obvious solution. *So much for having a special gift*, I thought. *I could have thought that up on my own without bothering to meditate.*

Because my only clue was my companion's appearance, I decided to go to the library's children's section, figuring there would be more illustrations there. With any luck I might find a similar image. When I got to the appropriate area, I was faced with a wall of books about Indians. All those bindings looking out at me were daring me to choose one. They all looked alike.

I randomly selected a book. As I pulled it out, I noticed that the cover had a picture of the headdress that my Indian companion wore. I leafed through the pages and there he was, beautifully illustrated. I couldn't believe it! The first book I selected was the one with his picture! My Indian was a Lakota elder. Feeling very strange about finding this answer so quickly, I took the book home and made a photocopy of the black and white illustration in his honor. It was the first time I knew anything about Indians; I never had seen any in Ohio where I had grown up.

I called Foxes with the news of my discovery.

"Hi! My Indian is a Lakota medicine man," I said proudly.

"How do you know that?" Foxes countered.

I explained to Foxes how I had found the book with my companion's illustration in it.

"That doesn't make him a medicine man," Foxes barked.

"Well, he's a Lakota elder. A chief. I know that for sure by the way he's dressed," I answered. I wished that my book had more information about Indians. I had been so surprised to find the picture so quickly that I had left the library right away.

"Now you have to find out why he's with you. Let me know what you find out," Foxes hung up the phone.

Am I ever going to impress this man? I wondered, as I said good-bye to no one. I wasn't sure I wanted to find out why a Lakota elder was my companion, although I had become more comfortable seeing him next to me. He began to feel reassuring; I knew he meant me no harm. I was pretty sure he wasn't like the man who had marched into my office while I was doing my healing meditations and had urinated on my face.

My Lakota elder had been around long enough without frightening me for me to begin to trust him and want to find out more about him. The problem was I had no idea how I could find out why he was there. It was one thing to look up a picture in a book, another to figure out why I was seeing this vision.

MELANIE TO THE RESCUE

To continue work on my healers project, I went to interview Melanie Noblitt-Gambino, a wonderful healer and teacher. She is a graduate of Rosalyn Bruyere's Crucible Program for Healers and an ordained minister in the Healing Light Center Church, which is the equivalent of certification in Bruyere's organization. Melanie was going to give me a healing as a demonstration.

We began with a conversation about healing in general and then soon I was up on the massage table, ready to receive some energy from Melanie. I felt wonderfully comfortable as she skillfully asked me probing questions to bring out issues that I needed to work on.

"Strange things have been happening to me," I explained. "At Theo's workshop I saw the spirit of a deceased woman. And now I 'see' a Lakota elder next to me all the time," I explained as I motioned to what I thought was my invisible companion.

"Yes, right there next to you," Melanie smiled. She saw my Lakota elder, too. I was flooded with relief at the confirmation that my companion was really there, and that I wasn't the only one who could see him! It made me feel even more comfortable with him; I wasn't just imagining things.

"What's his name?" Melanie asked.

"I don't know," I answered, shocked at the question.

"Why don't you ask him?" Melanie continued.

"Talk to him?" My mind went spinning out of control. This was too much! Melanie expected me to be able to hear what my companion said. What if I didn't like what he said? I was terrified.

"Go ahead. Ask him his name. I'll listen too," Melanie encouraged.

I thought I heard something like "Tonka," but I felt embarrassed to say it out loud. Tonka was the name of a toy manufacturer, not a Lakota elder. I was too shy to say anything or even recognize that I was "hearing" something.

"It begins with a T. Go on and say it," Melanie urged. "Ta . . ."

"Tatonka," I muttered, thinking that I was speaking gibberish.

"Tatonka! That's great!" Melanie cheered. "Tatonka. That means 'buffalo' in Lakota."

"It does?" I said in wonder. I didn't know anything about Indians. How could I have invented a name that actually meant something in Lakota?

"He wants me to call him Tonka for short," I said. Melanie made me feel that all this was wonderful and exciting.

With Melanie's encouragement I asked when Tatonka had joined me, and I "saw"a photo of myself as a young child, about four years old, with an Indian chief dressed in a manner similar to Tonka's. I had forgotten that picture. We had been on our family vacation, and I was sick, as usual. My mother always insisted on stopping at every roadside attraction. This one had something to do with Indians. We stopped, and even though I was feeling sick, she made me stand next to the Indian chief for a photo. Melanie laughed as I recounted this story.

"He says you thought you were stopping for the photo, but it was really to pick him up. He is your guide," Melanie explained.

"My guide!" I exclaimed. I never even thought of that. Why hadn't Foxes suggested that to me?

"You're an open channel, just like me," Melanie said. "That means that you can hear and see the other side, the Spirit World."

So that's what's going on, I thought. I was amazed, but had to admit that I *had* seen that deceased woman at the memorial service organized by Theo. I understood now that Tonka was part of the same Spirit World. Melanie made all this seem perfectly normal. There was nothing frightening or bizarre. Instead, I now felt it was a wonderful gift.

"When you're an open channel, you can pick up higher frequencies, similar to an animal's ability to hear things humans can't. Now that you're open, you need a gatekeeper. That's someone in the Spirit World who can keep spirits from talking to you unless you want to hear them. Before I had my gatekeeper in place I was constantly hearing messages for people and trying to deliver them," Melanie laughed.

That rang true for me, too.

"That happens to me sometimes," I told Melanie. "I just feel that I have to tell someone something. I have to give them a message. I never thought of it in those terms before."

"It's important information that the spirits want to get through any way they can," Melanie said.

"Right. The words usually don't mean anything to me, but they have a profound effect on the person I tell them to. I also feel terribly agitated until I deliver the message. One time I kept feeling I had to tell a young woman named Jane, 'You are perfect despite the circumstances of your birth.' Talk about a weird thing to say. I thought the message was really strange because I knew that the woman, who was about twenty-five years old, had had a normal childhood and her parents were still married," I told Melanie.

"The situation doesn't always make sense," Melanie agreed.

"When I told Jane, she dissolved in tears and spent the rest of the day crying. Later she told me her tears were very cleansing, and she felt much better. Months later I found out that her parents, who were struggling students when they were young, had gotten married when Jane's mother got pregnant. This woman had always felt guilty about ruining her parents' lives."

I also understood what my recent meditations had been advising me. I had signed up for a weeklong intensive workshop with Rosalyn Bruyere. The date was coming up soon, and I had been concerned about what would happen there. My healing with Theo had triggered the unhappy memory of my childhood molestation. Bruyere had such tremendous energy I couldn't imagine what other horrible things might come up at her intensive. My meditation question recently had been "What should I expect at the intensive?" The answer I would "hear" was *Be careful of the voices.* I hadn't understood what this meant at the time. Now I did.

"Why don't you ask Tonka to be your gatekeeper?" Melanie suggested.

"Tonka can do that for me?" I asked, wishing I had had him in place before that horrible spirit had stomped in and peed on me.

"Sure," she laughed.

"That's great. In meditation recently I was asking what to expect at Rosalyn Bruyere's intensive. I kept getting a confusing message about voices there," I said.

"I know about that. You really need your gatekeeper in place before the intensive. Before I had my gatekeeper in place, I was running around at one intensive delivering messages to people from their guides. It was crazy. Now, go ahead and ask Tonka if he'll be your gatekeeper," Melanie continued.

I asked Tonka to be my gatekeeper. I "heard" him say yes. I could feel his protection around me like a warm coat.

"Now ask Tonka to take three steps behind you," Melanie instructed. I did, he moved back, and I suddenly felt much lighter. Melanie said I had to let Tonka know when I wanted to communicate with spirits, otherwise he would keep them all out. I guess he had already been doing that until I said I wanted to "see" the deceased woman at Theo's ceremony.

Melanie suggested that I probably always had the ability to be an open channel. I was reminded of my meditation experience in France, when my spirit began to leave my body. I had shut down that capability at the time.

"I remember an imaginary friend I had as a child. We had so much fun together. It was right after my best friend, Janie, moved away, and I was very lonely. My mother was so concerned about me and my imaginary friend that she took me to the doctor," I told Melanie.

"That friend was probably a young spirit who had passed over and just enjoyed playing with someone her age. Unfortunately, people don't understand what is happening. They shut kids down that way," Melanie said.

"That was true for me. That visit to the doctor taught me that it was bad to have an imaginary friend," I said.

"Spirit didn't want you to stay shut down," Melanie laughed.

"I'm really glad about that," I said. "Another thing that was weird in my life was that any time anyone works for me, they find a partner and fall in love. Then they get married and usually move away. If they're already married they usually get pregnant. It's pretty annoying! I hired a forty-year-old woman to work for me as an office manager. She had been trying to get pregnant for fifteen years. Within six months she got pregnant and left. I was happy for her, but I had to find another manager. My cleaning lady just told me she was pregnant. What's all that about?" I asked.

"Love and fertility is in your aura. When people are close to you, that's what happens to them. It sounds like a pretty nice thing," Melanie said.

"Nice for them," I agreed. "But tough on me because I always have to replace those people." I laughed with Melanie.

Feeling confident and at peace, I left Melanie. The long drive back home was more like a trip with Tonka down memory lane. We reviewed my life and how he had helped me. He was there when I had phlebitis as a fifth grader and missed almost the whole school year. He was the one who had warned me that I would go to the hospital, but that everything would be fine. Although I had never been away from home, when my mother came in my bedroom to tell me I would have to go to the hospital, I hadn't been shocked or afraid; I already knew. Tonka was there in the hospital with me, encouraging me to hang on as the hospital staff thinned and thickened my blood daily.

Tonka was there when my parents and I were in that car accident. He showed me how to get out of the smashed car and encouraged me to climb up the cliff in the rain to get help for my parents.

All those times I had wondered how I had managed to survive. I now realized that my survival in every case was due to Tonka's aid. I remembered when I was trapped and being assaulted in a rapist's car. Tonka was the one who had whispered to me to stay calm; he told me what to say and what to do and especially when to make a run for it. Tonka led me through the woods to a house, where a kind woman was right out front unlocking her door. She let me in and protected me. I owe my life many times over to Tonka.

People often ask me why my four children all have names beginning with T: Tania, Tristan, Terence, and Talia. I never had a satisfactory answer, but now I understood that it was my higher self who wanted to honor Tonka. Tonka has been helping me for so long and with so much patience. I am eternally grateful, and I will always try to be worthy of such a noble guide.

THE TEST

Because of all the time we were spending on the phone, Foxes and I decided to meet again. Once more I was driving the many miles to his retreat. This time I listened to a tape by Rosalyn Bruyere about chakra healing, and I enjoyed every minute of the drive. On the way up I heard a warning from Tonka: "There will be a test." I had no idea what he meant.

When I arrived, Foxes was in his filthy, dilapidated kitchen with Suzanne, the new tenant who had moved into the house subsequent to her interview the first evening I was there. I sat in the kitchen, disappointed. In fact, I was seething because Foxes was ignoring me and talking on and on with Suzanne, complimenting her on the great muffins she was making instead of working with me as he had promised.

I thought he was being downright rude. I had just driven two hours to get there, and I was being ignored! As Foxes poured out the coffee grounds after serving us all coffee, he stopped to read them. Yes, that was one of his talents too. Suddenly he swung violently around and stared at me.

"Why did you come here?" he snarled.

Startled, I muttered, "I thought you were going to help me with my research."

"How's that?" he barked again.

I was appalled and shrank back in my chair. He seemed like a wild animal ready to destroy me. "Like we were discussing over the phone. You invited me. That's why I came," I mumbled.

"All right. Let's do it right here," he bellowed. He marched into the living room, grabbed a Bible, opened it at random, and began commenting on the passage at hand. Grimly I started taking notes. Slowly the chilly air between us warmed up, and we began to enjoy the same intimacy we had experienced over the phone. His words were catalysts that allowed me to develop my own understanding about the universe and my place in it.

At one point I finally got up my courage to ask Foxes, "Do you know your guide?"

"Yeah, I do," he answered.

"Who is your guide?" I asked.

"It's none of your business," Foxes answered.

"The Lakota elder I see next to me is my guide," I announced.

"Oh, so you think that's your guide?" Foxes said, with just a hint of interest. "How do you know that?"

"Well, I communicate with him," I announced, hoping that finally Foxes would show me some respect.

"What makes you think you communicated with your guide?" Foxes asked skeptically.

I was dumbfounded. Foxes seemed so rude and unfriendly in response to this wonderful ability I had discovered. Melanie had been so encouraging and supportive.

"Melanie heard him, too. His name is Tonka," I said defensively.

"You should never tell anyone your guide's name, if it really is your guide's name," Foxes continued. "What's his tribe?"

"Lakota," I answered proudly.

"I know that. What's his nation?" Foxes barked at me.

I didn't know, but I "heard" and then said, "Sue."

"That's right. The Lakota are part of the Sioux Nation. Who were their archenemies?" Foxes asked.

I had no idea. I "heard" and said, "The Crow."

"That's right," Foxes intoned. He continued his questions about Indians. I "heard" the answers and repeated them to Foxes. I was amazed. Foxes, knowing my complete ignorance about Native American culture, was finally satisfied that I could really communicate with my guide. *So this was the test I had been warned about,* I thought, *and I passed with flying colors.*

In that moment my whole experience with Tonka was confirmed as being real and not at all imagined. I also gained confidence in my ability to contact spirits. I had just proven the reality of this gift to the person I trusted most in this field, and to myself. I could always count on Foxes to be brutally honest. On the long drive home, as I was "talking" to Tonka, I realized that if I could talk to him, I could also talk to other spirits, or people who had passed over.

When I got home I tried to contact some relatives who had passed over. To do this I needed to shift into what I discovered to be an "altered state." I had to have complete quiet, and then I could summon the spirit and ask Tonka to allow me to first see it and then to hear it. Gradually I learned that the spirits would communicate with me in ways other than words. Sometimes I could "see" a still image, something like a photograph. Other times I could "see" a whole film clip.

I practiced more by contacting a couple of Georges' relatives in the Spirit World. This made him very uncomfortable, so I didn't pursue it. I think my ability was a threat to his Cartesian way of thinking.

Tonka introduced me to Rachel. She has been another of my guides, and has been with me from my birth. She didn't want to present herself to me because she had been disfigured in a fire; she thought I wouldn't like her with her burn-scarred face. Now that I can see her, I find her beautiful. She taught me, an awkward, unattractive child, to be gracious and beautiful. She guides me in my selection of what to wear, how to make myself up, and in social graces.

Rachel and Tonka have very different roles to play in my life, but both are important to me, and I am grateful to them both.

I found out from Tonka that we all have at least one spirit guide. For the most part they are relatives who have passed over. They have taken on the "job" of guiding us and try to help us make the right choices in life. They have a better perspective on things from their position in the Spirit World. They are not allowed to do anything for us unless we specifically ask for help. They can send us signals that appear in many different forms.

Sometimes it's a simple "knowing." Other times we might randomly look at the printed page of a book or newspaper and a particular sentence will jump out at us to bring special meaning. On other occasions we can be talking to a stranger who will bring us the answer to a question we were mentally asking. For the most part, we aren't open to these messages.

We call them coincidences and reject the information. Another term for this is *synchronicity*. As we become more aware of the world around us, and more aware of these messages, we are better able to interpret and accept them.

My husband and I were in the process of refinancing our home. We had a dinner party with some friends. It just so happened that those friends had had an awful time refinancing. After paying a fee to guarantee the rate for a month, the time it normally took to complete the paperwork, the company dragged its feet. Our friends had to engage a lawyer to recuperate their fee, and they ended up changing mortgage companies.

I told my husband that we needed to be careful. This was a message. We had also paid a guarantee fee, and the month was coming to an end. The mortgage company always seemed to ask for more paperwork when everything seemed to be complete. I finally told my husband to hire a lawyer. One letter from the lawyer and we got our mortgage refinanced immediately.

I wondered why Foxes had been so unpleasant about my relationship with Tonka. It wasn't just coyote teaching that made him so rough with me. He seemed to be angry that I could communicate with Tonka. Then

I realized why he had been so evasive when I asked him about his guide. It was probably because he couldn't communicate directly with his own guide! Melanie hadn't minded helping me discover my gift because she had the same gift. With Foxes, I had a gift that he didn't have, and I guess that irritated him. I decided not to talk to him about it anymore. He had so many other things to tell me about healers, and, besides, I loved to listen to him talk, and he seemed to love to talk to me. What other magical things lay ahead for me to discover?

7

The First
Spiritual Initiation

AFTER MEETING TONKA I became even more interested in my conversations with Foxes. He seemed too good to be true, making me feel wonderful most of the time and sharing my enthusiasm for healing. His energy was unbelievable! Plus, he was interested in helping me with my soul's project: to produce a television documentary on healers. I put Foxes on a pedestal as my healing arts mentor, and I gave him all my power. I gave him my energy, too, but he would take it and return it to me in spades because he had such boundless energy himself. He was very firm in his belief system, and I immediately bought into it. For me, his word was law.

Foxes explained to me that everyone has energy and wiring; that is the way the mind functions. If someone has lots of energy and bad wiring, they can't achieve much. The same thing is true for people with great wiring and low energy. The most successful people have high energy and great wiring. They get an idea and then have the intelligence and the energy to manifest it. According to Foxes I had pretty good wiring but low energy. I never could get my ideas off the ground. Although he never admitted it, I knew Foxes had high energy but I suspected his wiring was a bit faulty.

During our many meetings Foxes talked about his personal philosophy of the origin of healers, their history, and why they had been neglected by society for so many years. I wouldn't always accept his philosophy, and I often argued with him about it, but I always gave up in the end and accepted his point of view. We both looked forward to these meetings. Often I would go to his qi gong and tai chi classes after our work sessions. I never realized that he needed the power I gave him. In fact, I never realized I gave him my power until much later.

Why are we always looking for mentors? Why do we always need to put someone on a pedestal to tell us what is right and wrong? Why do we empower people in this way, stripping ourselves of our natural abilities to develop our own direct relationship with the Creator and establish our own belief system? These mentors can be anyone who tells us how anything should be done— a religious leader, friend, or relative. We always have a choice and an obligation to question everything. That's what this life is all about.

COYOTE TEACHING

I began to look forward to the ride up to see Foxes. It was an opportunity for me to meditate, communicate with Tonka, and reflect on all the new things that were happening to me as I opened up to Spirit. I no longer saw the filth in Heartbreak Hotel, and I looked forward to the gourmet lunches Foxes would make. He had plenty of time, because winter was off-season for construction.

As winter turned into spring and the rough branches bore delicate, gentle buds that blossomed into even more delicate flowers, I witnessed a change in Foxes. After initially being so considerate and caring, it seemed to me that Foxes increasingly treated me in a rough, almost rude way, berating me for not knowing different things about the world of healers. But how could I have known anything about healers or the Spirit World? When I debated a point with him, he would ridicule me for my beliefs and my foolishness for harboring such absurd beliefs.

When I would mention shyly how he wasn't very nice to me, he would say, "That's coyote teaching." Although part of what was happening *was* coyote teaching, another part of it was me assuming my familiar position as victim, unable to stand up for myself. I couldn't because I didn't have any more power, and the only energy I had was what Foxes would return to me after I gave it to him.

Although Foxes ultimately benefited many times from my ability to contact the Spirit World, I never felt that he really respected me. However, it was clear that he took me seriously. In my everyday world no one could contact spirits, and anyone who said they could was considered a freak or a fraud. My "chatter-mind," that helpful little voice we all hear that tells us we're wrong, was constantly telling me I was crazy. Meanwhile, the beauty and magnitude of pure bliss that I enjoyed by contacting the Spirit World encouraged me to continue at any cost. To me, part of that cost was accommodating Foxes.

One day I was particularly agitated and wishing very hard that Foxes would call, because we hadn't met in a while. Out of the blue the phone rang.

"What's wrong?" Foxes demanded, without even saying hello first.

"I . . . I was upset because we hadn't set up a meeting recently," I stuttered, surprised by his call.

"Okay. How about Tuesday?" he asked.

"That works for me," I replied.

"Good. See you then." Foxes hung up without saying good-bye.

This was a confirmation that we could communicate telepathically. He had "heard" my mental appeal for him to contact me, and he had immediately responded.

When Foxes called, he never announced himself. He would simply say "Hi," and launch into whatever was on his mind. I thought he must feel pretty sure that I could identify him from a simple "Hi." He was right, of course. To me it felt like a kind of ownership on his part to be able to do this. I have to admit, I rather liked the fact that he felt so comfortable with me. He had become my best friend and a part of my family, although I saw him only once a week, if that.

It's important to mention that Penney had pointed out to me during one of our first sessions how I gave my power to everyone around me. She said I had a lot of power, but that I was always eager to empower others and leave myself empty. She tried to get me to control my power and use it for myself. But even good-hearted Penney couldn't stop me from empowering her with my energy and depleting myself. This is a kind of codependency that leaves the dependent person empty and ultimately unable to function. And no one ever says thank you.

Not realizing I was divesting myself of my energy by spending time with someone whose agenda included me, I was extraordinarily blissful. I felt love everywhere. Once again Penney was right when she told me I would get stronger on my own, away from her. I didn't need or want a romantic relationship with Foxes. I was happy to be in his energy field discussing healing. That was my passion. At the same time I was breaking through so fast it made my head spin.

I began communicating with Tonka effortlessly, and I could contact spirits on the other side to help people heal wounds of loss. Although Georges wasn't on the same path, our relationship improved, thanks to my general fullness of love for everyone. I was so happy being connected to the Spirit World that nothing bothered me in the physical. I enjoyed frequent trips to Europe. For my birthday in February Georges and I went to Monte Carlo, where we had dinner with Prince Albert. It was a formal business event, not in my honor but, nevertheless, how many people get to celebrate their birthdays in that way? Georges and I also went to Paris and Cannes, and to Montreux, Switzerland. It was lots of fun, even though these were business trips. I loved staying in the finest hotels and eating the best food in the world. In my free time, I would be off in the Spirit World.

Foxes resented my trips, and he let me know it. As I was traveling, I began seeing Foxes' image in front of me all the time. I felt as though I could mentally communicate with him, and I did, even when I was in France. It seemed that we could read each other's minds regardless of where we were. My need to maintain contact with him encouraged me to empower him more and more, leaving me weaker and weaker. At his demand, Foxes became my coauthor on the television project, even though I was doing all the work. We would get together and talk for a couple of hours, and then I would spend hours and hours alone, writing the television presentation.

I believed I had to give all my power to Foxes to assure my opening to Spirit.

ANOTHER WORKSHOP

My second workshop about healing was with Rosalyn Bruyere, the internationally renowned energy healer. I had already chosen Bruyere to be part of my television program because of her excellent reputation. The equivalent of a diploma in energy healing in Rosalyn's organization, The Healing Light Center Church, is to become an ordained minister. This takes many years of study.

Two ministers, Theo Kyskostas and Melanie Noblit-Gambino, had built Rosalyn's reputation up to soaring heights for me; I was not disappointed when I met her. In fact, I was overwhelmed by her power, humility, and approachability. I was very shy about going to the intensive. This was a new experience for me. I was going to be away from my family for a week, alone. Of course there were other participants, but I had not gone off for a retreat without my family since my yoga experiences in Paris. I felt awkward and nervous.

The intensive workshop was to be held for five days in an isolated convent. The energy that Rosalyn and her partner, Ken Weintrub, brought to it was incredible. The participants were, for the most part, very high-level energy healers. They added to the energy level in the hall where we met. I felt overwhelmed and frequently had headaches, which I learned were common when one expanded one's ability to reach higher vibrations. My migraines were a direct result of adapting to much greater energy vibrations.

As I arrived at the somber convent, I silently thanked Melanie for helping me engage Tonka as my gatekeeper. He would keep out all the spirits who wanted to talk to someone on the physical plane. Even though I had contacted some spirits for people at home, I had decided not to mention this gift to anyone at the intensive. I wanted to keep a low profile because I felt so awkward; I was a television producer in the midst of powerful healers. Anyway, I imagined that all these healers were also open channels, like me. I was sure that most of them were clairvoyant and clairaudient and could converse with spirits as well.

Theo welcomed me warmly and made me feel comfortable immediately. I settled into my small room and then went down to dinner. The vast dining hall seemed forbidding. Other participants embraced each other with joy, but I didn't see anyone I knew, and Theo was stuck at the door welcoming new arrivals. Finally I recognized a few people I had met at Theo's workshop many months earlier I sat down with them.

One of the women immediately turned to me and said, "Oh, Alexandra, a lot has happened since I saw you six months ago. My mother died in a car accident. Can you see her?"

I froze. I hadn't wanted anyone to know I could do that.

"No," I mumbled. It was partially true. I couldn't "see" Linda's mother, but I did know for sure she was around Linda. I felt it. Linda cast her gaze down and sighed.

During the lecture that evening I was sitting about three yards away from Rosalyn, who was speaking, in the front of the large hall. Suddenly all I could hear was a woman's voice screaming, "I know you can hear me! Listen to me! I know you can hear me!" I couldn't hear Rosalyn's voice anymore, just a strange woman's voice screaming in my head.

Oh, God, I am losing my mind, I thought in a panic.

Then, on top of that voice, I heard Tonka warning, "Intruder! Intruder!" Strangely enough, Tonka's voice reassured me that something real was happening. I knew the woman's voice was Linda's mother. I tried to ignore her, but I couldn't hear anything else. Mentally I promised to communicate with her daughter later. The woman asked me who her daughter was. Unfortunately, in my excitement, I thought the wrong name. "Linda," she corrected me. "Her name is *Linda.*"

I wrote down Linda's name and promised to tell Linda I would connect her with her mother. Once again I was able to hear Rosalyn, and I relaxed. Nevertheless, several times during the lecture Linda's mother would return and ask me again, "What is my daughter's name?" I would answer her by circling Linda's name. Then she would allow me to listen to the lecture in peace.

Later that night I contacted Linda's mother for her. Linda and I sat in a quiet place. I relaxed to be able to calm my chatter-mind. Gradually, as I began to feel drowsy, I heard Linda's mother. Then I saw her standing slightly behind Linda.

"Linda, I love you! Don't worry about me. I didn't suffer in the accident. I went to the light right away. It was much better this way," Linda's mother told me. I repeated this to Linda. "Please try to understand," her mother continued.

Linda sobbed and nodded slowly.

"It would have been too much for me to go through. There was no point. Can you understand? The accident was a blessing. I don't want you to be sad," Linda's mother continued.

I certainly didn't understand what she was talking about. I asked Linda if any of this made sense to her.

"Yes, it does," Linda said. "My mother was going to undergo major surgery soon because of a health condition. The surgery was scheduled, but she died just a month before it in the accident."

This was important information for Linda. She understood that her mother's death was in fact a deliverance. The surgery wasn't guaranteed to be successful, and Linda's mother could have or probably would have suffered increasing pain.

Reflecting on what had happened, I realized that only God could bypass a gatekeeper, as Tonka had been bypassed. This was a sign to me that I had been given a gift, and I was expected to use it. No hiding my light under a bushel basket for me! But I was still concerned about contacting spirits in general. Would I be protected? If Linda's mother had gotten past my gatekeeper, couldn't others who might not be so nice? I explained to Linda that I was keeping a low profile and made her promise not to tell anyone about my gift.

As the workshop progressed, my mind was spinning. There was so much information about chakras and colors and channeling energy that I felt overwhelmed. Every healer attending knew all of this already and were merely perfecting their skills. I was a television producer, not a healer. *I don't need to learn all this stuff anyway*, I thought defiantly one night. Suddenly I heard a voice say, "Oh yes you do." There was no one in my bedroom with me.

I began to realize that my gift for contacting spirits was unique, and that many healers were striving to somehow develop this particular gift. Even people who are able to contact spirits rarely can do it visually and audibly. To not honor this gift was to insult all the people who so wanted to have it.

Ken practiced qi gong with us and led us in some guided meditations. Everything was so powerful. The qi gong series he and Rosalyn developed for healers is one that I now use every day. As Ken performed the qi gong series, Rosalyn would draw his aura. Together they developed a series of movements that balanced the aura energetically.

In an effort to to ground myself I tried to call my family on my cell phone several times, but I couldn't get through; the retreat's location didn't have good reception. It seemed that I was supposed to be on my own, experiencing all this strange stuff.

Rosalyn believes that naps are very important for the efficient functioning of the human body. During her intensives she always has the participants take afternoon naps.

I was taking our required nap in my room one afternoon when my cell phone rang. It was Foxes. I was amazed that he had gotten through. He just wanted to talk. It was beautiful hearing his voice. He missed me and wanted to know how things were going. At the workshop I had been so involved with everything going on that I hadn't thought about Foxes. My permanent connection to him had been interrupted, and he knew it. Maybe he felt me taking some of my power back as I became more empowered. I excitedly filled him in on all the things we were doing. Once again we were connected, and he was an intrinsic part of my opening to Spirit as I gifted him with my power.

The theme of the seminar was *Healing and Dreaming: The Marriage of the Mystic and the Mind*. Rosalyn taught us to build "rooms" in our minds. These rooms became very real places. Rosalyn encouraged us to decorate them as we wanted. In the afternoons we took naps and visited the rooms we had just created. At night we visited these same rooms and saw what Spirit wanted to convey to us. In the room designated for friendship, Foxes appeared. It was wonderful to have him there.

Rosalyn herself is so powerful and kind, very accessible and real. It was obvious that she loved us all. Her self-deprecating humor and her humility in the face of the remarkable healing that she has achieved for people is an example for us all.

At one point an eighteen-month-old girl was running around the lecture hall, laughing and talking to everyone while her mother tried to keep up with her. Rosalyn had a massage table up in front of the room. She called the little girl and her mother forward. It turned out that when the little girl was born, she had been diagnosed with brain damage. The neurosurgeons declared that she would suffer some kind of disability and offered only patience to the mother as the infant went into convulsions. The mother had no patience. She contacted Rosalyn, who worked with the infant, and the results we saw were amazing. The little girl was perfectly healthy now, with no disabilities. Rosalyn gave her a last treatment and pronounced her completely healed. It was a true miracle.

We learned to feel energy and channel healing energy to one another. At the end several of us were working on each other in groups. Not everyone in the group could have a turn because of time limitations. I very much wanted to have a healing by the group, and it proved to be an initiation. Once again I felt the light of God surround us. One of my favorite hymns, "Here I Am," kept running through my mind with these lyrics: *Here I am Lord. / Is it I, Lord? / I have heard you calling in the night. / If you lead, Lord, I will follow, / I will hold your people in my light.*

After the session I was very dizzy. One of the practitioners mentioned that it was a real initiation. The others agreed. Yes, something profound had happened.

On the last day of the intensive there was much joy and camaraderie. Rosalyn was sending us off with wonderful light and love. The good-byes we said were full of hope and happiness as we were all eager to take our lessons to the world.

A curious thing happened while I was saying good-bye to Jan Brugal and Katherine Baugh. Jan is a wonderful healer, full of light and goodness. Katherine, one of Rosalyn Bruyere's ordained ministers, had been kind and helpful. She had made me feel comfortable in this confusing and daunting healers' world.

To my and Katherine's surprise, Jan turned to me and asked me to contact Katherine's mother, who had passed on several months earlier. I hesitated, because I was still shy about my unusual gift. But seeing the hopeful look in Katherine's eyes, I couldn't refuse. As a message to Tonka, I thought, *Let her in,* referring to Katherine's mother.

Suddenly I began to tremble and sob. I threw myself on Katherine and gave her a big hug, patting her back. Appalled at my actions, I quickly pulled back and recovered my composure. It didn't take me long to realize I had allowed Katherine's mother to inhabit my body. I had channeled her in that moment. Katherine was in shock. Apparently her mother had Parkinson's disease, and before she died all she could do was hug Katherine and pat her back as I had done. Once again in control of myself, I asked Tonka to let me contact Katherine's mother so that I could "see" and "hear" her. Not only could I now hear things that she was saying, I could also see images that she wanted to show me. Katherine was delighted and healed by this communication with her mother.

The unsettling experience of having a spirit inhabit my body made me even more uncomfortable about contacting spirits for people. I worried that some bad spirit would inhabit me without my knowing it, or something equally horrible or worse would happen.

When it was over, Jan came to me and whispered, "You are protected in this work that you must do. Don't worry." For some reason I took her words to heart and realized that I needed to make myself available to contact spirits for whoever needed it. I knew Tonka would always protect me. That day's experience showed me I could channel and do it quite well.

Much later on I learned that when a spirit is channeled, it first appears in the last form it had before passing over to the Spirit World. That's why Katherine's mother "appeared" with Parkinson's disease. This is a form of identification for the person in the physical world. The deceased person isn't really caught in that sad state for eternity. When I contact a spirit, I always see it in a relatively attractive form. I only see the illness or accident if I mentally ask how the person died. Then I "see" the spirit's physical body at the point of death. This is never frightening; it is simply informative.

I have often thought about the coincidence of that moment when the three of us—Jan, Katherine, and myself—were together, when I understood that with my gift came the obligation to use it to help people. It's amazing how often we experience "coincidences" that we discount and choose to ignore. I like to think of what Dr. Bernie Siegel once said: "Coincidence is God's way of remaining discreet."

Rosalyn Bruyere's intensive was a hallmark experience for me. It's hard to put into words the profound difference it made in me as a person. I arrived there a frightened mouse; I left tremendously empowered. No longer frightened of my special connection with Spirit, I now rejoiced in it. Every time someone needed to contact a loved one who had passed over, I promised God to be available to help that person heal. I have tried to live by that pledge.

AURORA

An important person I met at the Bruyere intensive was Diane Foster Grella. At one point we were randomly partnered. It turned out to be the beginning of a beautiful friendship. Diane is a Reiki master, a certified hypnotherapist, an ayurvedic practitioner certified by Deepak Chopra, and is certified in EMF (electromagnetic field) Balancing. These are all different forms of alternative medicine that are available to people everywhere. They can be used instead of or combined with allopathic medicine. Diane's credentials are second to none, and she is an amazing, talented woman. In her down-to-earth way she has kept me in positive balance about the many gifts I have experienced with the Spirit World.

I was focused on my television project when Diane introduced me to a wonderful healer in Connecticut named Aurora. Aurora conducted a session on me. The basic teaching she gave is one that has stayed with me and still echoes as a guideline for enjoying everyday living.

What Aurora taught me was this: We begin with something we want to happen. In other words, we have an intention that we want to manifest. With that intention we attach expectations as to how we believe the manifestation of our intention will play out. For example, I want to produce a television project. That is my intention, what I want to have happen. Rather than do what I think I need to do to make that manifest, I begin to imagine exactly how things *should* play out. I attach expectations to my intention. I imagine where I will pitch the project and how it will be received. I end up being so convinced of the way things need to play out that I feel completely lost and rejected when it doesn't work out in the manner I expected. I then waste time feeling sorry for myself, or I just drop the project altogether.

Instead I should continue to put energy into my intention, but I shouldn't attach expectations to that intention.

I should pitch my project to everyone in a detached manner and accept the outcome without losing the intention. I should also be open to the information coming in. I should let the universe work things out without being upset by some strange side roads.

When things don't work out as we expect, we lose our energy through depression. We begin to believe it will never work out; too often we give up. The same thing holds true for communicating with spirits. When the spirits don't speak to us in sounds we want to hear, and they don't let us see them, we give up because the communication has failed to meet our expectations. It's as though we say, "I'm not going to communicate with a spirit unless I can see it and hear it speak recognizable words." We miss so much this way.

The other important guideline Aurora taught me was the difference between reacting to something and responding to it. When we react, it means we are not sure of our truth, therefore we have to defend ourselves and convince someone else they're wrong. We do this because we aren't solid in our own truth, and we are really trying to convince ourselves as we vehemently try to convince someone else.

For example, Tara believes in spirits; Martha doesn't. Rather than let Martha live in her own truth, Tara will try very hard to convince Martha that spirits exist, because Tara feels threatened by Martha's disbelief. Tara feels threatened because she isn't completely convinced herself. If Tara were completely convinced that spirits exist, if this *was* her truth, then she would respond to Martha by simply acknowledging that Martha's truth was different from her own. When we *respond* to something, we don't have emotion attached to the response. When we *react* to something, a trigger is hit and we have an emotional reaction. Once we are sure of our own truth, that emotional trigger no longer exists, and we can calmly respond with peace and detachment.

8

Getting Stronger

"HI, ALEXANDRA?" a tired little voice addressed me over the phone.

"Yes? Carmen, is that you?" I asked.

"Yes. You know that surgery I had a week ago to remove an ovary? I still haven't recuperated. I'm so exhausted. We'll have to postpone our lunch. I'm sorry," Carmen said.

Carmen and I were supposed to have lunch when I returned from the Bruyere intensive. We had planned it a month prior. I couldn't believe that she would endure surgery rather than see Penney as I had suggested. Carmen knew about my fibroids and how Penney had healed me. This made me realize that many of us are brainwashed into believing that the only one way to heal is through modern medicine. We don't even consider other possibilities.

"I just got back from an intensive with Rosalyn Bruyere. She is amazing! What energy, and what a fabulous teacher! She taught us to channel energy. We practiced it on each other. Would you like me to come over and give you some energy?" I asked Carmen.

Carmen is a very private person, so I was surprised when she eagerly agreed that I should come over. Carmen lay pale and subdued on her couch when I arrived, like a shadow of her former self. It hurt me to see her usually energetic, happy self crushed. Awkwardly, I did as Rosalyn had taught us. I placed my right index finger and thumb gently on Carmen's vertebrae, beginning at the coccyx or first chakra, and my left

95

index finger and thumb at the base cervical vertebra. Apparently the cervical vertebrae—the bones of the neck—model the seven chakras. As your right hand moves up the chakras on the spine, the left hand moves up the seven cervical vertebrae. At the end you put the right hand on the first chakra and the left hand on top of the head to send energy up and down the spine. This was the only technique I remembered from the intensive. When I was finished I instructed Carmen to take a nap, and I quietly let myself out the door.

The next morning the phone rang.

"Hi, Alexandra," Carmen sang. "Are you free for lunch today? You know, after you left yesterday, I slept for an hour. Then my son Thomas came home. I jumped up and drove him to his piano lesson. Then I went to Starbucks and had a coffee, just like I used to do. I had forgotten all about my surgery. And the best part is that I'm not tired at all. And I feel great today! Thank you so much!"

USING MY GIFTS

My family benefited from my new skill. On the soccer field one day my daughter Talia sprained her ankle right before halftime. She was carried off the field in tears. Her ankle looked bad, and she was in terrible pain. Georges was her coach, and he decided to pull her out of the game even though they really needed her. There was no way she could play when she was injured.

There on the sidelines I placed my hands on Talia's leg and channeled energy to her ankle. I tried to look as nonchalant as possible, as though I were just holding her ankle to inspect it. I was fervently praying to God to use me as an instrument of his healing energy. When halftime was over, to everyone's amazement Talia got up and, joining her team, finished the game. Her ankle was healed. It never bothered her again. And no one realized that I had just healed her.

Talia's piano teacher was a delightful older woman. Her husband was eighty and in declining health. When the teacher found out that I could channel energy, she asked me to help; every time I picked up Talia from her lesson I would channel energy to her teacher's husband. The poor man would smile at me wanly from a pasty-colored face as he sat down in a chair.

His back was so bent that he couldn't lie down on his stomach. I would stand behind him, gently laying my hands on his shoulders. After a while I would feel the energy coming back into my hands. Then I would know he was "cooked," as I came to call it. The difference in his face was striking. His cheeks would be rosy, and he would flash me a great smile.

Foxes also gave credence to my ability to channel energy. He had terribly painful knots in his shoulders because of his work; he had to carry cans of paint and other heavy materials. I used the same method on Foxes as I had on the eighty-year-old man. I simply lay my hands on Foxes's shoulders, channeled energy, and made the knots disappear.

"Aren't I good at channeling energy?" I asked Foxes one day as I channeled energy to his tight shoulders.

"You're okay," Foxes said. That was the closest he ever got to complimenting me. "I know another Alexandra who's a masseuse. She lives upstate. She's really amazing with knots in muscles!"

"I bet she isn't a beautiful blonde," I fired back.

"No, she's a beautiful brunette," Foxes retorted. "*She's* very gifted."

℘

Because of my early success channeling energy, I felt that anyone could learn to do it. My *real* gift was in conversing with the Spirit World. If you've got it, flaunt it, right? Well, maybe I wasn't ready to flaunt it, but I was ready to use this extraordinary gift, and I began to contact spirits for people. I realized I was clairvoyant, clairaudient, and clairsentient. I could see the spirits and hear what they were saying. I could also see a short "film" or random images that were presented to me from Spirit. It was very exciting. Sometimes I would feel something within my own body that would give me information.

What I see is a clear image that is superimposed on what everyone can see in the physical world. When I'm working, it might often seem as if I'm looking at an empty wall. I choose that background so that I can better see the images that Spirit is sending me, like watching a film projected against a background. If the background is neutral, it's easier to see. If there isn't a neutral background, I can focus in on the image from Spirit and blur out the physical world image.

Hearing is literally that. It is as though someone is standing behind my right shoulder and speaking to me. Sometimes the words flow easily and I have no problem hearing them. Other times I just hear bits and pieces of information. This is usually complemented by some visual support, like a film clip or images, to help me understand the message.

I also just *know* a great deal about my client when I'm in a session. This isn't anything I pick up through my senses; it is knowledge that is there, as though I have been my client's best friend and confidant their whole life.

One day I was rushing to catch a subway in New York City. About fifty yards away from me I saw a man collapsed on the floor, surrounded by people who were helping him. We made eye contact as I raced by. I didn't stop, because it looked as though many people were already helping. I wondered what had happened. On the subway I suddenly felt excruciating pain in my chest. I couldn't breathe. It was frightening. I was trying to figure out what to do when Tonka told me that I had asked what was wrong with the man collapsed in the station. This was my answer: The man had suffered a massive heart attack. Immediately my pain subsided, and I was fine. After that I was very careful about articulating what I wanted to know.

Because I was still shy about it, I would tell only select people about my gift, and inevitably that individual would be someone who could benefit from it. Tonka would indicate to me who needed a healing contact with a loved one in the Spirit World, and then I would mention to that person that I was a medium. Always the person would want a reading or to have contact made. This included many people whom I didn't know personally at all. For the most part I met them at workshops, often getting "randomly" partnered with someone who would immediately be grateful to find out I had this gift. It was what they needed to heal.

I was especially careful to keep my new world as a medium separate from my suburban mother world. Because I was still adapting to my gift, I simply wouldn't talk about it at all in my daily life. This meant that I never discussed it with my husband, and certainly never at social gatherings. This made Georges more comfortable.

On one occasion Spirit overrode my predilection to separate "home talk" and "spirit talk." I was at a business lunch with my husband. In my mind I was there for a free meal, barely following the conversation, when Tonka told me that I had to let our dining companion know about my gift. To Georges' horror, I told his colleague that I was clairvoyant. I thought Georges would fall off his chair. The colleague didn't blink an eye but said that he had lost his mother a few months prior (which was news to Georges) and that he was looking for someone with this precise gift. I was answering his prayer.

To contact a spirit, I'd first say a prayer and then sit in a quiet place with my client and slip into an altered state. The state of my body was changed. I calmed my chatter-mind and allowed my body to reach a state of deep relaxation, the same state people try to reach when they meditate. I won't venture into a scientific analysis of brain waves, but I know that scientific research exists that confirms this altered state. Then I began communication with Tonka. I asked Tonka to allow me to communicate with a certain spirit. I then heard the spirit's voice and saw the spirit appear, usually slightly behind and to the side of my client. The spirit's voice came to me from behind my right side, whereas my "chatter-voice" came to me from my left. This helped me distinguish between what I might be thinking and what I was actually receiving from the Spirit World. Gradually I learned to have confidence in what I heard from Spirit, even if it didn't make sense to me.

At one reading for a man whose mother had recently passed over, I heard the words "coffeemaker, small appliances." I thought I couldn't say such a bizarre thing to this man at a time when he was emotionally upset, but that's what I heard. I finally decided to override my chatter-mind, and I explained the situation.

"Please bear with me, but I keep hearing 'coffeemaker' and 'small appliances.' Something about forgetting to turn them off. Does that mean anything to you?" I asked shyly.

The man looked at me, stricken. "I'm totally obsessed with forgetting to turn off small appliances. Just last Saturday night I left a concert during intermission because I was sure that I had forgotten to turn off my coffeemaker."

"Your mother wants you to know that she's going to help you with this. She's going to watch over you and cue you if you ever really do forget to turn off an appliance before you leave your house," I explained to the man.

Who knew?

With my healing work I come into contact with many different people. A client by the name of Shirley was distraught because her brother had been murdered. Several months after the fact she was still tremendously depressed. I offered to contact her brother. I was a bit nervous about this because he had died a violent, dreadful death. I was concerned that perhaps the quality of his death had something to do with the energy around him now.

It proved to be a beautiful contact. He was in a beautiful place. He wasn't upset about his death, but was very philosophical about it, and he was glad to communicate with his sister. The spirit can "hear" the physical person's thoughts, but I always ask the physical person to speak out loud to make it easier for me to understand what I hear from the spirit.

Shirley asked her brother about different people he had known. At one point he began to swear when she mentioned a particular name. I was surprised at the sudden change in his mellow attitude. I asked her who this man was. It turned out to be the murderer. Shirley wanted to know if she should testify against this man, because it was emotionally draining for her to be at the trial. Her brother said she needed to go. It would be bad for the perpetrator to get away with this crime because he might harm others in the future. Shirley's brother didn't want revenge against his murderer.

Shirley continued her questions, "Should I give some money to Sarah?"

Her brother answered, "No. Shirley, you should hold onto the money. You will need it later. Sarah wants something else, anyway."

At that point I saw something that looked like a guitar, but it wasn't really a guitar.

"I see something that looks like a guitar, but it's different than that. What could it be?" I asked Shirley.

"That must be my brother's balalaika. Sarah actually asked me if she could have it. I guess he wants her to have it," Shirley said softly.

HOW LIFE WORKS

Contacting spirits has brought me some insight to the reason why we are here on Earth, and how this whole system works. Basically, we all begin as spirits residing in a different dimension, or vibration, that I will call

Heaven because all spirits are happy there, just like you would imagine. To refine our spiritual state we need to incarnate, to have our spirit enter a human body form. We then come to the Earth plane, or dimension or vibration, as you might prefer to call it. Before we do this we choose spiritual goals we want to accomplish during our lifetime on Earth. To help us do that, we plan a variety of challenges that will assist us in achieving our goals. These challenges are the awful surprises and setbacks that we suffer throughout our lives, and they are designed to have an effect on us that will modify and enhance our spiritual selves.

Before we are born we choose our family, our key friends and lovers, the circumstances of our birth, and where we will be born. Some of us can see quite clearly how certain family members present enormous challenges. Or we can choose to be born with illness or handicaps, or in a poor country that cannot provide us with much of anything. However, we also are capable of seeding our future lives with family and friends who will nurture us and help us along the way.

There is nothing like a spirit preparing for a new incarnation into the Earth body to think up some pretty wild challenges! We write a contract with God, the Creator, whereby we agree to live a lifetime of specific duration, comprised of the seeds and setups mentioned above.

However, the moment we are born, we forget all of this. We don't even know how to use our bodies. Just as we're growing into our bodies, things happen to us, seemingly out of the blue. Illness, hurt, love, and joy come into our lives in their own time and in their own way. We are faced with different situations whereby we have to make choices. The process of choosing is when we develop ourselves spiritually; nonaction is also considered a choice.

To make things more fun, we have a burning desire for something we can't identify. These are the spiritual goals we want to achieve but simply don't remember. It's like going to the store and forgetting your list. You try to remember what you had on that list. You know you're forgetting something, but what is it?

Spirit guides are like the person at home you can call who reads the list. However, even if you do remember that there is someone at home and make that call (or that request to your spirit guide), communication with the spirit guide is similar to communicating with a foreigner whose language you don't understand. Enhancing spiritual awareness includes developing a dictionary to learn how to understand that language.

Then, at some point, our contracts expire and we die. The timing of our death can seem plausible, or it can be a horrible shock that those in the Earth plane consider "untimely." Our natural death, be it by illness or accident, are part of our contract. At the moment of our death, when we pass over to Heaven, everything is prepared for us to go back to the light to live in peace and comfort. Back in Heaven we undergo an evaluation process and we are debriefed before we begin the process again. This is reincarnation.

A Siberian shaman who was addressing a group of Westerners at a conference recently began by stating, "Everyone here must have lived pretty good lives last time around to be living in the States right now."

A word on suicide to clarify the consequences of that sad action. *Our one and only obligation when we incarnate is to show up for life every day.* Along our path God provides us with several exit points where we could die through accident or illness, and we have a choice at that point to continue in the physical world or pack it in for this round. If we choose to commit suicide, we are in breach of our contract with God. Even if we have been given only a few weeks or months to live, the exact time of our death is still not subject to our own personal choice. When we commit suicide, it is a bad choice, and *nothing* is ready for our return. The path to the light is not prepared and obvious, and the person who commits suicide risks getting lost. Instead of finding peace in the Spirit World, the suicide victim might just continue to wander miserably, connected to the Earth plane for any number of years. Family members or friends can help suicide victims find their way to Heaven by praying for them. I have contacted people who have committed suicide, and thanks to the prayers of their families and friends, the suicide victim was able to find the path to the light and finally reside in peace in Heaven.

This enlightenment of our life story helps to make sense of many heretofore inexplicable things: babies who suffer horrid illnesses, children born into situations of torture and abuse. And it is important to remember that even if we believe that some spirits choose to suffer tremendously difficult challenges, it doesn't mean that we should not have deep compassion for them and help ease their burden. That is one of the important choices we have to make on Earth: Do we help others as we should?

The knowledge that we have chosen the challenges we have to face also gives us hope that we can make it through them. If we hadn't begun with the belief that we could overcome these challenges, we never would have included them in our contracts to begin with.

CHANNELING SPIRITS

When I was in my early twenties I saw an astrologer who told me that I was psychic, but that I should never channel spirits. She might as well have told me that I was going to sprout wings and that when I did I shouldn't fly too high.

Many years later, long after I had accepted my gift of clairvoyance, I remembered that long-ago warning. Just the fact that I had remembered it made me believe it was a warning I really needed to pay attention to. I became terribly afraid of channeling spirits until I attended Rosalyn Bruyere's Mediumship Level III Intensive.

Just being in Rosalyn's presence was energizing, nurturing, and enchanting. And I was among like-minded people with whom I could share personal experiences. It was heaven, and it was there I learned that I could channel spirits without fear.

I had been afraid to channel spirits because that astrologer long ago had told me it would be dangerous and I had believed it. This is an example of how we might pick up some information about ourselves, believe it, and create a ridiculous wall.

I prefer to contact spirits rather than channel them unless it is a much higher spirit, such as a saint. Instead of having my spirit leave my body and let another spirit enter it and speak directly through me, which is channeling, my spirit stays in my body and the deceased's spirit remains outside of my body, but nearby. At this point, I hear and see information from the spirit. Contacting spirits is more in line with Native American tradition. I only channel when I want to feel the presence of a much higher vibration. It can be quite beautiful. Also, I only do this channeling in the presence of a trusted friend who can later fill me in on what I might have missed. I don't completely leave my body so I am somewhat aware of what is going on. Otherwise I can get all the same information simply by contacting spirits.

Discernment of what is information from spirits and what is simply my chatter-mind is simple because my chatter-mind talks to me on the left and I hear spirits from the right slightly behind me. As far as knowing information and trusting that information, practice makes perfect. Now I can just tell what is my chatter-mind making up a story versus what is coming from spirit.

I have channeled some very beautiful higher spirits who have left me feeling wonderful.

A NEW WAY OF BEING

It was over an hour's drive to get to Melanie's house. I had left late, and now I was stuck in traffic. I felt frantic because I hated the idea of Melanie waiting. I only had thirty minutes to cover an hour's distance. The traffic stopped completely. When my frustration was about to reach fever pitch I heard, "We control time. You won't be late. Just listen right now."

After that followed some information about new gifts I was due to receive. While I understood that I would be gaining some new kind of power, I didn't really understand all of what I was being told. I did retain the fact that I no longer needed to shift into an altered state to reach the Spirit World, as I would, from that point on, always be open to the Spirit World and its many dimensions. This meant that I would never need to sit quietly in a calm place and enter into an altered state in order to communicate with spirits; rather, I would be able to communicate clearly with Tonka, or any other spirit, in any situation and from any place. In effect, I would be in an altered state all the time. Up until that time, when I communicated with Tonka in the car or anywhere else I had needed to shift into an altered state first. Only at the intensive had I been in a constantly altered state

Before I knew it the traffic was flowing again, and I arrived at Melanie's house right on time. It was amazing, and made me realize that time and space really are complete illusions.

9

Tracking Animals

"YOU'RE NOT GETTING THIS! How could you ask such a dumb question? It's a reflection of your programming. It's all those years of programming by your parents that have shut you down. Your mind is so closed that you can't even begin to see another perspective!" Foxes assailed me. "You need to get out in the field and meet more healers. You think you know something, but you don't know anything." Foxes stared at me and it felt as if he could see right through me.

"I'm willing to learn," I replied. "That's why I'm here. And I've been meeting healers in Manhattan."

"Healers in Manhattan? You have no idea what I mean!"

"Who should I meet?"

"Anyone that's not in Manhattan! Just do it!" Foxes ordered, sounding like a Nike ad.

"Can't you suggest someone to me?" I asked.

"No," Foxes answered.

"What about your teachers that you've been talking about?" I asked.

"They're all far away. I have their phone numbers, but they're always traveling. That won't work," Foxes said. Then he continued his tirade—his personal interpretation of healers and the history of their social persecution through time.

"As city-state societies emerged in different cultures around the globe due to the accumulated resources and wealth of the respective ruling classes, individuals found themselves disconnected from nature. Nevertheless, there was still a strong belief in natural healers among the commoners. These natural healers often lived away from city life, out in nature. If someone needed help, they would usually have to find a healer out in the sanctuary of the wilderness. Got that?" Foxes said.

"Yeah, yeah, I understand," I said.

"With the growing complexity of society, priestly orders evolved. At first they derived their knowledge from healing rites of certain tribal shamans, and learned their methods of herbalism and mystical practices, some of which still exist. The authority in power encouraged and provided for the priestly orders in return for political allegiance. In the beginning, the priestly orders were fairly pure. However, as these orders spent more time in the cities, separated from nature, they began to lose sight of their original truths. This corruption begins when people use only specific elements of esoteric knowledge, which prohibits individual spiritual inspiration. Is that too complicated for you?" Foxes asked.

"No, keep going. So the priestly orders weren't bad in the beginning, but got corrupted because they were away from nature, right?" I asked.

"That's right. You have to be in touch with nature. That's something *you* don't do," Foxes said.

"That's not true! I love nature. How can you say that about me?" I inquired.

"I suppose you can't know what you don't know. Just take my word for it, that you don't know!" Foxes said.

"Look, just keep going. I'll understand what I'll understand," I said.

"Gradually there was a more pronounced standardization of the practices of these 'holy men,' further extinguishing their spiritual knowledge. The priests then united with the wealthy class to become a powerful plutocracy. The people, through fear of grave punishment, renounced their beliefs and, through many generations, began to believe that anything not prescribed by the authorities was dangerous. That's when the shamanic healers withdrew from public view. All of this transpired throughout the last fifteen hundred years," Foxes said.

"So it was quite gradual," I echoed.

"That's what I just said," Foxes continued. "The survival of healers was now dependent upon secret 'cults' or underground countercultures that kept the philosophy and practice of their traditions hidden from the destructive forces of the new regime. Right up to the present day many still keep their arts secret for fear of persecution."

"Is that why you don't openly practice healing?" I asked.

"*I'm* not afraid of anything. I'm just not supposed to practice openly, that's all." Foxes' tirade was over. For the time being, anyway.

GETTING OUT IN THE FIELD

I thought healers in Manhattan were fine, so I didn't know what Foxes meant when he told me that I needed to get out in the field and meet more healers. The universe helped me in my quest by sending me a catalog of workshops, retreats, and wellness vacations from the Omega Institute in upstate New York. Their motto was "Awakening the Best in the Human Spirit."

The next time I saw Foxes, I brought the Omega catalog with me. I half-expected him to ridicule me for having a catalog in the first place and for bringing it to show to him. I was relieved to find out that he was familiar with Omega, had been there, and liked it. He immediately went through the catalog, pointing out workshops that he valued, and I was touched that he apparently cared for me enough to select the perfect healers' workshops for me to attend. I had visions of going to these workshops with him. What an energy trip that would be! I later realized that he was choosing workshops that he wanted to attend himself, alone.

MEETING MOTHER NATURE

The first workshop Foxes selected was to be held over a weekend. He was unable to go to it, but I was free, so I went by myself. When he said I needed to get out in the field to meet healers, I didn't appreciate that he had meant it literally. The first workshop was an introduction to tracking with Tom Brown Jr. Foxes wanted me to include Tom in my healers' show even though I had never heard of him. I also didn't see what a tracker had to do with healing. Foxes, however, was adamant about Brown's capabilities.

Although I appreciate an attractive garden, I was not by any stretch of the imagination an outdoorswoman. My Girl Scout camping experiences were few and long ago. My idea of a vacation in nature was a comfortable bed-and-breakfast. The idea of camping, much less animal tracking, had never entered my mind. I wasn't against it; I just didn't want to do it. All the bugs and dirt were just too much bother.

But since Tom was one of the teachers Foxes valued above all others, I knew I had to attend this workshop. *At least it's only a weekend*, I reassured myself. *How bad can it be?*

Foxes was unable to attend the workshop himself, so I went alone. Dutifully I read *The Tracker*, Brown's book about his experiences in the New Jersey Pine Barrens as a young boy, and about being educated in Native American ways by an Apache scout. I loved the book, although the prospect of searching out animal tracks in the mud didn't excite me.

As the workshop approached, Foxes got increasingly nervous about it and feared I might make him look bad in front of his mentor. He yelled at me and scolded me about the proper way to act: I was not to ask any questions and I was supposed to be very careful about my every move. Foxes was so emotional about this that his instructions were confusing and contradictory.

I tried to analyze what I was doing. On one hand I was trying to make Foxes happy by attending a workshop led by his hero. But what if Tom Brown Jr. expected me to draw animal tracks? I had no aptitude for drawing whatsoever, so the whole thing might just explode in my face; I felt as though I might jeopardize my whole relationship with Foxes by accidentally doing something stupid. I couldn't have cared less about that particular workshop. And yet if I didn't go I would be slighting Foxes' hero. For all the wrong reasons, I decided to attend the workshop.

By the time I got to Omega I was a nervous wreck. I was leaving my family to be alone on a new experience that I really didn't want to have. What a mess! Feeling completely miserable and out of place, I was surprised to run into Melanie, who was there for the same workshop. It was as though God was smiling down on me and saying everything would be fine. Melanie welcomed me warmly, and then she kept her distance. This was her private time, and I needed to honor that. She was not there to be my teacher. I was glad that she was present, but I also instinctively understood that I would get more out of the workshop if I were on my own, not depending on someone else's help.

Following Melanie's lead, I sat on the floor in the front row, ready to drink in the wonders that Tom was sure to teach us. *Anyone Foxes holds in such high esteem must be pretty good,* I reminded myself, *even though he will be talking about animal tracks. Wasn't it this very conversation Foxes bored me with that first time he came to visit? There must be a greater message that I might get, if I don't fall asleep first. Maybe I should have sat in the back. . . .*

Tom began his lecture and talked about animal tracks and about scat, a polite word for animal poop. I couldn't believe that someone could look so intense and speak so solemnly about his scat collection. He also talked about how to find animal tracks in the mud as well as in other harder-to-track surfaces. I was perplexed. What did animal tracking have to do with Spirit and healing? Had I already missed the greater message? We were instructed to draw tracks and then feces. I prayed that we wouldn't be tested on what we were supposed to be learning. *At least I'm not falling asleep,* I comforted myself. I pretended to draw whatever Tom drew on the easel in front of us. I don't think anyone, even Tom Brown himself, would have been able to recognize my scribbles as any sort of earthbound animal. Drawing the poop was a bit easier, but who cares what animal poop looks like anyway?

Eventually we had to go outside to look for animal tracks. This was okay with me, because it meant I didn't have to try to draw anything anymore. Tom took us to an area where he had allegedly found tracks. You could have fooled me. I certainly didn't see any. Tom announced that he would find several tracks, and that we had to line up and file by to see them. The people in the front would stay next to a track and explain it to the other people coming by. I tried to get in the back of the line so that I wouldn't have to explain anything. On top of the general torture of it all, the sun was shining down on us unmercifully; the air temperature was ninety-four degrees. Showing a track meant lying down in the dirt under the burning sun for at least an hour while people filed by. I wasn't going to do it!

Spirit had another idea, and somehow I got stuck showing a raccoon track. In order to see it you had to lie flat on your stomach in the dirt. When it was shown to me, I couldn't see it. I didn't want to appear stupid, mostly in deference to Foxes, so after a couple of explanations, I lied and said I saw it.

"Oh, yes! There it is!" I lied enthusiastically.

But then I had to show it to other people as they slowly marched by. With as much authority as I could muster, I would gesture vaguely in the direction of the track and announce that it was a raccoon print. The sun was hot, I was lying in the dirt worrying about my fair skin getting sun damaged, and I was miserable. I hated being there. One person after another filed by. Some of the people didn't buy my description. I didn't like those people.

Troublemakers, I thought. *Why can't they just pretend to see this stupid track like me? It should be enough for them that I'm wallowing in the dirt like this! I wonder if these dirt stains will ever come out of my pants? And why didn't I bring my hat with me?*

One idiot was really giving me a hard time. Rather than hold up the line, he left and then returned, determined to see my raccoon track. Oh, surprise! He couldn't see the track. I couldn't see the track either, and I didn't care. *Just pretend you see it*, I prayed. *Just pretend you see it, and then we can all call it quits.* I had just about had it with this jerk when I stared again at the invisible print. However, this time I "saw" the whole raccoon as it was making the track. I could "see" the exact position of its body as the paw touched the ground. It was extraordinary; I *felt* its movement. A new world opened up.

From that moment on, everything changed. I was amazed by the world around me—a world that I had been ignoring. Nature had so many hidden treasures that I could finally see. The trees felt wonderful in their majesty. There was a beautiful balance in the world of all living things. Everything affected everything else. I realized that I had been missing all of this. It was as though I had blinders on, and now they were off. My perception of the world changed.

Even in my transformed state, I was afraid of approaching Tom Brown, because I didn't want to embarrass Foxes. Nevertheless, I was determined to speak to him at some point. When I asked Tonka if and when I should approach Tom, he told me that the time would come. As I was walking back to the meeting room after finally seeing the raccoon in its track, there was Tom walking alone ahead of me. Everyone else was gone. It was almost surreal to see him alone; he is usually surrounded. Tonka told me to go for it. I thought this would be a perfect time to ask

Tom about participating in my television show. I walked up; before I could say a word Tom turned to me and declared, "I hate TV." How had he known what I was thinking? He didn't even know who I was or what I did for a living.

I took a deep breath and began sharing the magnificent breakthrough about the raccoon track that I had just experienced. Tom loved that. Someone else joined us, and Tom slowly dropped back and to the side behind us. This was a surveillance technique that he later taught us. He was checking me out. I must have passed the test because he soon joined us again. He told me how frustrated he was teaching a weekend workshop; he had to squeeze a week's worth of classes into two and a half days.

It wasn't enough time for people to really get his message of awareness of nature and life. We must all look for the tracks and patterns around us because everything is related, and to understand ourselves we need to appreciate and understand all parts of our natural environment. Once we have that basic connection with Mother Earth, then we can open ourselves to Spirit everyday.

Tom's energy was amazing, his presence magical. By the afternoon session I was mesmerized.

As I continued to try drawing a mouse's paw print and poop, I eventually felt I was communicating with someone on a higher plane. I began to notice an old Indian standing next to Tom. It must have been Tom's teacher, the Apache scout Stalking Wolf, whom Tom called Grandfather. Stalking Wolf was standing by Tom's side, watching him proudly.

I never learned how to draw tracks well, and I'm not good at identifying them—scat either, for that matter—but I had gained a new appreciation of the world around me. I like to sit on the ground and feel the gift of the sun. I like to notice the tracks around me, both animal and human, even though I can't identify them all. I like to wonder why these things are as they appear. I want to know more and to understand more.

Tom told the story of an old fisherman who had never recognized the beauty of his world until he saw Tom honoring the different colors of the sand. For that old man, all sand was gray until Tom provided him with a different perspective. The old man was moved to tears when he discovered this splendor he had never observed before. He felt that he had lost so many years wearing blinders.

During his lecture Tom spoke about Jesus. Grandfather had pointed out to Tom, one day while walking by a church, that Jesus was not someone who stayed cooped up in a building. He went out into nature for his strength, and he invited his followers to do the same. It made sense to me.

As Tom suggested we do, on my way home, driving on tree-lined highways, I no longer saw walls of green as I had on my drive there. I saw the openings where animals made their runs. I thought about the leaves, about how they had grown during the couple of days since I had driven past them. I saw some deer recessed in a dark forest. All of it was magnificent.

At home, my backyard was now a wonderland of life in many different forms. There were larger animal tracks of cats and dogs and deer, but I also found the tracks and passageways of mice and birds. I felt myself an integral and important part of life. I felt I was one with the Creator, as we all are.

I called Foxes as soon as I got home. He wanted me to come to his place and tell him absolutely everything that had happened. I guess he was so sure I had messed up and embarrassed him somehow that he needed a detailed report, in person. As soon as I arrived at Foxes' house, he looked at me and said I had changed. He was right. I had changed. I didn't realize this was only the beginning.

10

Facing Down My Ego

I CONTINUED VISITING FOXES to discuss healers and the healing arts. Our meetings were still forums for him to sermonize on his personal beliefs about the universe and Life with a capital L. I remained a willing and captive audience. What he said helped me to later define my own point of view. With my new interest in nature, I was departing from my old world at a faster pace. It was good to be around someone who completely accepted nature and the Spirit World as a part of everyday life. In my Westchester existence no one did that. It would have been hard for me to develop my gifts without Foxes' support.

I didn't see myself growing, but he did. He even accused me one time of trying to "catch up" with him. I had no idea what he was talking about. I had no personal agenda except to understand the world of healers enough to produce a television show.

My frequent trips abroad with my husband seemed to increasingly annoy Foxes. I don't think he was jealous of my relationship with my husband; I think Foxes wanted to be the one doing the traveling. In the beginning of our acquaintance, he didn't have much work, and so he was very accommodating about my schedule. As winter turned to spring, however, it was getting more difficult for him to know when he would have free time, because the unpredictable weather dictated his schedule. I would get agitated if we didn't have our next meeting set up, and I often prayed for rain.

I noticed that Foxes was becoming more and more belligerent toward me, yet I accepted anything he dished out. I never stood up for myself; I continued to put myself in his line of fire again and again. It was as though I didn't have control of myself, and in my mind I absolutely had to maintain our relationship. But why?

What I didn't realize was that I had given Foxes all my power in the hope that he would help me realize my television project. I felt that without him I could never produce my important film. This made me even more frantic about accommodating him, until somehow he became the television production authority and I was demoted to being his helper. This was despite the fact that I had been in the television business for twenty years, and he'd never had anything to do with it until we met.

I had also empowered Foxes to control my convictions regarding my spiritual development. It was as though, on some level, I believed that without him my whole experience with the Spirit World would end. I wouldn't have any gifts unless Foxes was there to support them and me; my underlying fear was that I would end up a sad, ordinary, tired, suburban housewife if Foxes was not in my life.

My relationship with Foxes didn't feel right, but I no longer held my own power, so I returned to my familiar role of victim. I convinced myself that Foxes really did know what he was talking about in regards to television production, even though this was a completely new area for him. What I didn't see was that, once again and true to form, I had given my power away to someone, as I had done with my husband and with my mother. I was allowing that person to run my life, even though that wasn't particularly comfortable for me. I was caught in a very unhealthy pattern. Once I realized this, I began to wonder how I could extricate myself from its grip.

MORE PAST-LIFE REGRESSIONS

When I was at Tom Brown Jr.'s workshop at Omega, I enjoyed meeting new people. One day I sat down at one of the large round tables in the cafeteria with some people I hadn't yet met. People were always glad to include someone new. This group was discussing past-life regression. Sally was describing her experiences of past-life therapy as having liberated her from some unhappy traps she had been caught in. That sounded a lot like what I was experiencing with Foxes. I decided that this could be the means by which I could free myself, and I made an appointment with a therapist as soon as I got home.

Dr. Marilyn Gobel answered the door of her stylish midtown apartment. She was petite and very attractive. When I made my appointment I presented myself as a television producer compiling a documentary about healers. I said I was interested in learning more about past-life regression. She told me about her training in California and how she had worked in a mental hospital for a while. There she was able to heal some incoming patients in crisis because they had been caught in a past life. She would do the past-life regression on them and release them from that past-life trauma.

Finally Dr. Gobel suggested regressing me—what I had been waiting for! She always began by taking a new client to the moment of conception in this life. First she had me feel myself in the womb, which was an amazingly comfortable experience. She then asked me to listen to what was going on at the time of my conception.

I was absolutely unprepared for what I heard. Apparently a Frenchman who was my mother's boss, and for whom she carried a crush, had seduced her: too much flirting and one glass of champagne too many—Moët et Chandon, my mother's all-time favorite. When my mother finally protested, her boss ignored her. I was a product of rape.

Never in a million years would I have imagined this! Around the time of my conception my parents, although happily married, had not been living in the same place, so the possibility that this was true was entirely likely. To cover up this unwanted pregnancy, my mom calculated the months of her pregnancy from a time when it would have been possible for her to have conceived me with my father, and she always told me I was born a full month late. I believed that, even though medical people had told me that this was impossible. They were right. I think my mother almost fooled my father into believing that I was his daughter, but she certainly never convinced his mother. Evidently, unbeknownst to me, she had constantly reminded my father that I was not his daughter.

Finding this out made a lot of things fall into place—my childhood and the way different people in the family treated me, and why I was allowed absolutely no contact with my paternal grandmother even though my brothers enjoyed regular visits. It also made sense that my mother insisted I learn French when I was a small child. Although she never would have willingly betrayed my father, she nevertheless remained enamored of her French boss. When I was growing up she made many positive references to him. She even kept a banal business memo that he had once written to her. This discovery also explained my childhood dream to go to France and study there. I ended up marrying a Frenchman, carrying a French passport, and spending seventeen years living in Paris! Three of my children were born there. Until this point, I never knew what had drawn me to France.

To finish up the session on a positive note, Dr. Gobel tried to lead me, still in my hypnotic, altered state, to someone who loved me unconditionally when I was an infant. But there was no one. She continued through my childhood. Again I could find no one who showed me unconditional love. Then Dr. Gobel changed directions and tried to take me back through the past in search of a love connection—if not in this life, then at least in some past life.

Going back in time, I finally found myself in a past life with Foxes. We had loved one another unconditionally. I realized that I had never felt this kind of unconditional love in my present life from or for another person until I met Foxes, and he had triggered that past-life memory.

There is only one kind of love, whether it occurs between a man and a woman, parent and child, or simply between friends. That basic emotion is initially exactly the same; then we build a story on it. Meeting Jesus during the craniosacral therapy session had opened up my heart and had transformed me into a more compassionate and caring person. Now that Jesus had opened my heart, I was vulnerable to having a physical person trigger my ability to love unconditionally in my present life. Was the love Jesus showed me that of a friend or a relative or a lover? It was all that and more. I didn't need to qualify it. We don't need to qualify love! We shouldn't confuse what we do with someone we love with the basic emotion of love. We unconditionally love relatives, partners, children, and friends all the same way; we just don't express it the same way. Foxes, with his remarkable energy, had reconnected me with my ability to experience unconditional love. I learned to love everyone better. That's what happened at the healing he conducted on me when he filled the hole in my heart. It all made sense and I think it made me a better person.

The whole past-life regression experience was a Pandora's box opened. It left me with pieces of a puzzle that fit together, but were so painful that it took me weeks to get out of a severe depression. I couldn't tell anyone about the experience because my husband wouldn't understand a past-life romantic relationship with Foxes. I certainly couldn't discuss this with Foxes, who obviously didn't love me now. And I knew I didn't love Foxes in this life. I didn't yet understand the true nature of unconditional love.

However, I could share the theory of my conception with my husband. He was receptive and supportive of it and the pain it caused me, making it all seem much more plausible. This made me feel better about everything.

I described to Georges the many childhood events that corroborated this theory about my conception. Once, I was a child examining my face in the mirror, as children do, I smiled and found I could make a kind of dimple appear. In delight, I ran to my father.

"Daddy, Daddy, look! I have a dimple just like you!" I announced.

My father just looked at me briefly, then walked away. At the time I felt rejected, as though he didn't want me to resemble him in any manner. Now I understood why he had acted that way toward me; he hadn't really ever believed that I was his biological daughter.

During the week that followed my session with Dr. Gobel I went to New Orleans with my husband. One night I was tremendously uneasy, and I couldn't sleep. Something was coming up. Spontaneously, I saw a scene from a past life with Foxes. It was in Europe during the Renaissance. We were lovers, and I had stepped in front of him so that I would be stabbed instead of him. I physically remembered the fear of being stabbed, and then the release as I died and my spirit left my body. In spirit form I was filled with joy at the ultimate sacrifice I had made for my lover, in the name of love. What I didn't realize was that this past-life experience had been revealed to me to serve as a warning about the true nature of my relationship with Foxes.

After finally coming to terms with the real circumstances of my conception in this lifetime, I felt drawn to return to Dr. Gobel to find out more about my relationship with Foxes, in order to free myself of it and the addictive hold he had over me.

This time I had a definite focus. I briefly told her about my current relationship with Foxes and how he sometimes made me feel afraid. She decided to start at that point.

I lay down in her office and she quickly led me into a trance. I suddenly began making the guttural sounds of a cavewoman. The therapist encouraged me to speak English. Foxes and I were mates in prehistoric times. I was afraid of him, because he would occasionally beat me. Nevertheless, I adored him. I got pregnant with twins. I couldn't birth them, and as no one could help me, I was fated to die. Foxes knew I was dying; he had seen it happen to animals. I was suffering horrible pain, and I begged Foxes to kill me. He did. He suffocated me. As I was lying there in the therapist's office, I couldn't breathe. It was horrible! I thought I would die on the spot, and I tried to bring myself out of the trance by getting up. But Dr. Gobel wouldn't let me out of the trance. Then I, the cavewoman, died and my spirit rose above my inert body until I was able to look down upon it. When I came out of the trance I was shaken but otherwise fine.

Oddly enough, on my way home I was infused with wonderful memories of my life as a cavewoman. I remembered the way my people selected partners: the men chased the women at a time specified for just this event. A woman caught would then be the catcher's mate. I could run very fast, and this made me a more valuable catch. My future mate had to be very strong and fast, which ultimately enhanced others' perceptions of him. These memories were incredibly physically stimulating to me.

The revelation of this particular past life didn't improve my relationship with Foxes, however. I felt that he was becoming increasingly abusive toward me, but I was incapable of standing up for myself. He insinuated himself more and more into my television project, until it seemed as though he was trying to take it over completely.

As I continued my research, one healer I worked with told me that my relationship with Foxes was a mirror of my relationship with my mother. As a child, I felt I needed to be submissive to my mother in order to be loved. It was the beginning of a victim pattern. When I wanted someone to like me, I became submissive to that person.

IT ALL FALLS APART

My meetings with Foxes continued, but so did my trips with Georges. We were going to China! I love China. I had been there ten years earlier, and I was thrilled at the prospect of going back. This was definitely a trip not to be missed. I could tell that Foxes hated the idea of me going, although he never directly addressed the issue. Because we could communicate without words and over long distances, I understood how he felt. It must have been doubly hard for him to see me go when he was a qi gong master and knew so much about Chinese herbs.

When I returned from China in June, Foxes refused to see me. I had bought some Chinese tea for him, so I insisted on delivering it. When I got to his home he was very cool, but he invited me go to his qi gong and tai chi classes. That improved things between us, and we began working together again.

Foxes had highlighted in the Omega catalog a workshop conducted by John Perkins. It was called "The World Is As You Dream It." I signed up hoping Foxes would come, too. Rosalyn Bruyere would be at Omega that same weekend. Because Foxes hadn't met Rosalyn, he said he would come for a day.

I didn't hear from Foxes for a couple of weeks after giving him his tea, and my calls went unanswered. Tonka told me Foxes wasn't going to go to the Perkins workshop, and he wouldn't even show up to meet Rosalyn. I felt that without communication with Foxes, I couldn't do anything, either on my television project or on my own spiritual development.

Penney, the only person who knew how important Foxes was to me, said it was all about ego; my ego was in the process of being crushed. This was, according to her, a good thing.

I didn't see that at all. The only thing I knew was that I was miserable. I was angry. When I couldn't stand the anger and frustration anymore I went to the basement, where I spent hours smashing a piece of old furniture. The result left me in despair.

Penney told me that she couldn't help me go through my pain. I had to do that alone, and I understood that. We all have to go through our own pain alone.

As I walked alone through the darkness of my despair, I felt that my life was over because I could no longer produce my television project or, even worse, develop my spiritual gifts. I felt trapped. Who could I discuss this with? I was a mess. I spent the day in tears. Fortunately my young daughter had the day off from school. She didn't know what was going on, but her presence made me try to conceal my pain. I knew I had to get out of the house, so we went out for lunch. There again I had to leave the table to cry. It was horrible. I cried and cried.

Later in the afternoon, I almost decided not to go to the Perkins workshop. I had no energy or desire to do anything except die. The image of slitting my wrists kept filling my mind. It seemed like a relief, although I consciously knew nothing in my life demanded suicide, and there was no reason for me to be so depressed. I also knew that according to my spiritual beliefs, suicide was not an option. Nevertheless, my spirit was walking through the dark.

I thought I was having a nervous breakdown. I didn't realize it was a breakthrough.

Only later, when I became more adept at past-life regression, did I see that I had committed suicide in a past life because of a relationship with Foxes. That is why I had those awful visions of slitting my wrists. I wish I had had someone to turn to who could have helped me out of that at the time, but instead I just suffered alone. That is why I do a lot of hand holding with my clients. I try to be there for them emotionally, to make sure they don't ever get stuck in some bad place. I am always available to support them. Ultimately, though, everyone has to walk through the dark alone, even if there is someone standing nearby.

CREATING THE DREAM

On the drive up to Omega for the Perkins workshop, I tearfully called my husband to say good-bye. I was so depressed that I was sure I would have a fatal accident.

I arrived at Omega that evening and pulled myself together for the public, going through the motions of participating. The first exercise we did was to get rid of everything negative we've ever had in our lives. That was exactly what I needed. I sat across from my partner and blew out my pain and misery. It was a tremendous relief. My partner, a therapist herself, commented on the foul smell of everything I had expressed. The poor woman had no idea how foul it really was!

The next day was a building day. We were taught to find our individual *huaca*, or spirit connection. This can be anything at all. I somehow knew my two power animals were a grizzly bear and a black panther. The workshop participants randomly partnered. My partner was new to all this, and to her astonishment, she found the frightening brown grizzly bear that was my huaca. For me it was a confirmation of what I already knew.

My partner had come to the workshop to try to free herself from the pain of the loss of her husband to a heart attack three years earlier. I wasn't surprised. Almost every time I partnered with someone in a workshop setting, that person needed me to contact the Spirit World. Eventually I contacted my partner's husband for her. This brought her a tremendous amount of relief.

I also found my partner's huaca. It was difficult for me to see it at first, because I was literally in the dark. It turned out I was really underneath the branches of a huge tree, standing next to its dark trunk. As I tried to gain some perspective, I finally saw the large tree from afar. When I related this to my partner she was amazed.

"I have a large, magnificent tree like that at home. Its branches are long and full. They drop down to the ground. I love to go sit next to the trunk, underneath the branches where it's dark. That's where I seem to be able to find some peace," she said.

The huaca is a tremendous tool for connecting with the Spirit World. I have found huacas for all my family members, friends, and many clients. During one session my nine-year-old client's mother sat anxiously by as the little girl chatted happily about school and what she enjoyed doing there. I was going to find her huaca for her. I lay down next to the child, our sides touching completely. The mother sat near us. In my mind I asked to be told what the child's huaca was. A vision came to me of a strange animal with long hair. It looked like some kind of mountain goat. It seemed an odd huaca for this child born and bred in the northeastern United States. I asked again if this was the huaca. After all, I thought, a huaca needed to have some relevance for the individual. How could this suburban child relate to this bizarre creature that I couldn't even identify?

All of a sudden I "heard" the word *llama*. I wasn't even sure how a llama looked. Did they have long hair? I thought they had short hair. I decided to respect my information; always a good idea. When I told the mother and child that the huaca was an ivory-colored llama with long hair, they weren't surprised at all. Apparently every year they visited a llama farm in Vermont because the girl loves llamas so much! I never could have guessed it.

This incident brought with it some understanding.

In addition to confirming the fact that I should never question the information I receive, I realized that Spirit is really energy that is disembodied.

For us to be able to relate to Spirit, we need to have it present itself in a comfortable form. Everyone has objects, animals, or people with which they have an emotional attachment. Speaking to Spirit happens through the emotions. Therefore Spirit, or contact with the Spirit World, needs to be based on emotional connection and comfort.

There are two kinds of huacas, which can also be called *totems*. One is a power totem, which is always there to protect and guide an individual. Another is a mission totem, which is there to teach us something. It is possible to have several of each. My grizzly bear is a power totem. For a while I had a blue jay appear around me. That was a mission totem. When I looked up the spiritual meaning of the blue jay, I found it contained a message about great potential but dilettante approach. I needed to deepen my study and practice of what I learned. That way I could achieve my potential with the gifts I had been given.

During the Perkins workshop we did a great deal of journeying, or guided meditation. This is usually done to a drumbeat while the leader suggests places and events to the person journeying. It is somewhat similar to hypnosis in the sense that the individual goes beyond his or her conscious mind. Journeying takes one into an altered state where he or she can access other parts of consciousness or unconsciousness. This allows the journeyer to connect with Spirit, face issues, and tap into strength and healing.

Through journeying we identified our dreams. Before we began the journey, we were warned about differentiating dream from fantasy. A dream is a true desire that deserves to be made manifest and, in that manifestation, can help everyone. A fantasy is a simple whim that might seem like a good idea at a certain time, but its manifestation would not be in the interest of the greater good. Both a dream and a fantasy can manifest if intention and energy are invested. The manifestation of the fantasy, however, would lead to an ultimately unsatisfactory outcome.

John gave us the example of Jared, who was secretly in love with his friend's wife. Jared mistook this fantasy for a dream. He invested intention and energy in what he believed to be his dream. When what proved to be a fantasy manifested, Jared declared his love for his friend's wife, and she loved him in return. This, however, was devastating for her husband, who was betrayed by not only his wife but also by his best friend. The realization of her bad conduct rendered the woman terribly depressed. Jared ended up with the woman he loved but she was depressed about how she had treated her husband, and the husband, who had been Jared's best friend, now hated them both. Everyone was miserable.

As an exercise at the workshop, we were supposed to identify our dream, make sure it wasn't a fantasy, and then put energy behind it to have it manifest. My dream was to produce the television project about healers, but I was unable to imagine doing it without Foxes. I had put all of my energy into what I believed was my dream, manifesting my project with Foxes and being invited to promote it on television shows, again with Foxes.

The Perkins workshop was fabulous. John Perkins was incredibly charismatic, uplifting, and commanding in a good way. His joy was infectious. The drumming was intense. The fire ceremony was powerful. We combined the four elements—water, air, earth, and fire—and filled ourselves with the fifth element, energy. It was extraordinary.

In fact, Melanie, who was at Omega to assist Rosalyn Bruyere, ran into me in the café after the fire ceremony. She was astounded at how open I was, how full of energy. I remember going to bed in my small dorm room and not being able to fall asleep because of the bright light. I tried to find a light switch before I realized that the bright light was coming from me! It was reflecting off the wall from my body. I was truly in a state of bliss.

After the Perkins workshop I felt so empowered, happy, and strong that I believed I could conquer the world. It was a beautiful experience. It was also a sign to me how Spirit comes to us just when we need help the most.

Although I had sworn never to call Foxes again, a week after the Perkins workshop I called him. In my mind it was "the last call," but in my heart it was a new beginning. At the workshop I had put energy behind the dream of manifesting the television production with Foxes, and I didn't understand the significance of what I had done. When I asked Foxes why he hadn't shown up at Omega, he said he had misunderstood and didn't think he was supposed to go there at all. In fact, on his own accord, he immediately invited me up to work on the project. He also had a cameraman he wanted me to meet. For me this was the beginning of the manifestation of what I thought was my dream.

11

We Hit the Big Time

MY NEXT MEETING WITH FOXES went well. I decided to ignore his absence from Omega and his lack of remorse about not attending. For me it had been a far better workshop without him there anyway. I had walked through the dark, and I had made it through to the other side. I was exuberant and positive. My newfound energy fueled my determination to manifest my television project with Foxes.

One major problem arose when Foxes had me meet Jack, a coworker. At some time in his early youth Jack had been a cameraman. Foxes was convinced that we should work with him. This needed my approval. The fact that Foxes was consulting me on this indicated the power I had regained at the Perkins workshop. I met Jack, and as I interviewed him I quickly saw that he was not the man for the job. I didn't say this directly to him, but Jack understood, and he was furious. When I later told Foxes that Jack wasn't who we needed, he demanded that we use Jack. Rather than argue I left it open, agreeing that we might use Jack for some future camera work.

PITCHING OUR SHOW

Through my contacts in television, I set up a pitch for the project, arranging for Foxes to pitch the show with me as I had dreamed it. Just getting an appointment like that was very difficult if not impossible for someone without an agent. The universe tried to protect me from my folly. The day of one pitch meeting Foxes was late arriving to my home. He was supposed to meet me there; then we'd drive into midtown Manhattan together. I kept getting messages from Tonka that I should just go into the meeting myself, but I wanted to go with Foxes. I asked Tonka whether or not Foxes would eventually show up and Tonka said yes, he would. That was enough for me. I waited. Foxes did finally show up: two hours late. He had run into horrible traffic, and when he tried to stop to call me the phones were out of order. He claimed it was negativity working against our project. I chose to believe him.

The time allowed for our pitch was extremely limited because we had arrived two hours late. The meeting nevertheless went well, and the director of programming liked the project. I was excited; my dream appeared to be manifesting.

As I was driving us back to my house where Foxes had left his van, he began talking about Jack again. "We need to lock in a cameraman," he announced.

"We still have time to research that. There's a lot to do before we actually begin production," I said.

"What's wrong with using Jack? He's good, and he's available," Foxes continued.

"I really don't think Jack can handle the kind of camera work we'll need for this production," I answered.

"How do you know that? You've never seen his work, and you've never worked with him," Foxes said. "As usual you're just making blind assumptions. It's dangerous to be so closed minded."

I hadn't seen Jack's work because there was nothing to see, and I could tell Jack was not going to be an easy person to work with.

"I do have a lot of experience with television production, you know," I said.

"You think you know everything, but do you?" Foxes countered.

"What kind of person just makes arbitrary assumptions without any regard for the facts?"

It was obvious that Foxes wouldn't give up until I accepted Jack as our cameraman.

"Okay," I finally said. "We could use Jack to shoot something." I was determined to keep peace with my partner at any price.

"That sounds pretty good. We can figure out later exactly what he'll film," Foxes agreed. "In fact, maybe sometimes Jack and I will have to go out and film something on our own."

"What are you talking about? I have to be there for all the filming. I'm the director," I said.

"We're both directors," Foxes countered.

"You don't know what you're talking about. We can't both be directors," I said. "I'm the director."

"But just imagine that you're really busy doing something, right? And there's a healer around who *has* to be interviewed right away. Jack and I could do it," Foxes said.

"That would never happen," I said. "You can work all that out with scheduling."

I began to suspect Foxes of a devious plan. It looked as though he wanted to go off with Jack and shoot the film on his own. *How dare he?* I thought.

"Yeah, but just imagine if it did happen, right? You're unavailable, and Jack and I would go out filming together," Foxes repeated.

"Under no circumstances will any filming take place without me!" I said.

"What if you're too busy, or you're sick, or something else happens? Then Jack and I could go out and film this show," Foxes screamed at me. "That's all you have to recognize. That's all you have to accept."

How could someone who didn't have a clue about television production direct a remote shoot? All the way home, stuck in traffic, we screamed at each other. It was a nightmare. The more he said, the more I believed that he was trying to take over my project completely, to produce it without me. He insisted on being involved with all the decision-making and expected me to forfeit all control. He just wanted me to provide the money.

I wondered how far was I willing to extend myself to enjoy the moments of good energy I now rarely got from Foxes. I felt that he was using me and was trying to discard me. However, the prospect of losing his participation, and what I considered my driving force, was too much, and I finally let Foxes believe he had all the control he wanted.

I felt like a wretched coward. *What's wrong with me?* I demanded. *Why can't I control this mess?*

LEARNING TO TAKE ABUSE

At that point, Tonka reminded me of my youth and my mother's constant need to blame someone for everything. To her, anything bad that happened was someone's fault. Most of the time, I was the most convenient person. Sometimes this was pretty contrived, but it still worked for her, and I always buckled under and accepted the blame. One example: I was chosen valedictorian of my high school class, and even though I was terrified of speaking in front of a group, I forced myself to accept this honor. My older brother was living three hours away. My mother asked me if I wanted him to come to my graduation.

"Sure, that would be great," I said. I was lost in the excitement of my approaching graduation, and I had to go meet my friends who were already waiting for me.

"He might not be able to come because he has to work," Mom said.

"That's too bad," I said as I prepared the things I needed to go out.

"But you really want him to be there," Mom insisted.

"Well, if he can, sure. I have to go meet my friends now. See you later," I said as I walked out the door.

Mom was the one who *really* wanted my older brother to be there, and any excuse would work to get him back home for a visit.

At the graduation ceremony I saw my brother in the audience. My speech went well, although my mother hissed at me that I had said "thank you" twice. Everyone else complimented me on it.

Right before the reception that my mother had arranged for me, she took me aside and told me, "You're such a selfish brute! You insisted that your brother be here, so he quit his job to be able to come. How could you be so selfish!"

I was dumbfounded. I hadn't insisted that he come, but that didn't seem to matter. I assumed the guilt and felt terrible. I even cried all though my graduation party. It seemed that I could never do anything right.

THE MANIFESTATION OF A DREAM

Someone called and asked me to appear on a talk show as an authority on healers. I wanted to do this with Foxes. He was an integral part of my dream, and he was tremendously enthusiastic about this possibility. Fortunately for me, when the call came to appear on the show, I was out of town. When I returned, I arranged for us to be invited again, but we never were called. The universe was trying to protect me from myself.

Regarding our television project, although our first potential broadcaster was enthusiastic, it didn't work out. Foxes and I were hardly talking by this point, allegedly because he was so busy painting houses. It was summer, a demanding time when he worked as much as possible, like a squirrel gathering nuts for winter.

I organized another pitch and made sure Foxes could be there with me. This time he was punctual as he arrived at my house. We met the director of programming, and once again our pitch turned out to be very successful. We were ecstatic!

Rather than go directly home, at Foxes' suggestion we went to Chinatown to buy him Chinese herbs and have lunch. It was a hot August day in New York City.

In the subway Foxes noted suspiciously, "It smells like dead rats down here."

"That's because there *are* dead rats down here," I answered, remarking that I had become immune to the smell.

It was a magical, fun afternoon. At lunch we got fortune cookies. Mine said I would be rich, but Foxes refused to read his to me. I didn't care. I had never spent any time in Chinatown, and I loved following Foxes around the stores while he bought exotic things and explained to me how the different herbs were used. At one point he spied a sword that he wanted to buy. He loved to fence, and this was a great épée, complete with a red tassel that he immediately removed and gave me. I insisted on carrying the sword for him, because I was sure he would have been arrested otherwise. He already looked like an aggressive street fighter whom people tried to avoid. If he had had his sword in his hand, he would have cleared the streets in a second. We had a great time together, just as I had dreamed we could.

On the way home we began discussing the production of our show. I had assumed my office in Westchester would be our headquarters, which would save money. Foxes had other ideas. He didn't want to drive two hours to work. I opted to negotiate with him, rather than go with my gut feeling, so we agreed to look for office space at a place midway between our homes. I would do the searching, and then Foxes would take a look before we jointly committed to it.

One day, concerned about our project, I called Foxes to work out some details. We had to be prepared to begin preproduction at the drop of a hat.

"Hi, Foxes. I wanted to figure out with you how the production will go, and what we're each going to do," I said.

"I need to be involved every step of the way," Foxes said. "Nothing will happen without my approval."

"Good. I'll look for office space," I said.

"Okay, but I need to see it before you commit to it," Foxes said. "Remember, nothing will happen without my approval."

"Fine. I'll wait until you see the space. You've got to like it, because it's going to be your home away from home when the production gets started," I said.

"What do you mean?" he asked.

"You'll have to be there every day, probably for most of the day. That is, unless there is some location filming going on," I said.

"I can't do that," Foxes replied.

"Do what?" I asked.

"Go to the office every day. I have other things I have to do," he said.

"Okay. I'll just have to make some decisions without you then," I said.

"You can't do that! I have to be consulted about every part of this production," Foxes insisted.

"In the heat of production, you have to make decisions all the time. If you're not there, how can you be consulted?" I asked.

"You can call me," Foxes replied.

"First of all, you don't have a cell phone. Even if you had one, you know that cell phones don't work well up where you live," I explained.

"Look. I have things I have to do, and you'll just have to work around them," Foxes said.

"What could be more important than this production?" I asked.

"I have to teach my qi gong and tai chi classes, and there are other important things I don't have to tell you about. I have a life," Foxes told me.

"This project *is* my life," I said.

"In that case, I feel sorry for you," Foxes answered, and hung up.

With those words, I realized that the "project of my life," the healers show, would never manifest with Foxes.

As if on cue, two days later the program director who had been so enthusiastic called to tell me the project had been rejected.

I felt so sad I could have just as well had a dagger in my heart!

I called Foxes to give him the news. Mercifully, I got his answering machine.

"Foxes, I just got a call today about the project. The proposal was finally rejected. Please don't call me. I need some time. Good-bye."

I never spoke to Foxes again.

☙

It took time for me to regain and regroup my energy and power. I felt exhausted, but more than anything else I realized how I had allowed myself to be used. I had believed that this person at least respected my dreams and me, and I thought that he wanted to help me. But now it appeared that Foxes really was just out for himself and didn't care a bit about my dreams or about me. I felt certain that he wanted to take the project that I had worked so hard to put together and exclude me from it. Fortunately, he could never do that, and now that I finally understood the situation, I took ownership of my own power. I promised myself to listen more closely to Tonka, who had tried to warn me.

What I thought was the manifestation of my dream had been, in fact, the manifestation of my fantasy.

12

Picking Up
the Pieces

I WAS FEELING VERY VULNERABLE after my breakup with Foxes. I was afraid of what would become of my project, and of me.

One August night I took an evening walk with my daughter Talia, our miniature poodle, Zoe, and our 120-pound yellow Lab, Pal. It was late and very dark. As we walked the familiar street that went around a small wooded area and then a large round marsh, Talia was in a panic. The first problem was the bugs. She was overwhelmed by the mosquitoes. I encouraged her to continue. On the way there was a streetlight that always turned off and on sporadically. As we approached that corner, it turned off.

"Oh, no! That weird light just went off. Something horrible is going to happen," Talia moaned.

"It's nothing. Probably just some bored spirit having fun," I laughed.

"No, I have to go home. I'm sure something awful is going to happen. That was a sign; that was a warning," she moaned. "Let's turn around and go home!"

"That's ridiculous! We're going to keep going and finish the block," I said, even though the dogs also wanted to turn around and go home.

"No, really Mommy, I know something horrible will happen. We have to go home right away," she pleaded.

The night was moonless, and the warm air around us turned cold as we passed a part of the marsh that was always cold like that. I was sure that there were some unhappy spirits there, but I didn't share this information with Talia. Nothing was going to stop my walk.

"Did you see it? Did you see it?" Talia hissed. "It's so scary! Let's turn around!"

"No, I don't see anything. What are you talking about?" I said. I knew that Talia was also clairvoyant, and I wondered what she had seen that I had missed.

"Those things flying across the road! They're horrible! Let's leave!" Talia begged.

"Those are bats," I said. "They're just night birds. They won't hurt you," I assured her.

"No, no! They might fly toward us. Look, there are more of them!" Talia whimpered.

I began to feel very nervous. I remembered the recent story of a girl upstate who had died from rabies. They thought she must have contracted the rabies when a bat bit her. I hurried my steps over the rugged road in the chilly, eerie night.

"They're going to bite me. I'll get rabies and die!" Talia moaned. She, too, had remembered that story. "Please let me go back home."

"Stay with me," I encouraged her. "We're almost halfway around."

Every time the bats passed by, Talia would moan. The creepiness of the night almost became intolerable. I didn't like the bats flying around either. I felt the air around us change from warm to cold, clammy, and stifling. And now I, too, felt uneasy about the light that went off and on. Talia and I stayed on our course as we hurried home.

CREATING FEAR

The next night I took the dogs out on my own. No moon or stars were visible on this street that I knew like the back of my hand. I walked along and began to feel apprehensive as I approached the streetlight that usually went out when I passed it. This time it stayed on longer than usual, and when it finally turned off and plunged me into complete darkness, I was overcome with fear. All the discomfort I had felt the night before now came back. I worried about being bitten by a bat. All the bravado I had demonstrated in front of Talia was gone, now that I was alone. I began to say the Lord's Prayer, repeating it over and over as I walked through the dark.

The bats appeared again, flying all around me this time. I continued repeating the Lord's Prayer. It was the only thing that pulled me out of my abject terror. I continued my walk and felt the cold, clammy air engulf me. How strange it was that on such a hot night this particular place had such chilly air. Just like a morgue, I thought. I continued to repeat the Lord's Prayer. At three-quarters of the way around, I felt I couldn't say the Lord's Prayer again. I was becoming hysterical in my need to cling to those words. I began to sing "Amazing Grace." The rest of the way home I sang "Amazing Grace" over and over again. I felt better, and as I reached home, I felt triumphant. "I once was bound, but now I'm free," I sang, incorporating my own lyrics.

I realized that I had turned a perfectly beautiful walk with night birds (the bats) into a terror walk. I had been so engulfed in the fear that my daughter had shown me that I had incorporated it into my life. This was manufactured terror that I had allowed myself to create.

How often do we do this to ourselves? I wondered, *Create a situation of abject fear out of nothing?*

FINDING THE LIGHT

Once again the universe was watching over me and timed my painful transition to coincide with another John Perkins workshop. This one, "A Gathering of Shamans," brought several South American shamans together at Omega. Perkins' Dream Change Coalition organized the event. Once before, when I had been walking through the darkness of despair, John Perkins had lifted me up. I felt empowered just by the thought of going to the workshop.

On the drive up I realized that I had become a different person. The original title of my project was "Healers: Fact or Fiction." Now, for me, there was no question about the authenticity of healers. It was only fact. I had discovered my amazing gift of being able to contact the Spirit World. I had developed a great relationship with my Native American guide, Tonka. I could ask him questions anytime and receive answers. I was bringing great joy and healing to people by contacting spirits for them. These people I had helped now encouraged me to make my gift more available to other people, and this is something I very much wanted to do.

Still, I had a terrible hurt because of what had happened with Foxes. The hole he had discovered in my heart and filled up during our very first meeting was now back again. I had blindly given away my energy and my power, and now I had to build it up again. On top of that, I had known what was happening, thanks to Tonka's warning, and I hadn't listened, drugged by my ego's imagination and my pattern of being a victim. I had put out energy and manifested a fantasy, and now I was suffering the consequences. I knew I could create a new and better show about healers, and I knew that the energy Foxes had given me could be found again through qi gong. That energy was mine to keep, along with my power, as well as the gift of mediumship. These were all gifts from God. But who could teach me qi gong? Who could I confer with? Who would make me feel comfortable about communicating with the Spirit World?

At "A Gathering of Shamans" I was filled with excitement and energy that almost masked my pain. As a confirmation of the necessity for me to use my gifts, I met people who asked me to contact loved ones for them. It made me feel wonderful to see troubled faces become serene with the knowledge that the loved ones they thought they had lost forever were really in a beautiful place not so far away, just in a different dimension.

I sat at a table and told Sam, who was sitting across from me, that I was a medium. According to Tonka, he was the person I was supposed to tell. But the man wasn't interested! Other people at the table were very interested, but Sam didn't respond. I was confused. One woman at the table, Annie, was so adamant that I contact her father that I couldn't refuse.

Annie's father had passed over fourteen years earlier. I contacted him, and he told her to watch out for her job. She said she was thinking about changing jobs at the end of the year, and he said that wasn't soon enough. Then he gave her information about her love life. Annie thanked me and the following day presented me with a turquoise bracelet. I didn't want to accept it, because I didn't want to receive payment for using my gift. But

I saw that she would be hurt if I didn't take the gift she was offering so sincerely. Up to that point I hadn't received any monetary compensation for my work; I didn't think I should. Annie made me realize that I needed to make my gift available to more people, and that I needed to receive compensation for it. Several months later I heard from Annie about how she had been made a scapegoat at her job and humiliated, even though she had had the highest approval rating earlier that year. She had thought she was invulnerable. Now she was sorry she hadn't listened to her father. She decided to follow the rest of his advice more closely. Today she lives in Hawaii, where she is in a happy relationship and a fulfilling and rewarding job.

Meanwhile Sam, whom I had targeted, didn't want to contact anyone. For the weeklong duration of "A Gathering of Shamans," every time I saw Sam I felt pushed to ask him if there wasn't anyone he needed to contact. He always said no.

I began to worry that Sam would think I was stalking him. I told him I was married with four children. He just seemed to think I was crazy. On the last day I ran into him at the cafeteria.

"Hi, Sam. Looks like this is your last chance to find out who wants to speak to you," I told him.

"I guess I just won't find out. I have to meet some people for lunch," Sam answered flatly, walking away.

Spirit kept instructing me to insist on making this contact for him.

"Well, that would be a real shame. What about after lunch?" I insisted.

"I have to get home right away. It's a long drive," Sam said. "And my wife is waiting for me."

"It wouldn't take long," I continued.

"How long?" Sam asked, impatiently.

"About ten minutes," I replied hopefully.

"Okay. I'll come to your table, and then I'll take just ten minutes to find out who this spirit is," Sam acquiesced.

We perched on a secluded picnic table on the great lawn at Omega. It was a beautiful day. An hour and a half later Sam and I said good-bye. I had contacted his grandfather for him, a contact so powerful that it changed Sam's life forever.

Throughout his youth, Sam had been continually sexually molested by his older brother. This experience had rendered him meek and fearful; he had become a permanent victim. Sam remembered his grandfather as a strong, powerful man. Knowing that he had his grandfather's strength helping him now, Sam felt tremendously empowered. His grandfather also brought Sam important information about his life, complete with suggestions on how he could improve it. Sam's powerful grandfather knew that this was his opportunity to communicate with his grandson and bring tremendous healing. That is why he, through my guide Tonka, insisted that I make contact for Sam. When we parted, Sam was a different person. In addition to being absolutely delighted and grateful to me, he was transformed by the empowerment he had received from his dead grandfather.

A few months later Sam e-mailed me about the significant, positive changes that had occurred in his life, thanks to his grandfather's help. A year later Sam called me so I could again contact his grandfather, this time while Sam was in Atlanta and I was in New York. I don't know where the grandfather was, but I could see him and hear him perfectly as I spoke over the phone with Sam. That was the first time I worked over the telephone. I hadn't wanted to try it before, because I didn't want to disappoint anyone if it didn't work. Fortunately it all went very well. I often work over the phone now.

HOW TO HEAL AN ACHING HEART

Although I was happy to help all these people, I still felt pain in my heart because of my breakup with Foxes, until beautiful Maria Juana Imberla from Ecuador healed me. She is about four-feet-five and doesn't speak a word of English. Maria Juana had been blind for several years during her youth. It was then that she "learned" to be a healer, and then suddenly at age eighteen she regained her sight. Now she works with her husband, Antonio. Maria Juana began her session with me by praying to Imbabura, a mountain in her homeland, and to Jesus Christ, who appears to her as a dove.

I am a very modest person physically, so I felt very uncomfortable undressing in front of Antonio and the interpreter, but I had decided to go whole hog for the healing. I was determined to be healed! Gingerly I rubbed a white candle over my body, and then Maria Juana made her diagnosis by examining the candle. Through the interpreter she told me that I carried my spirituality like a heavy weight instead of enjoying it as I should. I stood naked in front of her and Antonio as he took several swigs of alcohol into his mouth and sprayed them all over my body, to purify me. I wondered what my Westchester friends would think of me now as I shivered. Then he rubbed two raw eggs in their shells all over me. This, too, was way outside of my comfort zone. *What was I thinking when I decided to do this healing?* I thought. The eggs were supposed to absorb all the toxins from my body. Both Maria Juana and Antonio were praying fervently the entire time. Then Antonio rubbed a mixture of flower petals and alcohol on my body. By this time I had surrendered to the experience and simply waited for it to end. Maria Juana had me lie down on the floor, then she massaged my belly. She had picked up on the fact that I had a tilted uterus without me mentioning it. At the end of the healing, I received instructions not to wash for three days, and Antonio placed a carnation necklace around my neck while Maria Juana gave me a glass of juice with carnation petals in it, along with a cookie.

Through her interpreter I asked Maria Juana about my aching heart. "No problem," she announced. I just needed to mix some crushed pebbles with a bit of my hair burned to ashes in some juice. Within minutes Maria Juana had gathered the necessary pebbles and crushed them. Then she snipped some of my hair and burned it. She put these ashes and the crushed pebbles in a cup with some orange juice, gave it a stir, and handed it to me to drink. It worked! The heavy pain in my heart disappeared, never to return. I have shared this remedy with others who have used it to relieve their aching hearts.

In a daze, not knowing what to do with myself following this strange healing, I slipped into the back of the lecture hall to catch the end of whatever lecture happened to be transpiring. Various shamans were taking turns holding seminars, explaining their healing modalities. I had barely sat down when John Perkins, who was leading the seminar, suggested that people either partner up or be silent and alone that day.

I turned to the closest person sitting next to me and asked if he wanted to partner with me. He said no, he wanted to be silent, and walked away. At this point, everyone was either partnered or had left the room.

No problem, I thought. *I'll just meet up with someone at lunch.*

In the cafeteria, after getting my food, I found a table with some friendly looking people, settled in, and began eating. When I turned to talk to the person next to me I was told that this was a silent table. I sighed and gave up. By default, I accepted the message the universe was sending me and stayed at that table and was silent. I decided this was a lesson in *codependence,* and I needed to enjoy my *independence.* My heart was free from pain, and I was completely liberated from any attachment to Foxes. The universe was preventing me from falling into my old codependent patterns. I was forced to heal in a new direction.

I realized that, in general, I didn't spend a lot of time alone. Later, as I sat by myself, I was glad not to be with anyone else. People around me were talking, but I decided to keep my energy for myself. I even did qi gong to increase my energy. I slept and relaxed on a wooden lounge chair. It was heaven. The sun shone on me, and I remembered when Jesus brought me his open loving heart. I had enjoyed that so much.

In my meditative state I heard God tell me that for me nothing was random any more. Everything and every person in my life and on my path would be there for a reason. I had to be very present and try to understand the meaning of each encounter.

After dinner Tonka suggested I go to the sanctuary. I followed a road that became a trail in the woods. It led up and up. As I followed this dark trail I saw before me shiny stones or prints that reflected just enough light for me to be able to see the way. I wasn't on the main trail at all, but I didn't feel lost. I only felt frightened once, when what looked like a big, white, seated poodle appeared on the left. It was just a stone formation.

And isn't it a little ridiculous to be afraid of a big white poodle anyway? I chided myself, remembering my night walk with Talia. I had to make sure I didn't let myself fall into a mindset of fear.

I followed the shiny stones and reached the sanctuary. Once there, I began to meditate, and I heard a spirit voice tell me that forever more I would be led on my path. I didn't ever need to be afraid again.

THE MISSION

My black-panther guide suddenly appeared as I meditated in the sanctuary and told me he would lead me on a long trip during the next journey.

The drumbeats that accompanied the following day's journey

allowed me to fall into a deep trance. I didn't listen to the words of the guide at all, because before the first word was spoken, the black panther took me far, far away, past the red planet into the bright white light. An extraterrestrial-type face was sort of visible. Somehow I was talking about fear and my desire to accomplish something profound, although exactly what that was, I didn't know. The extraterrestrial said I couldn't do what I wanted to do because I was afraid. I began to beg and insist I could do it, that I wasn't afraid.

"I will do it! I can do it! I'm not afraid anymore!" I insisted.

He wasn't sure. I insisted that I wanted to do this. I could do it, and I would do it without fear. Finally he agreed. I didn't know what all that was about, but it felt extremely profound. I was filled with determination to accomplish some kind of important mission.

That night John Perkins led a group initiation ceremony. It was then that my mission became clear to me. One of my favorite hymns that we sing in the Presbyterian church, "Here I Am," ran through my mind. *Here I am Lord, / Is it I, Lord? / I have heard you calling in the night.* Over and over the song sounded in my head, just as it had during the initiation at Rosalyn Bruyere's intensive.

Finally, my ultimate mission became clear. I do what the Lord tells me to do. Growing up Protestant, I had always been religious, but this was over the top! I was overwhelmed with emotion. It was as though a curtain had been lifted and I could see my life's path. The movements of the workshop's initiation ceremony echoed my emotional impressions as I walked through the symbolic arch. I was patted with leaves, purified with smoke, and *camayed* in the same way as Antonio had purified me with alcohol. Then I got a candle and blew into it three times, silently repeating the personal mission I devised. "I do what God tells me to do, and I listen for instructions." I threw my candle into the fire and danced around with joy. Then I joined the circle and continued dancing until the drumming stopped and everyone left.

Alone again after the ceremony, I followed the path through the woods to the sanctuary. Even though it was pitch black I could see the stones again lighting my way, and I was not at all afraid. At the sanctuary I meditated. In God's eyes all creation is equal, and we are all loved in the same way. The number of people at this gathering whom I helped with my gift was impressive. It seemed that every person I came into contact with I either delivered a message to or empowered in some way. This is what the people themselves told me. I could see how I was fulfilling my calling from God in gratitude for the gift I had received, the gift of mediumship.

At the workshop I got a broader sense of life in general. The prophecies that were made about the destruction of mankind can be changed and are being changed. People like me, by their intentions, change the course of events. Mother Earth will always survive, but she will shake us off before letting us destroy her. I felt in complete harmony with the universe. My heart was repaired. I felt whole and one with God and the universe, tremendously solid, grounded, and complete.

I thanked God for this life and all the wonderful adventures I knew I would have. My heart was full of love for everything. I looked at the inside of my dorm room and I felt love for the wood that made the rudimentary shelves. I felt love and compassion for the metal chair that had served so well that it carried nicks and scratches from use. I looked at my shoes and marveled at their kindness in protecting my feet. I saw my clock, which reminded me of Paris and a visit with my daughter Tania, who had been living there at the time. How well the clock has served me, and how fortunate I am to have daughters like Tania and Talia and sons like Tristan and Terence.

It was in the middle of all this euphoria that I could face the memory of my healing by Foxes. I realized that, subsequent to my healing, the spirit in the form of a man who had walked in with heavy boots and urinated on my face had been Foxes. It was a warning that Foxes would take control and abuse me. I hadn't interpreted it as a warning at the time, and certainly not a warning about Foxes. How could the person who I thought had opened so much joy in my life cause me so much pain? I wasn't angry or hurt anymore. I felt indifferent toward him, but nevertheless fragile. It would take time to wholly integrate the reality that I was completely alone, and that I didn't need to depend on anyone to realize my dreams.

I returned home full of joy and energy. I had completely recaptured my power, and I was now comfortable with it. I was conscious of wanting to never give it away again and of never letting someone take it, either. This was a very important step for me, and I realized that Foxes had played a very important role in its unfolding.

13

A New World Opens Up

REPAIRED HEART OR NOT, one of the many reasons I was sad about losing contact with Foxes was that I missed his knowledge about Native Americans. I knew virtually nothing about the subject, despite my cherished guide, Tonka. Now I thought I had no way of learning more. Books were not the answer. I wasn't sure about asking Tonka for such information, because it seemed inappropriate in the context of my Westchester life.

Once again the universe presented me with what I needed. At "A Gathering of Shamans" I met Joann Morgan, who was very knowledgeable about Lakota tradition. She suggested I read the book *Black Elk Speaks*. She also mentioned that Wallace Black Elk, the author's son, would soon be facilitating a sweat lodge at Rowe Conference Center, a wonderful retreat in the Berkshire Mountains.

NATIVE AMERICAN CEREMONY

Suddenly, life had a new focus for me as I found a way to experience Native American life without Foxes. I registered for the sweat lodge and read *Black Elk Speaks*. The only experience I had had with sweat lodges was from having seen one at Foxes' place. Foxes and I never talked about it, even though we sometimes discussed Native Americans. I never questioned whether I should participate in this sweat lodge or not. I knew I had to do it, and Tonka encouraged me.

I noticed that many people at "A Gathering of Shamans" talked about vision quests. I didn't feel drawn to spending four days in the wilderness alone, much less without food or water. I had never even camped out. After attending Tom Brown's workshop, carried away by my enthusiasm to connect with nature, I spent one night in a hammock in our backyard. I have to admit that I had felt a bit afraid during the night, and the next morning I was covered with insect bites. So much for the outdoor life!

At the end of October I went up to the Rowe Conference Center to participate in my first sweat lodge. I had learned that a sweat lodge represents the womb, and the stones inside represent semen. Within the lodge, as people confront the darkness and the heat, they have an opportunity to get rid of all the negativity they have been carrying and struggling with. Cleansing occurs through sweating and emotional release. When participants leave the lodge, they are reborn, fresh and pure.

❧

As I drove up alone to the conference center, I reflected on how important it was to never give your energy or power away. It is yours, for you and your path. You can channel energy through you to help others, but you should never give yours away.

Sometimes a person can be unaware she is giving her power away because she and the recipient share the same goals and agenda. (Both men and women fall into this trap.) The person believes that she is promoting personal goals by giving the recipient her energy and power, because it looks like the goal will be met with the synergistic help of the recipient. But what usually happens is that either the recipient takes all the glory for achieving the goal, or worse, changes directions midstream to achieve a different goal. Then it is really hard for an energy- and power-strapped person to achieve any goals herself.

Another thing I discovered is that although I thought that giving my energy to people around me would make me more attractive to them and make them like me, it doesn't. Without my own energy I'm a dependent weakling. What's attractive about that? Feeling my own energy, being strong, I have more energy to intentionally channel to others while refilling myself at the same time. That's how charisma works.

The first night at Rowe I met some women who had participated in many sweat lodges over the years. They seemed to take me into their circle. During Wallace Black Elk's presentation, I was mesmerized by his words. It seemed that I was learning more from just being present than by intellectually processing his talk. Taping or taking notes was forbidden. In the Native American tradition, information is passed on verbally, with the understanding that we will retain what we are supposed to retain.

The next day was spent learning about Native American ceremony and how to make prayer ties that we could take with us into the *inipi*, the sweat lodge. The prayer ties are made out of small squares of cloth into which a pinch of tobacco and a personal prayer are placed. The ties are taken into the lodge and hung above the participant. The number of squares and their color depends on the person facilitating the lodge.

In a secluded wooded area, an auspicious spot had been chosen to build the lodge. Around the lodge area variously colored strips of cloth, "robes," had been hung in the trees. Each of the colors represented a specific thing. The area around the lodge was "smudged": sage was burned over hot coals, creating smoke that is believed to purify and remove any bad energy that might be present.

A Lakota sweat lodge is made of saplings that are bent and tied together to form a dome-shaped structure. Historically, this structure was covered with animal skins; however, in this day and age blankets and tarps are used instead. One side of the lodge is made in such a way that people can enter. A heavy flap of blankets and tarps serves as a door that can be opened, then closed when everyone is in the lodge.

Directly in front of the entrance to the lodge is the altar, which varies according to the spirit that is "planted" for that lodge. It might be a buffalo spirit or that of some other animal or bird. In line with the door, on the other side of the altar, is the sacred fire. This is a huge bonfire where stones are heated for the lodge. To build the fire, stones are chosen and then carefully stacked and surrounded by logs. A firekeeper is in charge of putting together the stones and fire and maintaining the fire throughout the sweat.

The stones, "grandfathers" as they are called, are collected from the surface of the earth. The pourer is in charge of pouring the water on the hot stones inside the lodge. For this particular sweat, the pourer was Wallace Black Elk, who is also referred to as Grandfather. In the course of the sweat lodge, the door is opened four times to bring in more stones. Some medicine men allow people to leave the lodge between doors. Others, including Grandfather Black Elk, don't.

Because of Grandfather Black Elk's popularity there were many people attending the sweat lodge, and we had to divide up into two groups to participate in two consecutive ceremonies. I ended up in the second group. I watched the first group line up to go into the lodge, the women first, in long cotton skirts and cotton tops, and the men in shorts or swim trunks lined up behind them. As I waited for my ceremony to begin, I spoke to other people who were there for the first time.

"I don't know if I'm going to do the lodge after all. I'm so nervous about it," one woman said to me. "It's going to be really crowded, and you know, it's completely dark in there. I know that Grandfather Black Elk doesn't like to let people out before the end. Can you imagine being stuck in that small, crowded space?"

As a matter of fact, I could. Just then I conveniently remembered that I was claustrophobic. What perfect timing. I remembered how I once had had to leave a guided tour of ancient catacombs under a village in southern France because of my claustrophobia. Those catacombs hadn't been as confining as the sweat lodge would be. I also remembered experiencing the choking feeling of being caught while climbing a tiny stone staircase leading up to la Sainte Chapelle in Paris. There were so many tourists that I couldn't move up or down the stairs. I was filled with panic and almost fainted before the line finally began to move again. What was I going to do, trapped inside the sweat lodge?

Another woman there commiserated. "This is the second time I've come here to participate in the sweat lodge. I couldn't do it then, and I don't think I can this time either. . . ."

As we were lining up for the lodge I scolded myself, *Now look what I've gotten myself into! What to do? What to do?* I watched some people break away from the line. *I could do that, too,* I thought. But I knew I had to go. I took a deep breath and crawled into the dark, smoky lodge.

There were people sitting in front and on both sides of me. I couldn't move an inch, but I felt fine as we were asked to pray out loud for someone while glowing stones were brought inside the structure.

I was wondering about seeing spirits when suddenly a woman's face appeared directly before me. Behind her I saw a long crystal that was lit up. I recognized this vision as being from a ceremony in Atlantis. This spirit woman kept trying to get my attention.

"Look at me. Look at me," she repeated. I tried to focus on her, recognizing her as someone I had known a long time ago, perhaps in Atlantis. I asked for my guide Tonka. He told me that he was there, protecting me, but that I needed to focus on the woman; she would get me through this ceremony.

I wondered what he meant by that comment, since I felt that so far I had been doing just fine!

Then the door was closed and the lodge became completely dark. Grandfather Black Elk poured water on the hot stones. As the suffocating steam rose, the terror of claustrophobia gripped me.

"You are facing your fear. That's what you asked to do," the spirit woman told me.

I didn't really remember asking for that, but I guess I must have. Now I had a past-life recall of being in a prison cave deep underground. My limbs were broken, and I couldn't defend myself as rats ate me alive. I wanted to pass out!

"Look at me! Look at me!" I heard, as again the spirit woman appeared to have her face almost touching mine. I focused on her beautiful, peaceful face and welcomed the calm surrender she brought me.

The spirit woman kept me steady. The person sitting next to me wasn't so lucky; she wanted to leave. Someone told her to lie down. Because there was no room, she had to lie in my lap. Now I had no room at all! But rather than freak out, I focused on the spirit woman who gave me silent strength and support and I felt fine.

For the rest of the time in the lodge, in the dark, I saw many fluorescent, amoeba-like shapes floating around, as well as many faces. Later on I was told these were *cachinas*, free-floating energy beings. This demonstrated to me that spirits can appear to us in many shapes and forms.

I came out of the lodge feeling reborn. It was a personal victory for me, not only because I overcame my claustrophobia, but also because I participated in something that had previously seemed so foreign. I survived the ordeal! My new friends—Betsy, Marilyn, and Judy—spoke of having participated in other lodges. In fact, they were planning to attend another lodge the following weekend that Wallace Black Elk was scheduled to pour in upstate New York, and asked if I would be interested in going with them. I was amazed that people participated in several sweat lodges on consecutive days. I couldn't imagine doing that. I thought I might lodge again in about, maybe, a year at the earliest. I certainly wasn't ready to lodge again the following weekend.

It also bothered me that the next lodge was taking place so close to Foxes' territory. Hadn't I come to Massachusetts in hopes of meeting people from a different part of the country? I was surprised, too, that my new friends were from that same area at the foot of the Adirondacks. What if I ran into Foxes there?

Betsy spoke of her recent vision quest. I was surprised to find myself asking her questions about this, as if I were personally interested in the mechanics of "going up on the hill."

I felt wonderful as I drove home. I believed that it would probably take me quite some time to digest this profound experience and the knowledge I had gained and would continue to glean from it, and I was in no hurry to experience another lodge right away.

But, a few weeks later, when I got an e-mail from Betsy, I realized that I was desperate for more contact and information about the Lakota culture. Betsy told me that Wallace had postponed the sweat lodge in New York and that one would take place in a week. I eagerly wanted to listen to Grandfather Black Elk speak, and the sweat lodge ordeal would be the price I was prepared to pay for it.

SWEAT LODGE HEALINGS

My second lodge experience was nothing less than extraordinary. I spent the evening before the event, and the whole next day, listening to Grandfather Black Elk talk about Lakota culture and his insights into the world at large and the universe beyond.

At that time my mother was ill and hadn't been communicating with my brothers and me about her illness. Some friends of hers in Ohio e-mailed that she was hiding in her room with a sign on the door that read NO VISITORS! Whenever either of my brothers or I called, she always said she was fine. Whenever I tried to question the staff at her assisted living facility, they told me she was fine, too.

I asked Tonka about what was going on. He told me that she had skin cancer on her face, and that she had recently undergone a surgical procedure that had disfigured her. According to Tonka, Mom was waiting to have reconstructive surgery before going out in public. As usual, she had ordered the staff to keep her family uninformed.

Before the lodge I asked Grandfather Black Elk if I could do anything for my mother. He told me to make a certain number of prayer ties and bring them into the lodge with me. I sat alone as I made the prayer ties and fervently prayed for my mother to recover and share the news of her physical condition with us. Even though I realized that she had wanted to die before, she was my mother, the one who had nourished me and given me life. I felt I wanted to return the favor. I was hoping that this time she might even change her mind and decide to embrace life. I took the prayer ties into the lodge with me, and I hung them above my head. This lodge was even more crowded than my first had been. People were seated in front of me, in back of me, and to both sides. Surprisingly, I had no problem with claustrophobia. I called Tonka to make sure he was there. He appeared, told me I was fine, and that he had other things to do. I was surprised, but instead of feeling abandoned, I was impressed by his power and that he was such a necessary part of this lodge. Then I opened my attention to see what was happening inside the black lodge. I saw wonderful lights in magical, Miro-type shapes, which were different from the amoeba shapes I had seen before.

One of the messages I received during the sweat was that I have been given great power to heal through my hands, but that I must use this power discreetly and not promote it for the time being. Instead I should promote my ability to contact spirits. Many will be jealous of me, I "heard." That is why I have been surrounded by jealousy my whole life— to learn how to deal with it.

My daughter Tania was on my mind. She had been facing some challenges recently. I had so wanted her to benefit from the lodge experience that I called her spirit to be with me. Suddenly a vision of Tania appeared.

She seemed confused to find herself in the lodge. Then the vision disappeared. Later on Tania told me that at the moment I had called her spirit to the lodge she was with a client in Seattle. She was walking with this client when she almost fainted, and the client had to catch her. It must have been at that moment that her spirit was in the lodge. She quickly regained her composure as her spirit returned to her body. I guess it was worth it because the issue she was dealing with was resolved.

A couple of months after that sweat lodge, my mother sent identical letters to my brothers and me. She told us about the skin cancer she had suffered on her nose and the disfiguring surgery that had ensued. Now she was in remission. She even sent us copies of the oncologist's report. I prayed my thanksgiving to God the Creator, who had brought this wonderful healing to my mother. I also prayed my thanks to Grandfather Black Elk, who had facilitated my prayers of healing.

After the lodge, I asked Betsy for more details about her vision quest. I was increasingly interested specifically in the Lakota vision quest. I was beginning to realize that going on a vision quest would be important to my spiritual growth, and thought I would probably have to travel to South Dakota, home of the Lakota Sioux. Betsy, however, directed me to the firekeeper for Grandfather Black Elk's sweat lodge, a man named Glen Gordon.

I staggered out of the sweat lodge to face frisky, clear blue eyes and a big, white-toothed grin, which contrasted with the soot-darkened face of Glen as he smiled at me. He was helping people out of the lodge.

Glen was standing next to a pail of water, and I was pretty thirsty.

"Could I have some of that water?" I asked.

"Why, ya shore can," Glen said with a smile. I reached for the ladle to get some water. "Course ya don't mind that I peed in it, do ya?"

I stopped middrink as Glen laughed, "I'm just jokin' with ya!"

"Hi, my name's Alexandra."

"Nice ta meet ya, Alexandra," he drawled, as he thrust out an equally soot-covered hand for a friendly handshake. His southern accent reminded me of sweet, syrupy pecan pie.

"I heard you know something about vision quests," I said.

"That might well be," he answered.

"Could you tell me about them?" I asked.

"We're goin' to be havin' some sweats up in my lodge soon. Everyone's invited, 'n that includes you," Glen said. "It's right here in the Adirondacks. Matter o' fact, your timin' couldn't be better 'cause Jake's comin' over from South Dakota to do the pourin'. Yep. That's as good a time as any to be learnin' 'bout vision quests."

"Did you ever do a vision quest?" I asked.

"I shore did. Did it right here in the Adirondacks. Best experience of my life," Glen replied.

14

We Are All Related

MY EXCITEMENT ABOUT THE SWEAT LODGE seemed to be infectious. My son Terence and his girlfriend, Ellen, were enthusiastic about joining me. It was exciting to share my spiritual experiences with members of my family who were also opening up to Spirit. Since we had shot *Around the Corner* and *Heavy Breathing,* Terence and Ellen had continued to pursue meditation and investigate alternative medicine. I spoke of the sweat lodge as a great opportunity to break through different barriers, such as transcending my claustrophobia. Because they are both actors, Terence and Ellen welcomed this opportunity for a new experience.

Ellen said, "It sounds like fun!"

"It's a profound experience. It's positive and life changing, but I wouldn't call it fun," I commented, wanting to make sure they wouldn't be disappointed.

We drove up to the Adirondacks together, and we were deep in the mountains by the time we arrived at our destination. People were gathering in anticipation of the event, the sacred fire was burning, and it was cold outside on this November night.

Glen greeted us with enthusiasm and warmth. "Well, how ya doin'? It shore is nice to meet Alexandra's son, and, o' course, your friend here. We're glad ya made it up here. Are ya goin' to lodge with us like your mom?" We immediately felt welcome.

"That's what we were planning to do," Terence answered.

"Well, that's just great. I always say, 'The more the merrier!' By the way, Alexandra, Jake's inside right there in case ya wanted to talk to him. Ya know, 'bout what ya were plannin' on," Glen said.

"Oh, right, right. I was going to ask him about vision quests," I explained to Terence and Ellen.

"Now's a good time to do that," Glen said.

FOLLOWING THE CREATOR'S LEAD

I left Terence and Ellen to discover the sacred fire and the lodge in the woods while I went to talk to Jake Sitting Buffalo, the medicine man, who was inside the ramshackle garage that Glen called home. Jake was sitting by himself; a couple of people were at the other end of the room fussing around a stove.

"Jake?" I asked. He nodded and invited me to sit down.

"I'm interested in doing a vision quest," I ventured. Although that's what I told him, there was no rush as far as I was concerned.

"You have to talk to the gatekeeper first. That's Glen outside. He decides if you can participate, and then you talk to me. You offer tobacco and a gift to follow to the gatekeeper, and if he agrees, then do the same for me," Jake instructed.

Embarrassed and a little relieved, I said, "Oh, I don't have any tobacco with me. I guess I can't do this right now."

A voice from the other end of the room said, "There's a gas station down the road where you could probably find some tobacco."

A gas station with tobacco out here in the middle of nowhere? And why doesn't that person just shut up? I thought. *Now I have to go look for tobacco.*

I said, "Oh. Okay. I'll go see if I can find some." I left feeling very confused. I had no intention of organizing a vision quest for myself right then and there, but I didn't want to seem like an idiot either. I would let Spirit guide me.

Sure enough, the one store in the area was a gas station that sold tobacco. After purchasing some, I walked back through the woods to the lodge. The sacred fire, piled high with stones and wood, was ablaze with flames that were over seven feet tall. The fire seemed to welcome me as I approached. Except for the crackling of the huge fire, everything was still.

As I approached the lodge, I felt peaceful. I found Glen alone next to the lodge.

"I would like to do a vision quest," I said, and offered Glen some tobacco.

Gravely Glen accepted the tobacco. "Ya do realize that a Lakota vision quest is a serious commitment?"

I heard myself say, "Yes. I understand that, and I want to do it."

"It's not just a one-time deal. Ya gotta commit to doin' one every year for four years, with one additional year as a thank you," Glen continued.

"I really want to do the Lakota vision quest, and if that means doing it for five consecutive years, that's what I'll do," I heard myself answer.

"Ya *do* realize it means goin' out into the woods for four days without food or water, right? They take yore shoes so ya can't leave yore spot 'til they come back and get ya. Yore out there by yourself with nothin'," Glen said.

Once again I heard myself say, "I'll do whatever I need to do. And I know I can do it. I *know I have* to do it."

Glen sent me back to Jake. As though in a dream, I offered Jake some tobacco and asked him to facilitate a vision quest for me. He told me to make a strand of twenty-one prayer ties and fill the strand with prayers for my quest. In a dream state I made my prayer ties. By the time I finished, everyone was entering the lodge.

Terence was seated among the men, away from Ellen and me. When the lodge began, the nature of it felt very different from the last one I had attended. Right away I felt challenged, but I knew I had to be strong for Ellen. It was a much hotter lodge than Grandfather Black Elk's. At one point, when the door had just closed, Ellen screamed, "My hands! My hands, they're burning!" I calmed her down, and she realized that her hands were very hot but not on fire. I encouraged Ellen to lie down on the ground and cover herself up. I felt like doing the same but didn't want to look weak in front of her. At one point the scorching steam hurt so much I turned my face toward the wall behind me for an instant. Searing pain burned the back of my neck. I turned my face back toward the center and felt some relief. Many people were lying down and moaning.

What's going on? I thought to myself. *And just what am I getting myself into?*

When the door was finally opened and we could leave the lodge, everyone staggered out and fell to the ground, exhausted. I was deeply concerned about the severe conditions that we were experiencing, but Terence had seemed so proud of me when I was making my prayer ties, I felt I couldn't walk away from my commitment to do this vision quest.

When I had collected myself enough to face other people I checked on Terence and Ellen. Terence had apparently screamed throughout the last door. He had tiny blisters on his ears. I was grateful that I hadn't heard him over the sound of the drumming and singing. I never could have stayed put if I had heard his screams.

There was a feast after the lodge. This was supposed to be the fun part, everyone breaking bread together and laughing a lot. Everyone was laughing, all right, except Terence, Ellen, and me. We huddled in misery. Terence was miserable about his experience in the lodge, and Ellen was upset and crying about Terence's blisters.

I was furious with the way everything had gone and at the lack of sympathy we received after the lodge. However, I didn't say anything about how I felt. We finished dinner quickly and left.

The ride home in the middle of the night was animated, thanks to Terence's unending, angry commentary about his horrible experience. Rather than participating in a sweat lodge, he sounded as though he had just been boiled in oil. I apologized to the kids for dragging them into this nightmare.

I tried to put a positive spin on the situation and spoke in healing terms. Fortunately the drive home took over two hours, which enabled Terence to retrieve his remarkable sense of humor.

"And these blisters on my ears! I don't need any red balls on my ears! I'm not a Christmas tree!" Terence said. "And you never told me that I should lie down in the lodge. Thanks loads. Good job, Mom! Just as it began to get hot, I remembered the Indiana Jones movie where he goes into the tunnel and has to lie down on the ground or else get chopped up by the swinging axes. But did I do that? No! I sat up straight like a real he-man! My ears really hurt! This sucks!"

"Maybe Spirit was trying to give you a message to listen better," I suggested.

"Well, excuse me, but Spirit must have missed my ears and hit around them instead," Terence retorted.

The last half-hour of the ride Ellen and I were laughing hysterically at Terence's hilarious remarks.

"And Glen. Is he Gomer Pyle or what?" Terence laughed.

"I know!" Ellen giggled in delight. "He could be on TV."

"Well, ya jus' kinda crawl in here, 'n jus' relax—as you get burned to a crisp!" Terence imitated Glen, finishing with a flourish in his own voice.

The next day Terence was amazed—all his blisters were gone.

It turned out that Jake is a Heyoka medicine man and that he poured an extremely hot lodge using at least 101 stones. Grandfather Black Elk had used only forty. I felt pretty stupid, and I felt sad for Terence and Ellen, and for myself, too. What was worse for me was that I had just committed myself to do a vision quest in April with this same medicine man. The prospect of spending four days out in the wild without food or water seemed like a walk in the park compared to participating in Jake's sweat lodges.

I called Glen to discuss my situation. He seemed charming and supportive of the lodge and as I spoke with him the concerns I had seemed to disappear. He confirmed that Terence's blisters were a lesson. He also helped me figure out my own lesson about *my* blister: in the sweat lodge the spirits are gathered in the middle around the hot stones, and when I had turned my face away, I was being disrespectful to them.

"Ya never turn your back on Spirit. I shore never wanna find myself doin' that," Glen explained to me. "But don't the sweat make ya feel powerful now? Jus' look at ya! What can scare ya after one of Jake's sweats?"

It was true. I did have a feeling of strength that I hadn't felt before. Even Terence and Ellen in their final analysis thought it was a beneficial experience. Another positive for me was that Jake's wife prayed to the Creator, Christ, and Holy Spirit in the lodge. Because I am a practicing Christian, her prayer meant a lot to me, especially hearing it in the sweat lodge.

IT'S NONE OF MY BUSINESS

Tonka encouraged me to continue on the vision quest. I even went back to Penney to have a healing in the hopes of getting her psychic impression of this quest. I mentioned how challenging Jake's sweat lodge had seemed for me. She said that lodges in general would do nothing for me, but the vision quest would make some definite positive changes.

I still had issues that bothered me to the point of hampering my life, and I wanted to do the vision quest in order to try and resolve them. My main problem was that, for some reason, I would often stop myself from following through on any action. I would think of something to do, and rather than just do it, I would reflect about it and, most of the time, think myself out of it. I was also overly concerned about what people thought of me. This fear contributed to my inability to take action.

In a conversation with Glen, I mentioned how difficult it was to follow my newly discovered spiritual path in Westchester, which was so conservative. "It must be easier for you to do what you want up in the Adirondacks," I told Glen. "You don't have to worry about what other people think about you."

"Well, I'd say it's all purdy much the same ever'where. I jus' consider that someone's opinion of me is jus' none of my business," Glen said.

"None of my business?" I questioned, appalled. "If it's about me, of course it's my business."

"But it's not *your* opinion. It's someone else's. Right? It really has nothin' to do with you," Glen countered. "Ya wouldn't be wantin' someone to try takin' 'way your opinion from ya, would ya?" Glen continued in his friendly drawl.

I thought about this. It was true that, to some people, I would appear a certain way regardless of what I did. I couldn't change their opinion of me. They owned their opinion, and I owned mine.

Someone's opinion of me is none of my business.

That statement became a mantra, liberating me from a lot of self-censoring. Nevertheless, I still had much further to go to be able to "speak my truth."

GRANDFATHER DON CARDINAL

I was trying to learn as much as I could about vision quests and Native American ceremony when I heard about Grandfather Don Cardinal, a Cree Indian with remarkable powers. When he was a young boy his mother already knew that he was different. He demonstrated his ability when he was a teenager. At a horse ranch several people were trying to round up some horses from a pasture. No one could control the horses. The group gave up, waiting for reinforcements. Don's mother asked young Don to help. He went out into the pasture, sat among the horses, and meditated. The animals began to gather around him. When they were all gathered, he stood up and walked to the barn. The horses all followed him in.

I flew up to Winnipeg to meet Don Cardinal.

At the Winnipeg airport, I recognized him right away. He had a light about him that was unmistakable. I stayed with Don and his partner, Allison, for four days in their lovely home in the country. Outside it was fifteen degrees below zero.

I spent most of my time listening to Don as he told me about Native American culture. Grandfather Cardinal is a soft-spoken man. His gravelly voice rocked me gently with wonderful and moving stories about his people. His narrative also told of unspeakable abuse and genocide experienced at the hands of white people. I was ashamed to be a member of the race that had massacred so many in the name of personal greed, and I was angered that such injustice continues to exist today. Their families separated, their culture prohibited, and their religion abolished by law, all indigenous people in North America need our support to help them retrieve their dignity and live decent lives.

While Grandfather Cardinal was softly talking about choices people make and why, I thought I would ask a personal question. I was still feeling a bit uncertain about contacting spirits for people. Casually, I asked Grandfather, "How do you know if you are on the right mission?"

"You know what your mission is!" he yelled at me. "You know what it is. And if you say you don't, you are in *denial!*"

I was in shock; this was the first time he raised his voice in my presence. But he also caught me off-guard in the way that he had read my mind and understood my confusion about what I was supposed to do with my life.

At that moment I clearly understood that I was a messenger. Regardless of whether I was contacting spirits or producing a television show, I was bringing a message to the world. Suddenly it all fit together perfectly. It was an epiphany that brought me a great deal of comfort.

Grandfather Cardinal also lovingly spoke about the sacredness of the vision quest. It is an exquisite opportunity for absolute, direct union with the Creator. All the trappings of life—food, water, comfort, amenities—are suspended as complete surrender to the Creator opens incredible and otherwise unattainable benefits. When you receive the call to do a vision quest, this unique communion with the Creator should not be missed.

By the time I flew back to New York, I knew I had to do the vision quest. It was an honor that I couldn't refuse. I began to prepare the required 405 prayer ties and my robes.

GOING NATIVE AMERICAN

By the beginning of April, however, I had become very nervous about the vision quest, which was to take place in a mere three weeks. I told few people about this strange adventure that I was going to undertake. Those I did tell told me I was crazy and that I would die if I didn't drink water for four days. While part of me wanted to do the quest, part of me was horribly afraid. I thought they would have to carry me down from my sacred space in the woods because I wouldn't be able to move.

On top of the ordeal of the vision quest I had to go through Jake's hot sweat lodges first, as well as a naming ceremony, where I would be given a Native American name. Before you can receive a name, a medicine man had to decide that you needed one. Jake decided I needed a Lakota name. I felt very honored, especially because even Glen didn't have a name. I thought that probably Tonka was responsible for giving the message to Jake that I should have a Lakota name. There would be a sweat lodge to get the name, another to be purified before the vision quest, one more of only two doors before going up on the hill, and finally one full sweat when we returned from the vision quest.

Generally the questors ask people to support them in prayer during the quest. I asked Terence to be close, to support me during my vision quest. He agreed, and Ellen ended up coming with him. When we arrived, Glen invited us to get settled in the loft above his garage.

Terence, Ellen, and I dragged our things to the garage. A ladder leaning against the side was the only way to get up to the loft. Terence teetered on the unstable ladder as he carried our bags up. I tried hard to forget my aversion to heights as I climbed up to inspect our new sleeping quarters. Large cabinet doors provided entry to the slant-roofed attic.

Several sleeping bags were spread out on some loose plywood that had been put down as flooring. This was quite a change from the four-star hotels I stayed in when I traveled with Georges.

MY NAMING CEREMONY

When Jake arrived from South Dakota I found out that I needed a brand new star quilt for the naming ceremony and another brand new one for the vision quest. Things had gotten confused with all the orders from different vision questors so that Jake had only brought one star quilt for me, and Jake said I had to use that one for the naming ceremony. It looked as though, despite all my preparation, I wouldn't be able to do the vision quest after all. Just at the moment when I had a perfect excuse to back out, I became determined to do my vision quest, and no one and nothing would stop me from completing it!

But where would I find a star quilt in the middle of upstate New York? Even if I had to find one in New York City, I wouldn't have known where to look. Once again, Glen came to my rescue.

"There's a department store jus' in the town down yonder, Alexandra. I believe I saw some there not more than a few days ago. I bet they still have some, if you wanna look."

I was amazed and relieved and happy to be able to move forward with the next step of the process, my naming ceremony, which turned out to be a really beautiful experience. I wore moccasins and a long beige dress printed with a Native American pattern. This was a far cry from my usual soccer mom outfit. I looked very native.

In the evening during the sweat lodge, Jake received three possible names for me, each of which brought a special power with it. I then was allowed to choose the one that I liked best. I chose Wambli Shakha Waste Wiyan, Good Woman Eagle Claw. It carries with it wonderful power that I am proud of and respect.

The next morning I prepared everything, including special food for the ceremony. At noon, with everyone watching, Jake conducted the naming ceremony in front of the lodge. The late April day was magnificent and the whole surrounding forest seemed to participate in this sacred event. I felt the presence of the Native American grandmother from the

Spirit World whose name I shared, Wambli Shakha Waste Wiyan. Wrapped in my star quilt over my dress, I felt a surge of connection with Mother Earth and the Spirit World when the sacred eagle feather was tied to my hair. Jake was becoming my brother, and my new sister, Betsy, the woman I met at my second sweat lodge who had informed me of this lodge in the Adirondacks and the vision quest possibility, tied the feather for me. I was doubly blessed.

"You look right purdy with that feather in your hair," Glen told me after the ceremony. "I like that dress, too. Just right for your namin' ceremony."

Following the ceremony we shared a wonderful feast that I provided for everyone. The weather was so perfect that we sat around the sacred fire and enjoyed just being alive.

I felt that I was on my way to becoming a stronger, more self-assured person. I now felt Indian, inside and out, despite my fair skin, blue eyes, and blond hair. I had stepped out of the social stereotype that had been my prison, emotionally and physically, for so many years. It was about time! I had now become a bridge between the Native Americans and the white people. I understood that it was my responsibility to help people connect with nature, that through understanding of native ways, this could be accomplished. This would also help bring all peoples together to live in harmony.

THE VISION QUEST

Around noon, we did two doors of the sweat lodge. Terence and Ellen bravely participated in this ceremony. They realized that beyond simply supporting me, their participation would also help them break through walls that confined them. After the lodge, we vision questers wrapped ourselves in our brand new star quilts before walking in silence up the hill to the places we had chosen a month earlier within a designated area. These places would be our personal altars wherein we would stay for four days without food or water. Each one was far away from the others. We came to mine first. I indicated that I had put tobacco everywhere over a twenty-five-yard-square area a month prior. Jake then designated a two-yard by three-yard area within that larger space. This would be my altar, where I would stay for four days. I was impressed by the location Jake had chosen for my altar. It was the exact place where I had sat a month prior with my dog Zoe and thought, *Here I'll sit during my vision quest.*

I stood and held my *chanupa*, my ceremonial pipe. The chanupa represents the owner's life and must be treated with utmost respect. When it is shared with someone, it is the ultimate expression of friendship. Glen and the supporters placed the stakes in the ground and wound the string of 405 prayer ties around my altar. Then they left, and all was silent. I was resolved to stay for the full four days no matter what!

I looked out at the gorgeous view. Right away I noticed two eagles soaring and swirling above. Then a third flew by. The weather was perfect—not too hot, not too cold. An eagle came and sat on a tree near me. I couldn't believe it. It just sat there for a while and then left.

Then I was attacked by mosquitoes. I hadn't thought to bring any insect repellent, but I don't think it was allowed anyway. These were going to be pretty long days if I was going to be the local bug restaurant.

I remembered the Lakota expression *O mitakuye oyasin,* "We are all related." I began to pray fervently to Tunkashila, the Creator.

Please Tunkashila, Creator of all, please help me make my relatives, the winged insects, and all insects, honor what I'm trying to do. Please have them leave me alone, I prayed fervently.

During the rest of the quest not one single bug came near. This was even more astonishing because there was a rotting log, a natural habitat for crawly things, in the middle of my space.

After witnessing the retreat of my relatives the insects, I was happy again until I was consumed by a horrendous migraine. The pain was excruciating. I wrapped myself in my quilt, hiding my head. It was all I could do to tolerate the pain. This was an unexpected turn of events. I prayed my pain would stop and that I wouldn't vomit, as I sometimes did with a migraine, because that would dehydrate me even more. I heard a voice, perhaps Tonka's, order me to stand. It told me how to arrange my three blankets and how to wrap myself in them. It was beginning to get cold. I huddled miserably in my blankets.

The voice ordered me to turn over. Painfully I rolled over and discovered the most beautiful sunset; to see it was an enchanting gift. As the sky darkened I must have fallen asleep, because suddenly I opened my eyes, just as I was about to roll off of my altar and down the mountainside. I was such an inexperienced camper that I had chosen a space that was on a pretty steep incline. I found a way to prop myself in place by using a couple of bushes. Feeling somewhat secure, I looked up and saw the most magnificent sky lit up with stars.

The next morning I woke to an amazing sunrise. These beautiful sights were short reprieves from my main occupation—trying to tolerate my head pain. I drifted in and out of sleep, and I couldn't think because of the pain. I spent another night in agony. My only moments of peace were when I looked at the magnificent sky. Whenever I could, I would stand and hold my chanupa. During a Lakota vision quest the quester is supposed to stand and hold the chanupa for the entire four days and nights.

This second night was freezing cold. I had visions of a couple of physical people I know, but nothing significant. The next morning my head was covered, as usual, in an effort to tolerate the migraine. A bird, one of two I had been listening to off and on, came into my sacred space, next to my head, and chirped loudly, which I ignored.

The bird's chirps became louder and it proceeded to beat its wings against my tarp, making an incredible noise in the early morning quiet. I knew I had to pay attention. I slowly uncovered my face. As I pulled away the covers to look out, I felt the pain of my headache peel away.

It was a glorious day. I got up and, with my chanupa, I honored the four directions and prayed. The day got warmer; by noon it was hot. I had no shade from the afternoon sun. It was incredibly humid, and I was very thirsty. Despite the heat, I got different messages about my life and specific projects. My guides were present throughout my fast.

This third day was full of visions of a life that would be exciting and satisfying. It made me very happy and able to deal with my dry lips and thirst. I wasn't very comfortable lying or sitting on the ground, but it didn't seem to be an issue for me. Somehow physical comfort was unimportant to me now. I saw a little squirrel and a pheasant. I prayed for my family and for others. Toward the end of the day I could hear the drums and singing voices from the sweat lodge as the nightly ceremony was being conducted. I looked forward to that moment every evening. I felt happy that I had made it through most of the vision quest.

That night the overcast sky hid the stars. I felt especially uncomfortable, and my body screamed once again for a nice bed. I was being sorely tested this last night.

When I woke up on the last morning, I felt great. This was the end. I had made it through alive! I got up and honored the four directions with my chanupa. As I was waiting to be picked up, I saw a cloudy image of a beautiful woman to my right in the distance. I thought she must be White Buffalo Calf Woman, who brought the sacred ceremonies to the Lakota people. Tonka had told me I would see her. Then she disappeared. A white buffalo calf appeared in her place and ran through the woods in front of me from right to left, disappearing in the distance. It was breathtaking.

I watched two eagles soaring happily together, and soon after that Terence and the others came to get me. I felt full of energy. We questers covered our faces as we walked down to the lodge. Inside the cool lodge, we sat for an eternity. Finally we were given a little sage tea and some fruit. Jake asked if we wanted to do two doors of the lodge or four. I wanted to do only two, but because everyone else agreed to do four doors, I did, also. One of my fellow questers asked for a towel. Jake didn't like this, and berated the person for being a sissy. That made me too embarrassed to ask for a towel, even though a towel would have afforded me cover under which I could hide to protect myself from the very hot steam. The result was that my friend got a towel but I didn't even ask for one. I had failed to speak my truth.

I was very worried as the sweat lodge began. In all, we had 182 stones! I asked my guides Tonka and Rachel what to do. I heard that I should try to go to one of the rooms that Rosalyn Bruyere taught us to create with our mind. I managed to find a room, but I couldn't stay there. As the second door began, the heat was unbearable. Nothing I could imagine would take me away from that painful heat. I was praying with all my heart and soul. I promised that I would give up television production if the Creator wanted me to. I would do anything to be delivered from the searing, burning heat. Then Rachel tried to calm me. (Rachel's face had been badly scarred in a fire.)

"You won't be scarred," Rachel told me. "It's okay. You're just experiencing being burned at the stake. This is from a past life, when you were a medicine woman. You were wrongfully punished. They caught you and burned you at the stake."

In my mind the flames engulfed me in unbearable pain, the exact pain from my past life in the fire. I prayed to leave my body so I could get away from this past life experience, but I couldn't get out of my body no matter how hard I tried to imagine myself looking down from above. The next thing I knew I felt Karen, who was sitting next to me in the sweat lodge, pushing me, telling me to exit the lodge.

I mumbled to her, "I'm going to stay for the four doors."

"It's over. It's over. I have to get out. Everyone's getting out!" Karen insisted.

I clumsily made my way out. I could barely walk. In a stupor, I sat down outside the lodge on a log. I felt a kind of sharp thud in my body, and then with a rush my mind came back screaming, *This man is crazy! You don't need to burn people! I'm never doing another lodge with him. He's insane! If I have to do another vision quest, I'll do it with someone else.* I took some dirt in my hands. I said my name to myself, *Alexandra Leclere.* Cole, a fellow quester, came up to me and whispered, "Call back your spirit." That was what I had just done.

I was wet from the sweat lodge. My face, arms, and legs were burning. I wanted to sit on that log forever, but I was concerned about Ellen, who had been in the lodge with us. Would she be okay? As it turned out she was fine. Slowly and painfully I went to change my clothes. My face, neck, forearms, and knees were burning. I don't remember the evening meal very well. Terence and Ellen seemed to be enjoying the celebration.

Because my face was so tender after the lodge, I couldn't wash it. I couldn't wash my hair either. I looked a sight, with matted hair and a dirty face. One of the women at the lodge, Jocelyn, who had a tremendously annoying way of speaking to people, came up to me. She stared at my face closely, really inspecting it. I was too exhausted to push her away.

"You look so beautiful! Your face is dirty, and your hair is a mess, but you look so beautiful!" she said in wonder. "Why do you look so beautiful?"

She was seeing the light that was radiating from me. Exhausted, I went to bed early.

That night I tossed and turned in pain and anger. I couldn't understand why I had gotten injured in the sweat lodge. I had horrible blisters everywhere: on my forehead, forearms, knees, and especially on the right side of my neck. One of my fellow questers admitted to having left her sacred space to go down to the creek to drink water. I had honored the whole quest, and it seemed I had been penalized. Why? I finally fell asleep after I inched close to the entrance to the loft from where I could see the stars.

The French say, *"La nuit porte conseil,"* "The night brings counsel." It did. I understood what had happened. My goal for my vision quest was to learn to speak my truth. The first thing I did after coming down from the hill was to betray myself twice: The first time I had agreed to stay for four doors when I had been given the option to leave after two; the second time I didn't ask for a towel even though I wanted one.

I honestly believe that part of me died in that lodge that day. It was the hesitant, self-censoring part of me that didn't want to make waves or bother people. It was a horribly painful experience, but the blisters I received would remind me to speak my truth. I felt renewed and positive. As the blisters healed, I noted with interest that a big pocket of liquid came out of a blister near my throat. I understood now that it was what had been blocking my ability to express myself.

I asked Jake about his take on my blisters. He just said, "Yeah. That happens sometimes. It was something that was bad and had to come out. It happens to me sometimes, too."

FACING LIFE AT HOME

When I got home, Georges said I had incredible light emanating from me and told me that I was more beautiful than ever.

A couple of days after my vision quest I had to visit my mother for her eightieth birthday. I was concerned about how I looked. Although the redness on my forehead was gone, the blisters on my arms had turned into angry red spots, and I had a large wound at the base of my neck. The top layers of skin had come off, and what was underneath was very tender. I put aloe juice directly from a plant on it, and then some plastic wrap to protect it. I was sure my mother would notice all this. She did.

I told my mother about my vision quest and how meaningful it was to me. In the past I wouldn't have thought of sharing such an experience with her, because I wouldn't have chanced her disapproval. Now I spoke freely about my adventure. To my surprise, she was very supportive. She pulled out a Native American sweater she had and put it on. She even gifted me with a star quilt for my next quest.

The final test for me was to speak my truth in front of her friends. Meeting my mother's friends has always been tremendously challenging, because Mom would always furiously accuse me of saying or doing something wrong in front of them. This time I was just myself. I felt great, and even enjoyed the gathering! Mom was very pleased, and everyone had a good time. I even told her friends about my quest. They were a bit taken aback, but beyond saying that they would never do that themselves, they didn't criticize my participation. They admired my stamina.

It felt wonderful to speak my truth in front of my mother and have her respect. It was the acid test that confirmed my breakthrough.

Another milestone was meeting with the minister of our Presbyterian church and my co-moderator of the deacons. Yes, I was not only an elder in the church, I was now the co-moderator of the deacons. In fact, I felt concerned that perhaps the two religious traditions had to be kept separate. It was in the lodge when Jake's wife prayed to the Holy Trinity that I realized how much we all are related. There should be no reason not to combine religious beliefs regardless of what they are.

With this in mind, I began to bring these two important worlds together. I blew into the minister's office overflowing with energy and light.

"Hi," I beamed. "I just got back from a vision quest where I spent four days in the woods by myself with no food or water. It was fantastic!"

Both the minister and my co-moderator simply looked at me, confused.

"Why would you do that?" my co-moderator asked.

"It brought me closer to nature and God, and now I'm incredibly happy and full of energy," I enthused.

"I think we could all use more of that," the minister said. The co-moderator agreed.

They were amazed, but more than that, they appreciated the incredible change it had effected in me. I was glowing, radiating love.

15
Broadening
My Mission

WHEN I RECEIVED INFORMATION about an upcoming intensive workshop with John Perkins, I was disappointed to read that it would take place immediately following my vision quest. *The vision quest in itself should be enough,* I thought. Tonka had other ideas. He counseled me to sign up, so I did.

Before the vision quest I had no idea why Tonka wanted me to go to the Perkins intensive. Though I wanted to feature John Perkins in my television project, I hadn't considered doing a promotional tape, a tape that would visually present how I planned to produce the show about healers. During my vision quest, I understood the need to do the promo for my project, and this intensive was a great opportunity to begin filming it. This is a good example of intentions and expectations, and allowing the universe to let things manifest in ways that we might not expect. I took a digital video camera with me, along with the courage to ask John Perkins for his permission to tape the intensive.

This intensive took place at a monastery in Florida, once again combining all my religious beliefs. The first night there I went to dinner with a group of workshop participants. It was wonderful to be among like-minded people. Many were familiar with vision quests and were enthusiastic to hear about mine. I also met some people who were interested in contacting loved ones who had passed over. I was flying high, feeling wonderfully confident and grateful for my gifts.

Samantha, one of the participants, asked me to contact her sister Ashley. Although Ashley had died fifteen years earlier, Samantha had never gotten over the loss. I saw that Ashley was next to Samantha. In fact, Ashley told me she is one of Samantha's guides. I wondered to myself how Ashley had died. I saw in my mind's eye an automobile accident. Later I asked Samantha how Ashley had died. Samantha said in a car accident.

Ashley gave Samantha some tips about how to have fun. Apparently Ashley had always been the wild one who would draw Samantha out of her shell. Since Ashley's death, Samantha had led a quiet and joyless life. Learning that Ashley was in a good place, Samantha began to look at things differently. The day following our session, Samantha told me that after Ashley died, Samantha used to wake up in the middle of the night and think, *Ashley's gone!* Then she would cry. Now, when she woke up in the middle of the night, she could think, *Ashley's here!* and she would be happy and relieved. Gradually Samantha was able to sleep through the night in peace.

❧

The intensive was a mixture of lectures, which I filmed, and exercises and journeying that, rather than film, I experienced. I enjoyed the journeying very much, although some journeys were quite difficult because I faced issues that I preferred to ignore. These were all things that I was better off identifying and removing; they concerned injustices I had endured as a child. Often I had taken these incidents and used them to unconsciously create walls for myself, preventing me from doing what I really wanted to do. With those prison walls gone, anything was possible.

At one point we practiced shapeshifting. This is the ability to change emotionally and/or physically. In one exercise, we were supposed to shapeshift into a large snake. I never particularly liked snakes, and I wasn't interested in shapeshifting into one. I would have preferred becoming something like a panther, but that wasn't an option. We could choose between a cobra or an anaconda. I chose the cobra, remembering cartoons depicting a swami playing the flute while a cobra slunk up out of a basket. Focusing on this stereotyped image reconciled my snake discomfort to the extent that I was able to participate in the exercise.

As the drum beat and I put forth the mental intention to transform myself into a snake, my whole body began to slither and writhe in unusual ways. It was moving on its own to a different master. I didn't feel that I was channeling a spirit; I felt that I was in touch with the essence of the snake. The goal of the shapeshift was to be able to shed an old skin and slide into a new life. This was exactly what I needed. It was even symbolic of my peeling skin from the last sweat lodge.

Snakes have been given a bad rap. They actually symbolize eternity, representing both the male and female in one entity. The tail represents the male and the mouth the female. So an image of a snake that forms a circle by holding its own tail in its mouth is a symbol representing eternity. The snake as a totem represents rebirth, resurrection, initiation, and wisdom.

My interviews with people at the intensive were wonderful. John Perkins is so charismatic and exudes such joy. His teachings about the Shuar people from Ecuador bring wonderful understanding of Pachamama (the Shuar word for Mother Earth) and a real connection to joy. He taught us to "walk like a Shuar." This is similar to the Native American fox walk that Tom Brown teaches. It is an experience in sensory awareness in which every fiber of the mind and body is attuned to everything around. All the senses, including the sixth sense, are engaged to transform a simple stroll into a Shuar walk through a magical world. Joy is an important gift that John brings into his workshops. His enthusiasm about life in general and his vision of a world living in peace in a sustainable fashion is a wonderful and inspiring example for us all.

We are all familiar with the five senses: seeing, hearing smelling, tasting, and touching. The sixth sense is the ability to feel things energetically.

Everyone can do this. For example, if you stare at the back of someone's head in a theater, that person will turn around and look at you after a while. That is the sixth sense at work. Your eyes send out energy and the other person feels this energy and turns around. We can develop that sense to be energetically aware on many different levels and to perceive many different things, including spirits.

Among the people I interviewed was Ipupiara and his wife, Cleicha, both incredibly wonderful, generous shamans from Brazil. Ipu, as he likes to be called, healed a woman of cancer, and since then has been invited to perform his shamanic healings in a cancer hospital in Washington, D.C. I wanted to film Ipu demonstrating a healing on someone, a demonstration scheduled to happen during a workshop lecture. I set up my tripod and volunteered to be the patient. At one point Ipu put a condor feather in my hand. The condor is a sacred bird in South America, just as the eagle is a sacred bird in North America. The feather vibrated and felt hot. Despite the fact that this was simply a demonstration and not a real healing, I was completely moved by the experience.

One night when I was sleeping and dreaming in my small monastery room, I looked out the window in my dream and saw a fierce bear. It was my huaca. I woke up sufficiently to remember my dream. In it my bear told me to practice more ceremony in the shamanic fashion. This is one of the typical ways that instructions comes to us from spirit—the messages are very eclectic and thought provoking. *Well that's nice, but what do you mean, shamanic ceremony? What kind? And where and when?* I wondered. I heard no answers.

Altogether it was a fabulous week. By the end I was exhausted but felt that I really was living my truth. The scab on my neck was almost gone, but the scabs on my forearms were taking more time to heal. I knew that the injuries were helpful. They were a daily reminder that I must speak my truth. They gave me the courage to go forward and do what needed to be done for my project and to contact spirits. I felt very comfortable and happy with myself. And I still do.

I felt so comfortable that my looks were unimportant to me. Before, I had always relied on looking perfect—my hair just right, makeup on, the right clothes—to empower me to do whatever I intended. In the context of this intensive, I was not in control of my looks. I had bizarre wounds on my arms, my knees, and at the base of my neck. Normally this would have kept me in a corner, hoping no one would notice me. Instead I was standing up next to my camera, in plain view of everyone. I also fearlessly approached strangers and people I considered to be authority figures.

The intensive ended with a shamanic initiation ceremony. I can see now that my vision quest served as preparation for this transition to becoming a shamanic healer. The ceremony was very profound. Nevertheless, I was having trouble identifying myself with shamanism; it's been given a bum rap by Christians. Then as I thought of Jesus I understood that he, himself, was a shamanic healer, someone trained in the mystical tradition of the Kabbalah, and I realized that shamanism was something wonderful to which we should all aspire.

USING MY GIFT

Back in my "everyday" life, I continued to develop my growing practice of contacting spirits for people. One of my clients mentioned a healing center, The Oaks, that was opening just ten minutes from my home. I first went there wearing my television producer hat to check it out. I interviewed Harold Osborn, M.D., who was running the center. In the course of the conversation I told him I was a clairvoyant energy healer. He didn't fall off his chair; in fact, he suggested that I join the practitioners who work at The Oaks. He said I needed to send in my résumé as well as letters of recommendation. That night spirit encouraged me by sending me a dream in which I saw myself receiving clients at the center.

After that, I had to be interviewed by the center's board of advisers. They turned out to be wonderful people who had a great deal of knowledge about clairvoyance. It felt wonderful to be with people who had the same belief system I did, and right in southern Westchester County! They encouraged me to set up my practice at The Oaks. My first public appearance there would be at the monthly healing circle. At the end of the evening I was invited to announce my gift and discuss my availability to practice as a healer.

That night, Gretchen, one of the women participating in the healing circle, began to cry. It turned out that she was observing the ninth anniversary of her mother's death, and I offered to contact her mother for her. Gretchen had been to a medium six years prior. After my session with Gretchen, two members of the advisory board interviewed her to see how I had done. Gretchen was pleased with the contact that I had been able to establish with her mother, and her articulation of this to the board members convinced them of my genuine gift as a medium. It also convinced me that I had to become more public in order to allow my gift to become available to more people.

As I continued to contact spirits, I realized that most people, once they know the deceased person is fine, become interested in their own personal welfare. They hope the deceased on the other side will become a personal spirit guide, someone who can give them knowledge or a vision that will help them in their own physical lives. A personal spirit guide can be anyone who has died, not necessarily a relative of the living person. But one needs to be careful when listening to advice from spirits. The spirit maintains his or her own personality and predilections when advising the physical person, which isn't necessarily a good thing. In other words, you don't get wiser just because you're dead. However, it also is the case that there are spirits who are more experienced and have freed themselves from any and all judgmental attitudes. I can count on Tonka to alert me when I need to be careful.

That is why I always begin a session with the Lord's Prayer, as well as with a personal prayer to bring the highest healing in joy to my client. For example, Carla asked me to contact her father. I did this, and soon Carla had questions for her father about her boyfriend. Carla's father unfortunately had a racial bias, and Carla's boyfriend was from a minority group that he did not like. As I listened to Carla's father explode about the impropriety of Carla's boyfriend, I also received information from my guide that the boyfriend was really good for Carla. I explained to Carla that her father, living or dead, would never accept this man for his daughter.

I also made it clear to Carla that she was much better off with her adoring boyfriend than without him. I told her that she was free to live her life to the fullest, enjoying the most happiness she could find, and she should not be trapped by her father's closed-minded opinions. In his own way, Carla's father was trying to give her the best, loving advice from his point of view.

On another occasion, a client brought me a photograph of her grandmother. Just as I was about to contact this grandmother, someone else, another spirit, appeared and told me to stop. Apparently that grand-mother would have brought unhealthy memories back to my client about her father. To have more input from her grandmother would have been destructive; it would not bring her "the highest healing in joy." With my client's approval, I continued contacting this other guide, who was eager to bring healing information. It turned out this was her spirit guide, there to protect her. The session was quite profound, and my client greatly ben-efited from it.

Before a session, I usually ask Tonka and the Creator what will hap-pen. One day as I was driving the ten minutes from my home to The Oaks, I heard from Tonka that I needed to journey my client. I didn't have a drum, but that didn't seem to matter. I was told that it would work out fine.

My client was an upper-middle-class devout Catholic who didn't know anything about shamanism. I felt a bit uncomfortable even suggesting that she lie down on the floor for this guided meditation. My chatter-mind, the one that second guesses everything, was overruled by my spiritual guid-ance. Without drums or music, I repeated the words as I heard them from the Spirit World. My client easily began a vivid journey, visualizing many things clearly. It was very exciting for me to see her recover her happiness and let go of her sadness as I led her on this journey.

After this I became bolder about smudging the room where I held my sessions in order to clear the energy there. I also brought my huaca sym-bols, the bear and the black panther, to better help me focus on my gifts. I felt increasingly comfortable about working with people. I was begin-ning to accept the fact that I am a shaman.

16

Following the Red Road

I HAD JUST GOTTEN BACK from picking up Talia at her dance class. As I walked the few steps from the car to the house, the telephone rang. I raced into the house to pick up the phone before the answering machine got the call.

"Hello." I breathed.

"Hi, Alexandra?" the woman said. "This is Brenda. We're having a PTA meeting, and we need you to take care of a reception for all the teachers. There's another volunteer available. I'll give you her phone number. I'd really like you to coordinate this. Can you do it?"

I grabbed a pencil and began writing. The dogs saw something outside and began barking. I strained to hear what I was being told over the phone. I had barely hung up and yelled at the barking dogs to be quiet when the phone rang again.

"Alexandra, Susan gave me your name. I just lost my father, and I would like a session," a woman's voice said.

I had barely hung up after making an appointment with Susan's friend when the phone rang yet again.

"Alexandra? How are you? This is Frank," a man said. Before I could answer, he continued, "We need you to head the membership drive for our TV station. You're on the board, and . . ."

Again I marked down what I was supposed to do. Mercifully the dogs finally stopped barking. I had just hung up and was beginning to wonder what I had to do next when my daughter pulled a paper out of her bag and handed it to me.

"It's my dance competition," she announced. "It's this weekend on Long Island. Can you go? Please? All the other moms are going. And can you drive? I don't want to go on the bus."

What could I say?

The phone rang again.

"Hi. I was calling about the minutes from our last meeting. Have you finished them? We need to send them out *now* so people get them before the next meeting," a woman said.

I thought about the one-hundred-plus copies of minutes I would have to copy, fold, stuff in envelopes, stamp, and mail out. How did I get to this place? When was I supposed to find time to commune with Spirit and practice shamanic ceremony? My life had become a mosaic of competing needs—other people's needs that I kept trying to satisfy. The dogs began barking again.

SUSTAINING THE CHANGE

About a month after the Perkins intensive, I found myself slipping back into my old life as a suburban robot. My burns from the sweat lodge were healed, except for slight red marks on my forearms. My home environment hadn't changed, and I was succumbing to the pressures around me. It seemed that my family and friends wanted me to be the same way I had been before. They seemed to tolerate my little forays into spiritual endeavors, but that was their limit. I wasn't supposed to *stay* that way. I knew I was a different person with wonderful new gifts, but it seemed to me that they didn't want to give me the time to develop them. As a matter of fact, they sometimes even seemed threatened by what I was doing, and this prevented me from following my path. And then there were all the commitments I had made to participate in volunteer organizations.

The single most difficult thing to do after breaking through a wall is to sustain the freedom and break old patterns of behavior. Even if we see a new and better way of doing things, habit and those around us who inevitably don't want us to change prevent us from integrating these important modifications into our lives.

One of my children told me in anger, "Life was fine until my mother turned into a psycho that worships dirt!" It was an interesting interpretation of what I viewed as an increase in personal freedom thanks to a spiritual breakthrough and contact with Mother Earth.

We have to constantly be aware of falling back into those habits and patterns. Chatter-mind, that nice little voice that cautions us and tells us we are doing things wrong, loves to keep to the old and beaten path, and relentlessly warns us if we try to initiate new patterns.

I had constant demands on my time from my family and others, but I didn't have the energy to face up to everyone. Maybe this is what Boris, the tarot reader, had been alluding to when he had read my cards and told me that I would have to break away from my family. In French there is an expression, *Nul n'est prophète dans son pays.* It means that no one is a prophet in his own hometown. I missed the catalytic presence of Foxes to bring me energy, although I didn't miss Foxes the person. I hadn't even thought about him for months.

Rather than build up my practice at The Oaks, I was sandwiching my clients in between my other obligations and, in the process, my spiritual self was becoming stretched thin. The only time I allowed myself to be with Spirit was when I was with a client. The rest of the time my life was, unfortunately, the way it used to be. The problem with that was that I wasn't happy. All the reasons why I wanted to change that life came back with a vengeance. Of course I didn't recognize what was happening. I just found myself in a rut, wondering how I got there, and wondering how I could get myself out of it.

A dream brought me information. I was in a busy area of a large, poverty-stricken city. I had a newborn baby whom I was breast-feeding. As I was walking by a dirty lake, I accidentally dropped the baby in. I immediately jumped in and saved the baby, and I woke up as I did so. It's obvious that the newborn was my new spiritual self. It needed a lot of attention and care. I realized I needed to carve out time for my spiritual development.

I had to recognize the gifts I had and become comfortable using them. I wasn't really sure what I could do with these gifts, even though I would hear occasionally that I was "all powerful," whatever that meant.

Another vivid dream found me in a shopping mall. I left a group of people and was by myself, feeling a little tired. A woman came up to me and said, "Alex, let me help you." She held on to me with one arm around me and with her other hand she pushed on a bone in my shoulder.

"Here. This took a long time to install," she said. I thought to myself, *She's an angel come to help me.* We walked around the corner and I realized I was going in a downward spiral. I broke away from her and woke up. A voice told me to write this down. The same voice told me that the message of the dream was that not everyone is an angel out to help me, and that I need to be careful. The new friends I had were like-minded people who could nurture my spiritual growth. The woman who presented herself as my friend was a symbol of all the people in my daily life who wanted me to stay just the way I was, to develop no more.

I also came to realize that breaking through personal barriers is a process. There are moments that are more intense than others, and sometimes when we feel we are on a plateau, not moving at all. The reality is that we are always moving, just faster at some times than at others. As soon as one major issue is resolved, there is another one to deal with. Fortunately, all of them are not equally daunting. This process of facing issue after issue doesn't stop until we pass into the Spirit World ourselves. It's like a long car trip. We can be bored and miserably count the hours or we can make it a fun adventure.

GRANDFATHER CARDINAL TO THE RESCUE

The universe presented me with an opportunity to get out of my rut. When this sort of opportunity presents itself, we have the option to take it or leave it; it's a choice. Spirit spoke to me through Don Cardinal, the Cree medicine man I had visited in Winnipeg. He was coming to Long Island to build a sweat lodge and facilitate a ceremony.

This was a great occasion for me to film the building of a sweat lodge, a perfect addition to my promotional film. Grandfather Cardinal and I had talked about me doing this when I was in Canada, but most Native

American ceremonies are considered so sacred and private that they are closed to the public. However, Grandfather Cardinal is powerful and has a mission to bring peoples together. He opens his ceremonies to everyone; he is not afraid of showing them to the world. He feels that through caring, sharing, and kindness we can all live well together.

Alone as always, I drove to Garvey's Point on Long Island. Secretly I hoped that I wouldn't have to participate in the sweat lodge ceremony, as I was still apprehensive about them. At the same time, I knew that Grandfather Cardinal was so kind and loving that he would never force me to participate if I didn't want to.

As I approached the wooded area, I began to relax. I felt calm and determined as I walked along a dirt path. It was wonderful to be outside in the forest again, even though it was raining. Grandfather Cardinal was, as always, tremendously welcoming and informational. He greeted me like part of the family. When I commented on the bad weather, he looked at me, surprised.

"There is no such thing as bad weather," he said. "Whatever the Creator provides for us is what we need."

It was a good philosophy that has remained with me to this day.

The filming went very well, and when it was over I spoke to Grandfather Cardinal about my painful incident in the sweat lodge following my vision quest. He was disgusted by it.

"It's not right to burn people. That's why I use forty stones, never 182. You don't need that many stones for people to be fixed up by Spirit," he said passionately.

He also said that if someone is nervous, they tighten up, and that makes the whole sweat lodge experience more difficult for them.

"The Creator is there watching you," Grandfather Cardinal told me. "He wants you to surrender, and then, when you do, you can be healed. He will provide for you what you ask."

Grandfather Cardinal also reminded me of all the tremendous healing that takes place in the lodge. He told me stories of people who had been discarded by modern medicine, because according to their doctors, their situations were hopeless. These people sometimes had been given just a few months to live. These same people found healing in the sweat lodge. Grandfather Cardinal had witnessed one old woman unable to walk, abandoned by doctors. She was carried into the sweat lodge. After four doors, she walked out. His words calmed me and encouraged me to try it again. I hoped this would help to lift me out of my rut and stay steady on my spiritual road.

As we entered the lodge, I was trembling. I was afraid I would freak out and scream. To my surprise, it was over before I knew it. I felt triumphant, cleansed of all the toxins of fear in my body. I was reconciled with the sweat lodge!

The next day I went back for a second lodge to honor Grandfather Cardinal and show him my gratitude for allowing me to film the ceremony. The sweat was difficult for me but tolerable, and by the end of the lodge I was relaxed. Even though I was more comfortable with Don Cardinal, I was attracted to the Lakota tradition, which was certainly due to Tonka's influence.

MORE SWEAT LODGES

At home again, the telephone rang. It was Glen. I hadn't heard from him since the vision quest.

"Well, hello there. How are ya doin'? Everything good for ya?" Glen asked.

"Things are okay," I answered.

"Well, there's somethin' good comin' that I'm sure you're gonna like," Glen announced in his southern drawl. "Jake's gonna to be doin' some ceremony up this way, and we're all lookin' forward to it. Thought you might wanna be a part of it, too. We'll have about seven sweats in a row in all. Ya know, one every day. It'll be grand. In fact, as a pipe carrier, ya otta be here."

It was true that before my vision quest I had decided to accept the responsibility of the chanupa, the sacred pipe. Prayers put into the chanupa bring rewards of all kinds to our lives, but it is also something that cannot be put in a corner and taken out only when you need something. It needs to be nurtured and brought to ceremonies. I had chosen to follow the Red Road, the path of Native American spirituality. Now I needed to walk down that path. Tonka was telling me to go there. My chatter-mind was screaming, *Stay away!*

Here goes, I thought. *The acid test. Am I strong enough to accept and use*

the gifts I have been given? Am I strong enough to walk the Red Road or not?
I took a deep breath. *Am I strong enough to face Jake's lodge?*

"I'd love to be there," I answered. "Just give me the dates." *I'll be there,
but maybe not in the lodge every day,* I thought to myself.

"You can stay in my loft. That's so's you don't have to go back home in
between sweats," Glen continued.

The weather was beautiful that June day in the Adirondacks as I drove
up to Glen's place in the woods. It felt wonderful to be away from
Westchester. Rather than feeling afraid or horrified when I got there, I once
again began to feel a tremendous peace. Glen greeted me warmly, as usual.

"There'll be a few of you up there in the loft. It'll be nice and cozy that
way," Glen said.

"Do you know if anybody snores?" I asked Glen.

He laughed as he watched me lug my bag toward the garage.

Later, I got ready for the lodge. I waited around the roaring sacred fire
until Jake said the grandfathers, the stones in the fire, were ready. It was
wonderful and peaceful.

As the ceremony began and we entered the lodge, some children vol-
untarily went inside. That encouraged me. The kids, however, didn't stay
for the four doors. My first lodge in this series was difficult, with Jake's
minimum of 101 stones. In between the doors I lay down on the floor of
the lodge, recuperating from the heat. During the door, when the water
was poured on the stones, I sat up, but I covered myself with my towel.
Tonka told me it would be a good lodge for me. I prayed to the Creator
for gentleness toward me. It was a challenging lodge. Surprisingly, however, it was easier for me than Grandfather Cardinal's lodges had been.
It's what is going on inside a person during the sweat that makes the
experience more or less difficult. The results were well worth it. I felt
invigorated and reborn after each lodge.

I spent each day in the kitchen, helping out. Gradually, I was bonding
with the other participants. I was no longer tortured by stress about anything from home. I enjoyed being so close to nature. I loved looking for
kindling and stacking the logs for the sacred fire. I loved sitting around
the sacred fire and the cook fire. I actually got to be pretty handy with the
cook fire. It was ironic how comfortable I could feel in such a physically
uncomfortable setting, eating off dirty plates with people who didn't

shower, and I didn't either! There was a water shortage, so we weren't allowed to use the showers. Glen said we were washing from the inside out. That must have been true, because no one smelled bad. It was okay with me; I was at peace and felt one with Spirit.

EUROPEAN VACATION

Returning home from a week of sweat lodges, I had very little time before Georges, Talia, and I were to leave for Europe. Our itinerary took us to St. Petersburg, Russia, the grandparents' homeland. My grandmother loved to tell me stories about the balls she would attend at the czar's palace with the royal daughters.

From St. Petersburg we traveled to Paris, where I worked with a woman by the name of Veronique who asked me to contact her recently deceased mother. According to Veronique, her mother had been practicing meditation quite regularly and had become very spiritual. One message Veronique received from her mother will stay with me forever.

The spirit said, "The only time we can advance ourselves is when we're on Earth. It's important to do a maximum to be advanced spiritually." This is an important message for us all, referring to the belief that we incarnate life after life until we reach Nirvana and free ourselves from this circle of pain. We have opportunities on Earth to develop our spiritual selves; it's up to us to act on those opportunities. Every step of my journey I was offered opportunities to learn more about healers, experience different types of healing, explore past-life regression, participate in Native American ceremony, and so forth. I had a choice whether to venture out into the unknown or stay where I was. Obviously I chose to seize these opportunities, and I am so grateful that I did! My spiritual self has advanced remarkably.

BACK TO THE SWEAT LODGE

Returning to New York, I was plunged into my own past-life garbage, which surfaced as depression. In retrospect I understand that I had to purge myself of these deep, dark, negative feelings of blame. These were remnants of a belief that somewhere in my essence I was profoundly bad. It was all part of my victim persona. To continue on my spiritual path, I needed to cleanse myself of the weights that were dragging me back to my rut. I tried to reach the healers I knew who had helped me before. No one was available. I would have to do this alone.

And so I did by following the Red Road. Jake returned to Glen's to do another series of seven sweat lodges. With Tonka guiding me, I shed the last of those horrible feelings. It was wonderful to sweat it out in the lodge. I learned more about walking the Red Road, following the principles of Indian life. As a pipe carrier I stopped drinking alcohol because alcohol has decimated the indigenous people in our country. Being half-French and having a French husband, giving up wine was pretty hard.

While I was in the sweat lodge I had a vision and a message. I was to make business cards with an eagle on them to represent my Lakota name. On them I was to describe my profession as Messenger. This I proceeded to do.

17

Keeping to the Path

ANOTHER GATHERING OF SHAMANS organized by the Dream Change Coalition was scheduled at Omega, and I wasn't going to miss it. This gathering was in two parts: one transpired over a weekend, the other the following week. I didn't feel I had anything to work on. I was going there to meet friends and relax.

Over the weekend we were supposed to sample presentations by all the shamans. Among them was a Buryat Siberian shaman named Sarangerel. She spoke with humor about her own road to becoming a shaman.

"Spirit wanted me to follow the path, would you believe of all things, of becoming a Buryat Siberian shaman, but I was resisting it. Are you surprised? Shaman, shaman? What's a shaman mean to a girl growing up in the Midwest? Then things started to happen to me until finally I said, 'All right, all right, already, I'll be a shaman!'"

Sarangerel went on to study with the Buryat Shamans in Siberia, where she was initiated and continues to perform shamanic healings as well as teach shamanism. At Omega, Sarangerel led us in a journey called "Meeting the Mother and the Cup." It began with the visualization of a frightening fire burning bright. I saw an image of my mother as a young gypsy flash by, as well as other faces I couldn't really make out.

Then a white light appeared around a beautiful blonde woman. I realized that I was that blonde! Someone gave me a drink from a cup. It was cool and nurturing. Suddenly, I was among angels. When Sarangerel told us to return to our bodies, I told the angels that I wanted to stay with them.

"You'll get here soon enough," they told me. "You have work to do now."

After this journey, most people left Sarangerel's presentation to see other shamans. I stayed on, fascinated. The next journey Sarangerel led was called "The Old Man with the Walking Stick and the Cauldron Transformation." I began my journey at my sacred place in the rain forest. I discovered this place at an earlier Perkins workshop when we were supposed to imagine being in the rain forest. I liked the place I had imagined so much that I have kept it as a mental haven where I can go at any time to find some instant peace. The panther, one of my power animals, had me ride on his back through the darkness. Below I could see the old man with the walking stick near a cauldron.

The panther dropped me into the cauldron. I was afraid, but the water wasn't hot, and I wasn't uncomfortable. I could see the panther watching, and the grizzly bear, also my power animal, must have followed us. It seemed like I waited forever. Finally I was transformed into a beautiful blonde dressed in white, just as I had been in the preceding journey. I was on stage and people were coming to me to be blessed. It all made me feel very powerful.

After the journey I spoke to Sarangerel about my experiences.

"These two journeys were rather strange for me," I began.

"You never know what will happen when Spirit decides to take you somewhere," Sarangerel stated. "So what happened to you?"

I briefly told her about the two journeys. "In both journeys I was dressed in white, and in the second one, my transformation had me on stage and people were coming to me to be blessed. Was this just my ego making me imagine that I was a great healer?" I asked Sarangerel. The two journeys were so flattering, I was sure my ego was doing some wishful thinking rather than listening to the message from Spirit.

"No. These are very powerful journeys. Just the fact that you drank from the cup and were transformed, and then that you were able to get in and out of the cauldron, is important. Many people can't do that. You have definitely been initiated. In our tradition, journeys like yours confirm that not only are you an accomplished shaman, but that you have been initiated to receive more power. Congratulations," she smiled and shook my hand. I was perplexed. Me? A shaman? Now I definitely had to accept it.

The second part of the workshop, a five-day gathering, featured a spectacular opening. We walked between all the shamans, who were lined up to greet and bless us. Following the intriguing journeys I had just experienced with Sarangerel, this was exhilarating. It felt like a celebration of my initiation.

Our first journey was followed the now-familiar "leave all the bad stuff behind" theme. I thought it would be easy because I was feeling so good. However, during the whole journey I heard from Tonka that I had to concentrate on the physical, which surprised me because I felt fine.

That same morning, after the opening journey, we were invited to sign up to have a healing with a shaman. I didn't think I needed one but realized that a little fine-tuning is always a good idea, and that I shouldn't miss this opportunity. I made an appointment with Jose Joaquin Penada and his daughter Soraya.

Almost immediately after I signed up, I began to feel the beginnings of a horrible migraine. Nothing could make that headache go away. I walked to the small cabin where my healing would take place, and as soon as I walked in the room, I began vomiting. An assistant who was organizing the appointments recoiled, while a nonplussed Jose Joaquin and Soraya began the shamanic healing on me; a healing similar to the one I had had with Maria Juana Imberla the year before.

When he completed the healing, Jose Joaquin told me I had to return the next morning for another healing. The assistant worried that there was no room in the schedule, but Jose Joaquin insisted I be fit in.

"Now you must get some newspaper and heat it up. Then you wear it around your middle. I'll see you tomorrow morning," Jose Joaquin told me.

I wondered if this was the shaman's version of "take two aspirins and call me in the morning."

I dragged myself to my dorm room and fell into bed, too sick to track down some newspaper. In this holistic retreat, newspapers were few and far between, anyway. Instead of sleeping, I tossed and turned in agony. I thought about going home, but what would I do there? And how would I get there? I decided to wait. The next morning I struggled to my appointment. Once again, the minute I walked in I began retching.

Jose Joaquin asked me, "The newspaper? Did you use the newspaper? Around the middle. You heat it up first."

I mumbled something about not finding any newspaper.

"I have everything right here. Don't worry," he assured me.

He and Soraya performed another healing. As part of it, he heated a flat stone and held it against my lower abdomen. It probably would have hurt if I had felt well enough to notice. After the healing, as Jose Joaquin was wrapping my middle in newspaper, I realized that my headache and nausea were gone. It was amazing. Obviously, something extremely toxic needed to come out, and now it was gone! I asked Jose Joaquin about it.

"Yes, you had something bad for a very, very long time. You needed it out," he explained. "Now you are good."

୨ଽ

My last journey at the gathering was led by John Perkins. With the rhythmic beat of a drum in the background, he instructed us, in our mind's eye, to climb an absolutely barren mountain. There was nothing there, but we had to keep climbing. We were alone, hungry, and tired. My mountain was made of crumbling dirt. As I climbed, I sunk in and had a terrible time. Debris would fall with my every footstep. It was painful, too, but I had a burning desire to get to the top.

As I looked at the other mountains around me, I saw one that was incredibly green. I had friends there, family and people who loved me. On the green mountain life was easy and comfortable, but I was on this other barren mountain climbing its treacherous path. I was miserable.

"Why?" I kept asking myself. "Why don't I go back to the green mountain?"

That was when I knew that I had a mission to accomplish. I knew I wouldn't be happy or well on the green mountain; it was an illusion. I was a messenger. I had to accomplish my work, my mission, and I realized that when I got to the top of the mountain I was currently climbing, I would feel fabulous.

HOME AGAIN

A few days later, when I was back at home, life was as complicated as usual. Once again my family and others were making demands, and I was teetering again on the verge of falling back into my suburban-housewife rut. I don't mean to denigrate the suburban housewife or househusband. Theirs are busy, thankless jobs that are rarely given proper respect; *I honor their work.* But when someone, man or woman, feels it necessary to change themselves, the people around them will not let them change easily.

In any event, due to the demands on my time as wife and mother, I wasn't honoring my spiritual development, and neither was anyone else. One of my few friends with whom I shared my spiritual path was going to an afternoon concert at Lincoln Center in New York City. Even though I really didn't have the time, for some reason I jumped at the opportunity to accompany her.

On the way to the concert I thought, *I must have completely lost it. Who in their right mind goes to a concert when there is so much to do? Doing this won't help me to stay out of my rut, or to develop myself spiritually.*

But the concert was magnificent. The healing power of music should never be underestimated. My whole being embraced the beauty of it. Listening to the Prokofiev piece at the end of the concert, my mind drifted back to the Perkins mountain journey. And although I was still sinking in the debris and sand on that barren mountain, I wasn't attracted to the green mountain anymore. In fact I didn't even *see* the green mountain! As I struggled up, I got a perspective of where I was. From above I saw that I was near the top and it was gorgeous. Just a bit more climbing and I would be able to tap into all knowledge.

Then I saw myself all in white with a white light around me. I was on stage in front of a huge audience, which I was speaking to. As I saw this, I was so confused by the image that I began to panic and feel frustrated. How could I get to that stage from here in this concert hall or from the confines of my suburban life?

Then I became aware of an old woman sitting next to me. She was having trouble adjusting her hearing aid for the soft and then suddenly very loud music. With all due respect to her difficulty, the scene was really very comical, as she would leap inappropriately out of her seat when the music suddenly reached a fever pitch. I began to laugh silently at this real-life cartoon from the *New Yorker* magazine. Life is joy interrupted by challenges and moments of sadness and despair. We should just take it as it comes with the confidence that Spirit will help us through.

STILL TRYING TO BE A TELEVISION PRODUCER

Full of energy and enthusiasm, I found someone I could afford to pay to edit my promo for the healers project. It turned out to be someone who needed healing. I wish I had known when I hired him.

Joshua had left a demanding but extremely lucrative job as a film editor in the advertising business because he couldn't stand the pressure. Two of his friends had suffered heart attacks while they were editing, both in front of Joshua. One died, but Joshua believed that he had saved the other one's life through his own gifts as a healer. However, he felt incredibly guilty that he had not been able to save his one friend's life. I realized that the universe brought Joshua and me together so that I could be a catalyst for him, helping him understand that it was not his fault that his friend had died.

Through this experience, I got a better understanding of the world of film editors and a clearer idea of my project. Joshua accidentally erased everything he had done on the promo, but he did free himself of any guilt attached to his friend's death. Unfortunately for me the tangible result of our collaboration was nothing.

This was a disaster! There were many television people who were waiting to view this promo. There wasn't enough time to redo it. I felt that I might as well give up, rather than see these people without anything to show them. The reality was I *had* to see them at an important meeting I couldn't miss. I was horribly depressed, anxious, and frustrated. I couldn't sleep.

Once again the universe rescued me. Glen called. His southern drawl sounded like music to my ears.

"Jake's goin' to be here this weekend. We're set to do seven days of sweats. We're goin' to be doin' some good sweatin'. Shore would be a shame for ya ta be missin' that. All of us up here are waitin' on ya."

I figured I could be sleepless in the Adirondacks as well as at home, so I went up for the two days before my big meetings. I was hoping to sweat the anxiety and frustration out. It was November, and the trees were well past their fall extravaganza. Everything looked gray except for the resilient, aptly named evergreens. Where did they get that resilience? From the moment I climbed the rickety ladder to Glen's loft, I felt wonderful. I surveyed the many sleeping bags and happily took a spot next to the door. I looked out at the beautiful starry sky, and all the negative emotions that had been plaguing me were gone. I slept like a baby.

As I was walking down from the lodge one evening, still in a meditative state, I "heard" that I had the power to heal people physically, not just emotionally. My first reaction to this news was to feel uncomfortable. I didn't like hospitals and felt very uncomfortable around sick people. How could I possibly help people I was afraid to be near?

The answer came strong and clear: I shouldn't worry about getting sick myself; I would be protected.

I thought this was interesting. I was ready for whatever Spirit wanted me to do. I prayed to be an instrument of the Creator's healing. *But can't I be a television producer, too?* I wondered.

Returning to Manhattan to face the executives who were expecting my promo, I was relaxed. Without any problem I met the important people awaiting me. It all worked out fine. No one was upset or angry or disappointed. Not even me.

TAROT READING REDUX

Still in all, I needed some outside confirmation that I was on the right path as a healer, and whether I should further pursue my television career. It's not the kind of question you can ask the average career counselor. *Why not try a reading?* I thought. I asked Penney for some suggestions. She gave me the names of an astrologer and a tarot card reader. I also asked for Boris's phone number.

I decided to have Boris do my reading. I wanted the brutal truth about whether I should continue to follow this crazy path of becoming a healer, and I knew that Boris would give it to me straight. Boris was the one who had upset me so badly, but I had to admit that he had been right on the mark. During the past two years I had emotionally and physically split from my family by pursuing the various spiritual opportunities that were offered to me. I had missed family events, including a wedding anniversary and birthdays. I was no longer dependent on anyone, even my immediate family, who had been my whole raison d'etre up to that point. I no longer felt that I had to prove that I deserved to be alive. I had walked through the dark contemplating suicide; I *had* faced armageddon. But I had survived as a strong, gifted healer. Tonka reassured me, telling me it wouldn't be a negative reading.

For this reading I met Boris in a busy West Side diner at lunchtime. This was the only place he could receive clients at that time. We ordered lunch even though I wasn't hungry, and I threw the coins for the I Ching. Boris discovered my I Ching hexagram to be number seven, the Army. He called this an "adult only" hexagram, which involves experience and risk-taking to get through repetitive problems. The waiter brought lunch and Boris took a couple of bites before he continued, pushing his plate to one side. I shuffled the cards and Boris spread them out in a pattern on the table next to our food.

"Here you are, the queen, a fire-sign woman," Boris pointed to the cards. I silently recognized the Leo rising in my astrology chart.

The reading went on to say that although I was surrounded by disaster, my great strength was my children. *He really doesn't mince words, does he?* I thought to myself. *And yet I asked for it!*

"They want you to know that you've done a great job with your children. They are your strength," Boris said. "The enemy is the future because you're afraid of it as though it were a game show with prizes and you think you might choose the wrong curtain. Don't worry about it."

My life is a game show?

"You have conquered a lot, but there still is dust and residual anger," Boris continued.

"You should write a book about your rebirth experience; it is something that needs to be written," Boris declared, unaware that I had already begun writing this book.

"You will experience a higher healing. You will do more and exceed your expectations," Boris intoned as he laid down more cards. "Aha! You have very strong healing power in your hand. I don't know if it's the left or right one. You can cure anything," he told me, not knowing that I was already working as a healer. "Your hand is like a sword cutting away negativity and illness around people. Hmm, yes. You are a goddess on Earth, performing miracles, very powerful, very powerful," he said matter-of-factly, as though he was reading the weather.

Wow! Me? A goddess on Earth performing miracles! Now this is my kind of Tarot reader!

Boris gathered the cards and put them aside for a moment while he ate his lunch. When he finished he told me I could ask some questions.

"Should I still be a television producer, too?" I asked. He laid out the cards, quickly answered "No," and then rapidly gathered them up again. This led me to believe they must have looked really bad for him to want to collect them off the table so fast. A man who had never hesitated to tell me awful things was refraining from telling me what he saw.

"You are supposed to be working on your book right now," Boris ended the reading. "Aren't you going to eat your lunch?" Boris eyed my untouched plate.

How could I possibly think about eating right now!

As I said good-bye and left the diner, I felt elated by the reading. It was a confirmation of what I felt I had to do; my own instincts had been telling me to write this book. My healing work felt right for me, and when I really thought about it, I realized that the television work was one big headache and it didn't appeal to me anymore. I had been doing it only because I thought I had to. Now I had a green light to write my story and continue to offer myself to the Creator to be an instrument of healing. I finally was accepting the fact that the universe had a different plan for me—one I had never imagined.

RESPONDING TO SPIRIT

This made me remember another time in my life when the universe guided me in a direction I fought. The universe wanted me to move from Berkeley, California, to Washington, D.C.

After graduating from Oberlin College, I was happily living a hippie life out in Berkeley. It was my first time away from Ohio, living in my own apartment. (Well, maybe it was only a room in a house where I shared the bathrooms and kitchen with other hippies.) Everything was beautiful, except that I had no income. Try as I might, I could not get any kind of steady work.

To get by I was doing Russian translations, substitute-teaching preschool, babysitting, and house cleaning. The last job really hurt my ego, because I had just received my B.A. Margaret, my best friend from college, was then living in Washington, D.C., and working for a senator. She would tell me how wonderful life was in Washington, and how I should come there and get a job; it would be a great opportunity. I resisted leaving my happy California home, regardless of the number of peanut butter sandwiches I had to eat because that was all I could afford.

I continued to suffer poverty and the bizarre humiliation of being rejected from one job after another. I didn't get the message from the universe that it was time for me to leave. The only other life I had known was in Ohio with my parents. That I couldn't return to.

I was raped in San Francisco, right across the Bay Bridge from Berkeley, and I finally understood it was time to leave. I thought Spirit had been a bit harsh, but it certainly did change my perception of the beautiful Bay Area.

I had needed to make a change. I wanted to go to India, but I had no money. Margaret not only promised that I would get a job right away on Capitol Hill, but that we would travel together to Europe and from there we would go to India. I moved to Washington in order to earn enough money to begin my travels.

My parents loved the idea. They were convinced I would have turned into a drug addict if I had stayed in Berkeley. Washington was only a few hours' drive away from them. They funded my move.

When I got to Washington, I found out that Margaret had lied; it was actually very hard to get a job on Capitol Hill. I shared Margaret's room in an apartment building filled with women, some of whom, like Margaret, were working on the Hill. All of them agreed how difficult it was to get a job in Congress, and I discovered how some of them had been waiting years to do so.

I tried to figure out how my best friend could betray me. Margaret explained that she thought she was being stalked by a man. Because we looked alike as twins, Margaret wanted me around as a decoy. It wasn't until many years later that I recognized the true balance of our friendship, and how this and other events were pure manipulation. I cared about her and therefore allowed her to order me around. I gave her my power and energy.

On my first Monday there I went to work with Margaret early in the morning. She directed me to the Senate Employment Office so that I could make an appointment for an interview. As the person in charge was looking up the next available date, some two weeks in the future, something made her change her mind and she suddenly decided to interview me right away. An hour later I had the names of two senators who were looking to hire a clerk. I couldn't believe it!

I went to Senator Robert Byrd's office first because it was on a closer floor. The job was in the press department. Byrd is a Democrat from West Virginia. Because I was politically very liberal, that was important to me. Two hours after walking into the Senate building, I was working for Senator Byrd's press secretary.

I had been hired so quickly that I immediately accepted the job and began work right away. I soon found out that Senator Byrd was a "Southern Democrat"—conservative and quite a hawk. This was not good because I, and all my friends, opposed the war in Vietnam. In fact, my alma mater, Oberlin College, was organizing marches on Washington to protest the war.

The trouble began when a new press secretary arrived. He made comments about the impropriety of my clothes, even though I was making great efforts to tone down my hippie wardrobe. This was at the time when pants were forbidden attire for women working on Capitol Hill. The press secretary told me the office was making bets on whether I would one day brush my hair before my arrival at the office in the morning. You see, I didn't curl it perfectly like everyone else. He once told me that a team was as strong as its weakest link, and that I was this team's weakest link.

I was stuck! I was embarrassed, and everyone at my job hated me. Fortunately, the four of us who comprised the press department were in a separate office away from the senator's suite. I don't know why the new press secretary didn't fire me. In Berkeley, life had been so easy and fun. Now I had walked into a horrible box! I felt that the only way out was to stay at the job and earn enough money to leave for Europe, quick!

To compound my tragedy, Margaret decided to get married and relocate with her new husband. That left me totally alone in a town I hated, and with no one to go to Europe with. Desperate to leave Washington, I convinced my parents to help me get a masters degree at the Sorbonne if I saved a certain amount of money. They never thought I could do it. Life in Washington would have been expensive, except that I didn't want to participate in any of it. I saved my money easily.

My work life was difficult, but I had a goal and I was going to achieve it. Paris was ahead of me. The press secretary made his derogatory comments, but I just ignored him. I actually got my revenge in a strange way. The press secretary and I had daily, violent arguments about the war. He seemed to be supporting it, but one day he admitted that he had been a Peace Corps volunteer in Thailand. It turned out that I was stirring up his true feelings about the war. He loved the Thai people, and he knew the culture well enough to realize that the domino theory, which was the basis for the war, was wrong. Our daily disputes brought to the surface his ethics and experiences in Southeast Asia. A press secretary is supposed to promote his boss and never consider his own personal ethics or point of view, which I was obviously pushing him to do.

When the war began to spread to Cambodia, the press secretary and I began to agree, much to his dismay! I remember how pleased he was when he showed me the address the senator had delivered on the floor, coming out against the bombing in Cambodia. There was a real celebration in the office. Byrd was against the bombing for financial reasons, but it was a step in the right direction.

By late summer I had finally earned enough money to go to Europe. The press secretary declined my offer to train my successor. He said all the mistakes would leave with me. Senator Byrd was surprised to see me leave. He felt he had a winning team and didn't want to lose any of it. His polls showed him winning over ninety-five percent of the vote in the upcoming election year.

Many years later, when the war in Vietnam was long over and historians were analyzing the course of events, it turned out that Senator Byrd's coming out against the bombing of Cambodia had had a major impact in changing the course of the war. A powerful hawk withdrawing his support of the unbridled war effort changed the tide. All of a sudden

I realized that I had been "placed" there in that awful job by Spirit. Had I not argued bitterly with the press secretary, he never would have felt compelled to convince the senator's chief of staff and the senator himself of the danger of spreading the war throughout Southeast Asia. From my vantage point at the time, I was a miserable little thing in a miserable job working for the enemy. I hadn't been able to see the big picture.

I have since reconciled with the Bay Area, and I still love Berkeley and visit frequently. I even met up with a high-school friend who arrived in Berkeley after I had left. He managed to get a job in social work, which I had petitioned for but had not gotten. I saw his life as one I might have had. Living on a small income, he had too many clients and could do too little for each one. His life was fraught with anxiety and overwork. Had I stayed in Berkeley and gotten his job, I never would have spent my life traveling around the world.

I think that Spirit works through us all the time. When things "fall" into place and we go with the "flow," it might not be fun at the time but, by our presence, we are doing Spirit's work.

18
Finding Joy

FOR MY NEXT VISION QUEST, Glen insisted that all the questors have a supporter at the lodge during the quest. Terence and Ellen had moved to California, and I felt that the rest of my family resented my weeklong absences and refused to help. I didn't feel comfortable asking anyone else in Westchester. I finally decided to ask a longtime friend, Rita, who lived in Manhattan. I had shared my experiences of breaking through with her, and she had benefited from readings I had done for her as she struggled through a difficult divorce. She was familiar with my sweat lodge encounters and seemed supportive of it as she, too, broke through to a better way of being. I called her up.

"Hi Rita. I need someone to support me during my vision quest. Could you?" I asked her.

"What do I have to do?" Rita asked.

"You just have to be in the Adirondacks near the lodge for the four days that I'm fasting. You know, when I'm up on the hill," I answered.

"I don't want to do a sweat lodge. I'm not ready for that sort of thing yet," Rita told me.

"You don't have to participate in the sweat lodge. You just need to be around the campsite while I'm up on the hill," I reassured her.

"Do I have to camp out? I can't do that," Rita replied.

"No. There are motels around. You could stay in one of those," I answered, knowing that Rita would never be willing to climb a shaky ladder, let alone spend the night in a sleeping bag in a loft full of strangers.

"Well, I don't know. It all seems really weird to me. And you won't be there. I don't know. Let me think about it," Rita ended the conversation.

I got home one day to hear this message on my answering machine: "Hi, it's Rita. I just can't help you with your vision quest. It's all too weird for me, and I'm feeling very fragile right now. Sorry."

Rita had been my best bet. It just brought to my attention how much I had changed, and how little I had externalized that to make the necessary adjustments to be with like-minded people.

Making friends with other healers wasn't easy. My gifts were a source of jealousy for other healers, and as I became a healer myself, I felt their resentment. Many of them had worked hard for years to arrive at the success they enjoyed. They didn't appreciate a Johnny-come-lately who seemed to be more talented and who hadn't had the same training. I found that I had to be quiet around them regarding my experiences, and that made me feel uncomfortable. Once again I was on my own.

ANOTHER VISION QUEST

I was happy up in the Adirondacks. A long time ago Penney had told me she saw me happy in a loft by myself. At the time I had imagined a fancy loft in the city that would apparently be my production office. It just goes to show how different reality can be from what we can imagine. Had Penney told me that I would be happy in a dirty loft above an old garage, I would have thought her crazy.

But I *was* happy. The sweat lodges themselves were challenging, but in a good way. We were going to do a series of twelve sweat lodges. In the middle of the series, eight of us would go on our vision quests.

I was stuck, and by now some of the people I knew from the lodge were already supporting other questers. I finally asked a young man named Abe to be my supporter. Tall, gentle, and young, he was a rather marginal lodge participant, showing up infrequently and always keeping to himself. He never spent the night, as the rest of us did. During the one conversation I had with him, he shared with me that he had been molested as a child. I told him I had been, too. In Abe's case, his abuse led him to drugs, and now he was HIV-positive.

Abe really got into supporting me. Suddenly he felt he had a mission, and this empowered him and turned him into a strong participant at the lodge. He learned to say my Native American name and helped me sing songs in the lodge. When we were supposed to prepare our sacred place for our vision quest altars, he helped me add moss for comfort. My new place was a far cry from the lumpy brush pile that I had slept on during my first vision quest. Even Jake said it was the best sacred place, a comfortable mattress in a perfect home. As Glen dug postholes for the supports that held the prayer ties, he accidentally pulled up some of the moss.

"Sorry to be redecoratin' here, darlin'," he quipped. "I see ya did such a grand job of it." He winked at me.

When we walked up to our sacred places, I already felt tired. The preparation for this vision quest plus all the work I had to do at home first had exhausted me. Abe took my shoes, and Jake stayed behind to tell me, "Be strong, sister. I know you can do it."

I felt so tired I had trouble standing up, and once again a headache set in. I prayed to be relieved of the pain and not suffer, as I had the previous year. The pain continued but was less violent and debilitating than before. During the night it disappeared.

Tonka warned me to prepare for rain. I wrapped myself in my blankets and tarp and prayed to stay warm and dry. I was warm and dry all night. The next morning the rain abated somewhat, and I realized the corners of my blankets were wet. It began to rain again. It rained for the rest of the day and night. It seemed that everything I had was wet, but I felt warm and dry. It was amazing to see my prayers being answered in this manner.

As I lay there, sandwiched in my tarp for hours, I prayed for everyone and I repeated the prayers I had put in my 405 prayer ties. In the afternoon the weather cleared and I saw an eagle. During the night it rained again. I was surprised there was no thunder or lightning. It was only later that I learned there had been a tremendous thunderstorm. I had never even noticed it.

The morning of day three I was terribly thirsty. I woke up and found my tarp was full of collected water. *Maybe this is a gift from Tunkashila? Maybe I should have some water?* I thought. I hesitated a while, deliberating. Finally I poured the water out. Then I found two more pockets of water and poured these out quickly as well. Later Jake told me that I had done well to resist this temptation. He said on his second series of vision quests he had taken food and water to hold as temptation.

"Only the strongest can face such temptation," he later told me.

Five gigantic turkeys waddled up the hill. It was funny to see them, so huge, following one another. The last one in line noticed me and kept turning its head to the right to look at me. It even stopped to scrutinize me, letting the others get a little bit ahead. They were south of me, walking west. Then they almost disappeared from view, but instead came rushing back, squawking as they flew directly over my altar.

There was no doubt this was a sign for me, a sign indicating abundance. I later found out that none of the other questers had seen the turkeys. In the afternoon it was really hot. The wet blankets kept me cool for a while. I saw two eagles fly by. There was a woodpecker who had decided to be my daily companion. It felt good to hear his efforts to find food in the trees. His message to me was *perseverance*. I heard someone shaking some stones. I heard this sound several times throughout the quest. No human being or animal was shaking those stones. It was a message from the stone people and Mother Earth that I now had the gift to hear messages from her.

Perhaps it was through the sound of those rattling stones that I understood about joy. We hold the key to our own happiness. We basically decide what will make us happy and what will make us sad. The more we open up to the Creator, the more we open up to finding joy and breaking through the walls that prevent us from seeing it and feeling it. The energy for joy comes from God. Because God is within each of us, we have everything we need to be joyful.

That night I prepared for rain again, because I saw the thunderbeings coming in. I was sorry not to have the great, starry skies of the last vision quest. I was tremendously excited that this quest was almost over, and I had made it through thus far. I encouraged myself to be strong. Thinking about Abe at the lodge eating and drinking for me really helped. I didn't feel hungry, but I was thirsty.

That last evening it didn't rain. At dusk, a bear came up to me. Tonka told me there was a bear next to me. I saw it, but its presence didn't affect me at all. I wasn't the least bit nervous or afraid. It was as though it wasn't there. The bear is one of my power animals, so it was a gift to have it visit me. Later on, the quester nearest to me told me she had seen the bear from afar heading in my direction and had been concerned for me. That was a confirmation that it was a live bear and not a vision.

The last morning I was awakened by a bird who landed behind my head and tweeted loudly. I opened my eyes but didn't move. I felt its beak on my head. It pulled my hair, let go when I finally moved, and flew to a nearby tree. It sat there and watched, tweeting at me until I stood up. Then it flew away toward the lodge. *Now there's an interesting alarm clock,* I thought to myself.

I had kept my chanupa dry during the entire quest. I held it proudly as I stood waiting for my friends to come and get me. We weren't supposed to look at the people picking us up, so my eyes were downcast. Suddenly I saw my sweet Talia's hand picking up sage from my altar, because I needed to leave my sacred space free of any traces of having been disturbed. What a lovely surprise! She had missed school to be with me. Terence and Ellen were also there to bring me down off the hill. The vision questors lined up and formed what Jake called a power line. Then Jake led the questors down the hill, followed by the supporters. I fairly floated with joy.

During the feast that followed the concluding sweat lodge, I learned that while I was doing the quest, Abe had eaten the foods that I liked in order to support me. He also sang songs and said prayers for me in the sweat lodge.

Later on my older daughter, Tania, came to support me. She left work early to make the long drive to spend a little time with me. I was blessed that my family members had surprised me with their collective presence.

TALKING THE TALK

Gradually I became bolder about going public with my gifts. It seemed to me that people would welcome an alternative to surgery if I could fix their problem through my healing. And if my alternative healing modality didn't work, they would at least have expanded their horizons to include the Spirit World. But what I thought would be a win-win situation was met with a lot of skepticism. In any event, I believed that at least people who knew me well would embrace my experience. At a dinner I hosted at home, my long-time friend Lydia surprised me.

There were eight of us seated around the table. I had prepared a multi-course, gourmet French meal. The table was attractively laid with fine porcelain plates and silver utensils. The food, too, was beautifully presented, which makes it taste better, in my opinion. Everyone was relaxed and enjoying the meal.

The conversation died down a bit, and someone asked me what I had been doing recently. At this point the whole table was looking at me. I took a deep breath and happily announced that I had discovered that I was a medium and a healer. Most people made interested and rather approving noises. I was beginning to feel comfortable about my announcement when Lydia lit into me.

"Well, as far as I'm concerned, that's all pure bunk," she stated. "None of that stuff really works."

I was taken aback by her impolite statement. Even though she might not believe in my gifts or the Spirit World, she didn't need to dismiss them so rudely.

"It worked for me," I said, and in a soft voice I shared my own story of being healed of fibroids.

"You'll have to do better than that to convince me of anything," Lydia sneered. "Getting rid of fibroids is nothing. I did that just on my own, and I'm certainly not a healer. When I discovered I had one, my gynecologist told me to stop drinking coffee. That's all it took. A couple of months later it was gone without surgery *or* the help of a healer. It looks like you just went to the wrong doctor."

I felt happy for Lydia, and I felt sorry for her, too. On one hand she was willing to try an alternate means of dealing with her fibroid before immediately resorting to surgery. I applauded her doctor for being so open-minded. On the other hand, she was unable to see beyond what a medical doctor would prescribe. Had a healer suggested she stop drinking coffee, she probably wouldn't have tried it. Lydia was unwilling to accept alternatives to standard medical practices.

I calmly looked at Lydia and said, "The gynecologist who told me I might drop dead in the street was yours, whom you recommended to me.

She was the one who told me, along with two other doctors, that the only solution for me was a hysterectomy," I said.

"You saw Dr. Lartin?" Lydia asked.

"The one and the same," I answered.

"Oh," Lydia mumbled. A door opened for her.

I remembered an incident that Melanie Noblit-Gambino had told me about. She was at a friend's family gathering when she met a man stricken with Parkinson's disease. His medication was no longer helping him. He explained how he was about to have experimental surgery so that his doctor could put wires in his brain. Melanie offered him a session of energy healing.

"Do you have scientific proof that a session will help me?" the man demanded.

"It definitely won't hurt you, and it might help," Melanie replied.

"No, I'm not interested in any of that weird stuff," he answered. "I'm going to listen to my doctor. He knows what's best for me."

The man remained attached to his belief that anything a doctor might do was superior to anything a healer might try. Unfortunately for him, he was willing to undergo invasive, dangerous, experimental surgery rather than try a healing experience that had no downside. I guess doctors don't need scientific proof that something works before patients are willing to try it.

Another "coming out" experience came to me in the calm setting of my Presbyterian church. At a church gathering in the basement community room, a rather "full of himself" gentleman walked up to me and said, "I saw your card at my yoga class. 'Messenger,' you call yourself. Am I correct?"

"Yes," I answered.

"And then you have something else on it: 'Healing through Contact with the Spirit World.' Is that right?"

"That's right. That's what I do. I'm a healer," I answered. *This man must have already practiced this line of questioning during the Inquisition*, I thought to myself. *In some past life!*

"Working with the Spirit World. Is that what you do?" he continued.

"That's right. That's exactly what I do," I answered.

"Spirits, and working with spirits—isn't that contrary to Presbyterian doctrine?" he demanded.

"Every Sunday we pray to the Father, Son, and Holy Spirit, right?" I responded.

"Yes," he answered cautiously.

"Well, there you go. Holy Spirit, Spirit World, it's all the same," I announced cheerfully.

He looked at me, a bit baffled, and then acquiesced, "Well, yes, I suppose it is." Looking confused, he wandered off.

I really do believe it is all the same.

One of my favorite hymns in our Presbyterian hymnal is called "Spirit"; it was composed by James K. Manley in 1975. The last stanza speaks to me.

> *You call from tomorrow,*
> *You break ancient schemes.*
> *From the bondage of sorrow*
> *The captives dream dreams;*
> *Our women see visions,*
> *Our men clear their eyes.*
> *With bold new decisions*
> *Your people arise.*

In church the following Sunday the minister read a sermon about Jesus healing a blind man. Jesus was treated badly and was questioned about the sanctity of his healing. It struck a chord in me. I faced the same skepticism and criticism. I thought of the number of times Jesus had been criticized because he was a healer. When we sang "God of Ages" I began to cry, and I had to walk home instead of drive in order to calm myself.

I began to realize how we create so much suffering around us when we allow our egos to exert control over others. Rather than be supportive of any kind of positive action, we question it first. A good deed is rarely accepted as such. We often look for the personal agenda behind everyone's action. The phrase "There's no such thing as a free lunch" comes to mind; anyone who might invite you to lunch surely has some hidden plan. We learn this in business, carry it over into our personal lives, and teach it to our children. Our egos let competition and jealousy enter into the equation, too. If the generous soul doing a random act of kindness is really doing just that, and doesn't have some ulterior motive, we often begin to appraise our personal status compared to the "goody two-shoes." Does that do-gooder make *us* look bad? Does that positive action usurp some of *our* power or control? Does it force us to change our worldview? Does it force us to change in other ways? Nobody likes change unless they initiate and control it personally. The do-gooder becomes a troublemaker.

Jesus was considered by some a troublemaker during his lifetime. I believe that one of the reasons that Jesus suffered the way he did was to show us the irony of a civilization in which we cannot accept random acts of kindness or be supportive of the people who bring them to us. After two thousand years, we still haven't learned that lesson. We become more aware of ourselves when we catch ourselves letting issues of jealousy and control poison us. We have to realize that it's not about one pie, and if you don't get your big piece of it, you won't get any. We have confused greed with joy. We tend to believe that if we have more then we will be happy, yet we all know that is wrong. Often more isn't better; it's just more.

Just like the fairy tale of the unhappy king who searches his kingdom for a happy man and finds that the happiest man is a shirtless beggar, we need to realize that our joy comes from inside. It is our point of view. Do we see the glass as half full or half empty? Are we aware enough to even know how we see the glass? Are we personally skilled enough to lead ourselves out of our sadness? Through self-awareness and meditation we can be.

If you go to a gathering of people and one person speaks to you and everyone else ignores you, will you consider the experience as negative? Or will you enjoy the beauty of that one encounter?

Can you accept the compliments that people give you, or do you discard them, refusing to believe them? And then do you remember verbatim all the criticism you have ever received? It is possible to live in the joy of abundance.

Are you miserable because you haven't found your soul mate? Have you given up hope? Rather than closing down your heart, it's time to open it up to the Creator. As you do that, and you stand strong in your love for yourself—because loving yourself is loving the Creator—then your soul mate will appear. This openness to love all is like a magnet that will attract loving people to you.

There is more than enough in this world to satisfy all our needs and to allow us to be joyful. The more we realize this, the better our world will be for us all.

WALKING THE WALK

These days my face is always smiling and I have a sense of joy and peace that I never knew was possible until I began to live it. My world is colorful and abundant.

Once, when I was channeling Mother Mary, she said, "If you are greedy, you will always be poor. If you are wealthy, you will always be rich." To me that means recognizing all the blessings I enjoy that make me feel wealthy. In other words, seeing the glass as half full, rather than half empty. That way I always have what I need. If I let myself worry about not having enough, and I am greedy, I will always feel poor. The baseline of need grows as we acquire more. Our appetites grow, and we believe we need even more than we initially thought. When will we ever have enough? I have learned to always feel wealthy, and Spirit has always provided for me, regardless of what it might be I believe I need.

The real bottom line is trust in the Creator. Put your energy behind your intention to trust the Great Mystery to provide for you, to help you manifest your dreams, and to accomplish your personal spiritual mission here on Earth. Often, when things don't turn out the way we want, there is the bigger picture to consider, a bigger picture that incorporates our larger spiritual mission.

We also shouldn't forget our basic mission on Earth. To understand our basic mission on Earth we just need to look at a tree. For it to complete its mission on Earth, it just needs to be—that's it! By its mere existence, the tree does what it's supposed to do. The tree has its personal agenda, too. It has a potential growth pattern that it attempts to achieve while it is facing challenges from weather, other trees, animals, people, illness, and so forth. Regardless of how far along the tree gets in fulfilling its personal agenda, it has completed its basic mission on Earth simply by being alive.

It's the same for us. We complete our basic mission simply by "showing up" every day. The rest is our personal agenda. We lose sight of the fact that we are already doing a good job just by keeping ourselves alive, and we get so attached to our personal agenda that oftentimes the only thing we succeed at is making ourselves miserable.

Trust in the Creator also means walking fearlessly. Remember that if you spend a lot of time trying to protect yourself spiritually, you are constantly living in fear. You must trust the Creator to protect you. If you should feel especially uncomfortable in a situation, you can pray to the white light of the Holy Spirit to enclose you, and you can imagine a beautiful white light descending all around you. In this way, you will be protected.

Although many of my references are inspired by my Christian faith, the Creator has no favorite religion. What I refer to as the "white light of the Creator" for my Jewish clients is the same white light of the Holy Spirit. During my healing sessions, Jesus turns up to help me regardless of my client's religion. All roads to the Creator are good, as long as they incorporate love.

I once participated in a workshop that combined shamanism and energy healing. The participants came from a variety of religious beliefs, some quite conservative and exclusive. The evening ceremony honoring the four elements ended with us remaining in silence until the next morning's gathering. When we could all talk, everyone enthused about the fabulous experiences they had enjoyed. That is, until they put labels on their experiences.

"My experience is best expressed by the passage in the Torah that . . ." began the conservative Jew.

"No, no, no! It was an experience that Jesus spoke about," declared the devout Catholic.

Before it turned into a free-for-all, I reminded everyone about the nature of the experience. It had been beautiful for everyone. Why ruin it with labels? Couldn't everyone just enjoy their own experience and define it in their own way for themselves?

That's exactly what we did and everyone was happy.

When Spirit told me to turn no one away, I panicked. What a huge responsibility! And I would have to be with all those sick people! Nevertheless, I have followed Spirit's advice. Through me, Spirit has healed people with physical and emotional problems. This includes heart conditions, thyroid conditions, and aches and pains in various parts of the body. One of my clients was a kidney transplant survivor who had been given two months to live. He was suffering from a second kind of cancer, considered inoperable. Two years after our healing session, he was still alive and doing well.

I have helped people find their light to continue their path in peace; I have contacted innumerable spirits for people. I have done this as an instrument of God's healing. Just like a flute, I make myself available and the Creator's breath comes through me to touch people. I am grateful to be of service in this way.

The first thing I always do is to reconnect people with their internal joy. It's like lighting a flame. Without that joy in our lives, how can we hope to sustain emotional and physical healing? It took me a while to find my joy. Now it is my turn to help others do the same. It is a job I welcome.

I have finally accepted the fact that the Universe wants me to be a healer and not a television producer. That doesn't mean I can't produce, but my main focus is my profession as a healer. This brings me joy and comfort that I never experienced in television. I'm free of anxiety and stress. When I am in a session with a client, I sit in the Creator's beautiful light and I feel unconditional love for that person. That is the same love that I feel for myself. It is what Jesus meant when he said, "Love thy neighbor as thyself."

I knew my life would continue to open more to Spirit, and that gradually my family and friends would understand and embrace what I was doing as they experienced the wonder of the Spirit World themselves. My path was and will continue to present challenges to me. Yes, the flute still needs to be cleaned further, and probably will always need some more work! But it's worth it as I walk this interesting, joyful, and gratifying path. I rejoice! I am thankful for it all.

YOUR JOURNEY

You are already on a journey, whether you are aware of it or not. Don't be alarmed! Being aware is not necessary, but it does make the journey a lot easier. My journey is no different from yours. The details may vary, but the basic emotional challenges that I faced as I broke through many walls are the same ones we all face. Look at my story as a road map. You can take different paths and turns, but you're still on the same map. Get used to it!

Gaining awareness of our situation and the situation of others around us helps bring emotional and physical release as we let go of our egos and surrender to the Creator. Our burden lightens, and we can shapeshift into a happier way of being. I never appreciated that it was possible to live in a constant state of joy, free of lingering anger and hurt, until I broke through to this amazing way of being. You can do it, too!

The help that I received from the Spirit World is available to everyone. It's all around us, trying to get our attention. You just need to trust in the Creator, and be aware of the messages that are constantly being sent to us.

As you open up to Spirit, mentors and teachers will appear to you. Penney, Rosalyn Bruyere, Melanie, and even Foxes were teachers that Spirit provided for me just when I needed them. Some of our best teachers are the ones we like the least. This is a wonderful thing and important to accept, even though some of our lessons are painful.

There is the temptation, however, to place a teacher or mentor on a pedestal, to give that person your power and your energy, and to try to hold on to your teacher as long as possible, at any cost. Many teachers understand this and do everything to empower you so that you can meet the Creator directly and get the information you need. Other teachers might be unaware that they are profiting from their students, rather than empowering them. This leads to situations similar to the ones that I experienced with Foxes. But I was also predisposed to being dominated.

The way to protect yourself from falling into a "worship trap" is to recognize whether or not the teacher places him- or herself between you and the Creator. Your whole journey is about empowering yourself to be able to communicate directly with God. You can ask questions about a message, or receive messages through a teacher, but this is only for clarification. Remember: *Omitakuye oyasin*—We are all related. There is no one better than you, and you, by the same token, are no better than anyone else.

Recently I met a nurse, Janet, who asked me what it meant to be clairvoyant, clairaudient, and clairsentient. She explained that her path led her to gradually open up to Spirit. She felt that this was a very private experience, and that she needed to separate it from her job. When she stepped into the hospital to work, she thought she left her openness to Spirit at the door.

One day something unusual happened. During her shift Janet entered a room and saw that a heavily sedated patient was asleep and restrained to the bed. Janet walked around the room checking the tubes and IV drips and monitors. She was unprepared to hear the voice of the unconscious patient follow her around the room, as though the patient was not only talking to her but was also strolling behind her. This experience frightened her.

At a holistic networking meeting, Janet shyly came up to me and asked what was going on. She was so resistant to combining her spirituality with her job that she refused to see what was happening.

I told her that being open to Spirit is something beautiful and useful and it could help anyone in any job, and could be particularly helpful in her hospital work. That is why her clairaudient ability manifested to her as she was working.

"Spirit speaks to us in many different forms," I explained. "Have you ever just known something without really thinking it through?"

"Yeah, sometimes I'm absolutely sure of something, and I really don't have any reason to feel so sure," Janet answered.

"That's Spirit communicating with us. Some people say it's their gut talking to them. It's really Spirit," I explained. "Have you ever glanced at a printed page and read just one sentence in the middle that answered something you needed to know?"

"Why, yes!" Janet exclaimed. "That happens to me all the time!"

"Good. That's Spirit communicating with you," I said.

"Really?" Janet inquired.

"Yes. Perhaps you have been at a gathering of people, maybe a meeting of some sort, and one of the people who you might not even know, out of the blue, answers a question you've had on your mind before you even mention it?" I inquired.

"Yes! And when I go back later and try to talk to the person about it, they have no memory of it at all!" Janet enthused.

"That again is Spirit speaking to you through another person," I explained. "As you open up to Spirit more and are ready to accept other ways to receive messages from Spirit, you will become clairaudient. That means that you can hear messages from the Spirit World."

"But the patient in the bed was alive. How could I have heard her right behind me when she was strapped to the bed and wasn't physically speaking?" Janet asked.

"Your patient's body was lying in bed, but her spirit was out of that body, following you around the room in a dimension that approaches that of the Spirit World. Because you are becoming clairaudient, you heard her voice right behind you," I explained.

"Someone's spirit can leave their body while the person's alive?" Janet exclaimed.

"Absolutely. People leave their bodies to protect themselves from pain and trauma," I said. "It's possible to do it during meditation also. We often do it when we are asleep. If someone wakes you from a deep sleep and you are disoriented for a moment, it's just your spirit returning to your body."

"And if I could see a spirit, that's clairvoyance?" Janet asked.

"That's right. Just imagine, maybe you could have turned around quickly and seen that patient's spirit behind you!" I said.

"Oh, that would have been way too weird for me," Janet said. "Just hearing the voice was enough."

"A lot of what we experience with the Spirit World depends on what we're ready to allow ourselves to perceive. You have to be open to seeing a spirit before you can actually see one," I said. "It's the same with hearing a spirit. Feeling something is another way of getting information from Spirit. That's called clairsentience."

"I guess I still have a long way to go before I'm doing all that," Janet said.

"Not necessarily," I said. "Sometimes these things open up quickly, sometimes they open up slowly, and sometimes they don't open up at all. The point is to be aware and available to get these messages from Spirit, however they are transmitted. They are always messages to help us live happier, better lives.

"You know, being a medium or psychic is similar to playing the piano: Everyone can learn to do it; some people are just more gifted at it than others," I explained.

I love it when people open up to the splendor of the Spirit World and all it can bring us. It's thrilling and comforting at the same time.

With Tonka near me I am never alone to face life's challenges. This morning when I woke up I heard the beautiful strains of Joanne Shenandoah, a Native American performer, singing my favorite song, "Feather from Heaven." I hadn't listened to that CD in months! The CD wasn't playing. It was a lovely gift from Tonka. The final verse expresses what Tonka's presence brings to me.

> *When the dust of death is settled in your voice,*
> *and you can say nothing at all,*
> *I will be there, water pure and clean,*
> *to wash away the silence within.*
> *I will be there, to wipe away your tears,*
> *I will be there to brush away your fears,*
> *Wash away the silence within.*

This is the way I want to make myself available to heal people. I have promised the Creator that for anyone who needs me, I will be there to wipe away tears, to brush away fears, and to wash away the sadness within. That sadness will be filled with pure joy.

Remember how you felt when you fell in love for the first time? It might have simply been an infatuation with a rock star. Everything was wonderful and no problem seemed insurmountable. That same sensation of falling in love is my reward for opening up to Spirit. It has taught me to fall in love with life every day. So can you.

The joy I have found is boundless and increases with every day. I invite you to open up and join me. Go ahead and risk doing the things you love. Make some waves! Will they really make such a difference on the ocean of life? You might end up enjoying your time here. Be daring and crazy. What do you have to lose? It's so great to feel like you've just fallen in love every day. The joy is definitely worth the journey!

Suggested Reading

Altea, Rosemary. *The Eagle and the Rose: A Remarkable True Story*. New York: Warner Books, 1995.

Andrews, Ted. *Animal Speak: The Spiritual and Magical Powers of Creatures Great and Small*. Saint Paul, Minn. Llewellyn Publications, 1993.

Black Elk. *Black Elk Speaks*. New York: William Morrow & Company, 1932.

Brown, Joseph Epes. *The Sacred Pipe; Black Elk's Account of the Seven Rites of the Oglala Sioux*. Norman, Okla.: University of Oklahoma Press, 1953.

Brown, Sylvia, and Lindsay Harrison. *Past Lives, Future Healing: A Psychic Reveals the Secrets to Good Health and Great Relationships*. New York: New American Library, 2001.

———. *The Other Side and Back*. New York: New American Library, 1999.

Brown, Tom, Jr. *The Tracker: The Story of Tom Brown, Jr., as Told to William Jon Watkins*. Englewood Cliffs, N.J.: Prentice-Hall, 1978.

Bruce, Eve, M.D. *Shaman, M.D*. Rochester, Vt.: Destiny Books, 2002.

Bruyere, Rosalyn L. *Wheels of Light: A Study of the Chakras*. Sierra Madre, Calif.: Bon Productions, 1989.

Coelho, Paulo. *The Alchemist*. San Francisco: Harper San Francisco, 1988.

Conte-Dubs, Tianna, N.D., and Janet Cunningham, Ph.D. *Love's Fire: Beyond Mortal Boundaries*. New York: Infinite Possibilities Productions, 2004.

Crow Dog, Mary, and Richard Erdoes. *Lakota Woman*. New York: HarperCollins, 1991.

Eadie, Betty J. *Embraced by the Light*. New York: Bantam Books, 2002.

Goldner, Diane. *Infinite Grace: Where the Worlds of Science and Spiritual Healing Meet*. Charlottesville, Va.: Hampton Roads Publishers, 1999.

Ladinsky, Daniel. *Love Poems from God: Twelve Voices from the East and West*. New York: Penguin Books, 2002.

Leyshon, Penney and Kathleen Spellman. *A Gift of Healing in a Handbook*. Bridgeport, Conn.: Oxccidus, 2005.

Myss, Caroline. *Anatomy of the Spirit: The Seven Stages of Power Healing*. New York: Three Rivers Press, 1996.

Mountain Dreamer, Oriah. *Opening The Invitation: The Poem That Has Touched Lives Around the World*. San Francisco: Harper San Francisco, 2004.

Orloff, Judith, M.D. *Second Sight*. New York: Warner Books, Inc., 1997.

Perkins, John. *The World Is As You Dream It: Shamanic Teachings from the Amazon and Andes*. Rochester, Vt.: Destiny Books, 1994.

———. *Shapeshifting*. Rochester, Vt.: Destiny Books, 1997.

Kübler-Ross, Elisabeth. *On Death and Dying*. New York: Scribner (reprint edition), 1997.

Ruiz, Don Miguel. *The Four Agreements: A Practical Guide to Personal Freedom*. San Rafael, Calif.: Amber-Allen Publishing, 2001.

———. *The Mastery of Love: A Practical Guide to the Art of Relationship*. San Rafael, Calif.: Amber-Allen Publishing, 1999.

Sarangerel. *Chosen by the Spirits: Following Your Shamanic Calling*. Rochester, Vt.: Destiny Books, 2001.

Siegel, Bernie S. *Love, Medicine & Miracles: Lessons Learned about Self-Healing from a Surgeon's Experience with Exceptional Patients*. New York: HarperPerennial, 1990.

BOOKS OF RELATED INTEREST

Shapeshifting
Shamanic Techniques for Global and Personal Transformation
by John Perkins

Bushman Shaman
Awakening the Spirit through Ecstatic Dance
by Bradford Keeney

Chosen by the Spirits
Following Your Shamanic Calling
by Sarangerel

The Dreamer's Book of the Dead
A Soul Traveler's Guide to Death, Dying, and the Other Side
by Robert Moss

Dreamways of the Iroquois
Honoring the Secret Wishes of the Soul
by Robert Moss

Shamanic Experience
A Practical Guide to Psychic Powers
by Kenneth Meadows

Shamanic Spirit
A Practical Guide to Personal Fulfillment
by Kenneth Meadows

The Shaman's Doorway
Opening Imagination to Power and Myth
by Stephen Larsen

Inner Traditions • Bear & Company
P.O. Box 388
Rochester, VT 05767
1-800-246-8648
www.InnerTraditions.com

Or contact your local bookseller